WHAT IS
SOCIAL-SCIENTIFIC
CRITICISM?

WHAT IS SOCIAL-SCIENTIFIC CRITICISM?

by
JOHN H. ELLIOTT

FORTRESS PRESS

Minneapolis

WHAT IS SOCIAL-SCIENTIFIC CRITICISM?

Scripture quotations, unless otherwise noted, are the author's translation. Excerpts from the New Revised Standard Version Bible are copyright © 1989 by the Division of Christian Education of the National Council of Churches of Christ in the USA and are used by permission.

"Diagram of the Research Process" (page 62) by Matilda White Riley is copyright © 1963 Harcourt Brace & Co. Used by permission.

"A Multivariate Matrix Model for Comparing Palestine Interest Groups" (page 66) by John H. Elliott is copyright © 1986 Scholar's Press. Used by permission.

Library of Congress Cataloging-in-Publication Data

Elliott, John Hall.
  What is social-scientific criticism? / by John H. Elliott.
    p.   cm.
  Includes bibliographical references and index.
  ISBN 0-8006-2678-8 :
    1. Bible. N.T.—Criticism, Social scientific.   2. Sociology, Biblical.   I. Title.
BS2361.2.E55   1993
225.6'7—dc20   93-22407
                                                                              CIP

The paper used in this publication meets the minimum requirements of American National Standard for Information Sciences—Permanence of Paper for Printed Library Materials, ANSI Z329.48-1984.   ∞™

Manufactured in the U.S.A.   1-2678

04   3   4   5   6   7   8   9   10

For
Bruce J. Malina
il mio amico e collèga
on the occasion of his sixtieth birthday
Ad multos annos!

Contents

Foreword

This very useful volume by John Elliott extends the program of this series, which is to deal with methodological and formal issues pertaining to the New Testament. The primary thrust of the book is to display the bearing that the social sciences have on our understanding of the texts and contexts of the New Testament, with due attention being given to theories and models. While the main interest of the volume is the social-scientific, there is also some comparison of this with social history. It has points of contact with other studies that deal with historical and rhetorical issues.

—Dan O. Via

Introduction: Two Scenarios

The aim of this study is to give an account of social-scientific criticism of the New Testament and its environment, the rise of this method, its practitioners and the foci of their work, and the details of the method itself, its presuppositions and procedures. We will conclude with a consideration of some recent assessments and a summary of its provisional contributions. Four appendices and a glossary of selected terms detail and clarify various features and terms of our discussion. Finally, two bibliographies list (*a*) exegetical and related studies along social-scientific or social-historical lines and (*b*) works in the social sciences and social history also mentioned in this study or recommended for further reference.

This study is written as a basic introduction to the contribution of social-scientific criticism to the several operations of biblical interpretation that are described in the Guides to Biblical Scholarship series. It is designed primarily for beginning students and general readers of the New Testament, but the interest of exegetical "veterans" would also be most welcomed.

Chapter 1 defines the method and the goal of social-scientific criticism and shows how this method relates to the other subdisciplines and operations of exegesis in general. The two chapters that follow it situate the emergence of this method within the recent history of biblical and particularly New Testament scholarship. Thus, chapter 2 explains how this method was developed to address questions that were raised but not adequately and systematically resolved by earlier exegetical approaches; and chapter 3 offers a chronological sketch of the rise of this method since the 1970s, together with a description of some of its major practitioners and examples of their work. Chapters 6 and 7 review and discuss representative critiques of this approach and estimations of its contributions to a study of the Bible in its original context.

The "methodological meat" of the study involves chapters 4 and 5, which give a description of the method itself, its presuppositions and its procedures. The biblical text used for purposes of illustration is 1 Peter. As will be evident, however, the method is described in such a way that it can be employed in the study of any New Testament or biblical text.

The various appendices summarize and illustrate in table form matters discussed in the body of the study. A glossary of selected social-scientific terms is provided to familiarize the beginning student with some of the technical vocabulary employed by social-scientific critics. Finally, two bibliographies are provided for readers who wish to acquaint themselves with the range of exegetical research along social-scientific lines and with perhaps unfamiliar but representative research of the social sciences upon which these exegetical studies have been based.

In order to illustrate the perspective and concerns that characterize social-scientific criticism, let us begin with two scenarios: the first, a slice of U.S. culture; the second, a page or two from the world of the Bible.

Scenario One:
Visiting the Strange New World of American Baseball

Your guest from Moscow has been with you in Oakland, California, for a week now. Rested and acquainted with the local shopping area, she is anxious to experience "something typically American." What could be more American, you think to yourself, than a baseball game, the quintessential American pastime? As fate would have it, the Oakland A's are at home and playing an exhibition game with the Japanese All-Stars. You drive to the Coliseum, park, buy your tickets and programs, and take your seats just in time for batting practice. Your friend, gazing around the Coliseum, watching the playing field for a while and the players taking batting practice, glimpses at her program, thinking that this piece of information will tell her all about what she is seeing. After a minute or two she turns to you with a quizzical expression on her face and says, "What's going on here? What is this game of baseball all about? What makes this event so typically American?"

What do you say? What will you tell her that will prepare her for the next nine innings, from the national anthem to the mass exit of some elated and some dejected fans? What is this game and how is it played? Is it really "play" ("Play ball!") of "the boys of summer," or is it serious business with millions of dollars at stake? Who are those nine/eighteen men (not women!) out there on the "grass" (artificial turf)? Why is that guy standing on a mound and continually throwing to a crouching guy with all that armor on? What are the players shouting to one another? What does "home team" mean, and why do the fans cheer more loudly for it than for the visitors? Do the players in the program have any special jobs, and is there any significance to the "batting order"? What are "runs, hits, and errors"? What does "Yogetchapopcornhere!" mean? What is a "diamond," a "rubber," a "sack"? What's the meaning of "homer," "strike out," "slider," "fast ball," "line drive," "steal," "sacrifice bunt" (human? animal?), "around the horn" (of the altar?), "goose egg," "three-zip after three," "seventh-inning stretch," "down to the wire," "rookie," "slump," "goat," "pennant race," "world series" (really the whole world?)? Why do the American and the Japanese players behave so differently? Why doesn't the program talk about Japanese "stars" (like your Mark and Terry), and why is *wa* ("team spirit") more important than *jinshugi* ("individualism") for them? If the A's are Oakland's team, are the players city employees? Does every U.S. city "own" a team? Who then are "managers" and "owners" (are the players bought and sold like commodities?)? What are "major" and "minor" and "bush" leagues, "American" and "National" Leagues (aren't they all Americans?)? Why do you sing the national anthem? Is this a political event? And so on. What does your guest need to know in order to understand the game of baseball, its routines and jargon, its role in the U.S. economy and politics, its incarnation of the myths and values of American culture?

These are questions about both content and context, matrix and meaning, details and the "big picture." American baseball is less than a civil religion (at least for some) and more than a game. To understand this "national pastime" in all of its ramifications, is it not necessary to put the specific details about uniforms, "lumber," and scorecards into an encompassing framework of society, big business, culture, and meaning?

Scenario Two:
Visiting the Strange Old World of the New Testament

In a late-night bull session on that perennially scintillating subject of sex and sexuality, one of your conversation partners remarks, "Christians have been plagued by the problem of sex from the very beginning. Just look at Paul's letter to the Corinthians!" The next morning you turn to the Corinthian letters, and after flipping through the early chapters of the first letter, you indeed come across large sections of material dealing with sexual issues, beginning with 1 Corinthians 5.

But what does it all mean? And what are you to make of these words about "immorality," "delivering offenders to Satan," "shaming," being "one with a prostitute," not "touching" a woman, "consecrating" a spouse, and the like? What makes a man's living in the same house as his father's wife "immoral" (1 Cor 5:1)? Or is "living with" a euphemism for "engaging in sexual relations"? Is "father's wife" a synonym for "mother," or does it mean "stepmother"? And how does one decide? Is this an instance of "incest," and what exactly constituted incest back then anyway? Why was Paul so shocked about the cavalier and "arrogant" attitude of the Corinthians regarding this matter? How exactly are the Corinthians to "deliver this man to Satan" and why? What has this to do with getting rid of leaven and "cleansing" and Christ as "paschal lamb"? Why is Paul so concerned about believers not associating with "immoral" persons, with in-groups and out-groups, and with excluding wicked brothers from the group? Are these people all members of the same biological family, or is "brother" used metaphorically? Why would the believers consider themselves "brothers" (what about sisters?), even if not related by blood? What has all this to do with believers pursuing lawsuits against fellow believers ("brothers") in the courts of nonbelievers (1 Cor 6:1-11)? Why are "sexual perverts" (RSV) or "homosexual perverts" (TEV, NEB) or "boy prostitutes" (NAB) or "effeminates" (KJV) or "male prostitutes" and "sodomites" lumped together with idolaters and excluded from the kingdom of God (6:9-11)? Why do the various translations disagree? What kind of behavior was envisioned here? How did Paul imagine becoming "one body" with a prostitute (6:16), and why was this incompatible with being "united with the Lord"? Why does Paul relate physical bodies and the social body and why around the issue of morality and holiness?

What about the "bigger picture"? Why was sexual behavior such a burning issue at Corinth (1 Corinthians 5–7)? What was its connection to the other matters Paul covers in his letter, such as idol worship and eucharistic celebration, freedom, and group solidarity (6:9; 8:1-13; 10:14—11:1)? Why are male- and female-gender roles, hair lengths, and hair coverings such a problem (11:2-16), and what has this to do with worship (11:17-34; 14) and the theological issues of death and resurrection with which Paul begins and ends his letter (1:18-25; 15:1-58)?

What must you know about the social institutions and cultural values and norms of that time in order to make sense of Paul's words—within

4

this letter as well as within the social world that Paul and the Corinthians inhabited?

Once again we are faced with a series of questions about specific details and larger context, particular problems of meaning and broader questions about the bigger social and cultural picture that shapes meaning. And what of the answers? How and where are strangers to Paul's world to find the "Frommer's guides" that can "fill us in" and "put us in the know"? What social and cultural scenarios are we to imagine for reading and making sense of the meanings being communicated here? What "maps" are available to enable us to detect the lay of the cultural and social landscape and thereby comprehend the whys and wherefores of the Corinthians' behavior and Paul's response? Were there in antiquity institutions like the game of baseball that embodied the values and worldviews of an entire culture? How much alike and how different are biblical and modern cultures, and what bearing might this have on an intelligent reading of the Bible?

Enter social-scientific criticism of the Bible and its environment.

1
What Is
Social-Scientific Criticism?

Let us begin with a definition. Social-scientific criticism of the
Bible is that phase of the exegetical task which analyzes the social and
cultural dimensions of the text and of its environmental context through
the utilization of the perspectives, theory, models, and research of the
social sciences. As a component of the historical-critical method of exegesis, social-scientific criticism investigates biblical texts as meaningful con-
figurations of language intended to communicate between composers and
audiences. In this process it studies (1) not only the social aspects of the
form and content of texts but also the conditioning factors and intended
consequences of the communication process; (2) the correlation of the
text's linguistic, literary, theological (ideological), and social dimensions;
and (3) the manner in which this textual communication was both a reflection of and a response to a specific social and cultural context—that
is, how it was designed to serve as an effective vehicle of social interaction
and an instrument of social as well as literary and theological consequence.

This definition indicates, first, that social-scientific criticism is a *subdiscipline of exegesis* and is inseparably related to the other operations
of the exegetical enterprise: textual criticism, literary criticism, narrative
criticism, historical criticism, tradition criticism, form criticism, redaction criticism, rhetorical criticism, and theological criticism. Social-
scientific criticism complements these other modes of critical analysis, all
of which are designed to analyze specific features of the biblical texts.

Inasmuch as biblical texts entail a diversity of dimensions, various subdisciplines have been developed over time to focus specific attention on
these various aspects. Thus textual criticism analyzes the Bible as a collection of texts and textual witnesses with individual and collective histories

of textual transmission. Literary criticism examines the features of the document as a literary (aesthetic) product shaped by both contemporary literary conventions and the genius of its particular author or authors. Historical criticism interrogates the text as a historical document influenced by and responsive to historical events. Form criticism and tradition criticism study the text as comprising particular forms and sources of communication with a history preceding that of the text in which they are incorporated. Redaction criticism analyzes the text as a creative combination and editing of previous traditions. Rhetorical criticism studies the text as composed and arranged to have a persuasive effect on its intended audience. Theological criticism studies the text as an articulation of beliefs about God, the sacred, space, time, the cosmos, good and evil, the human condition, and the origin, nature, and goal of life.

Social-scientific criticism, in its turn, studies the text as both a reflection of and a response to the social and cultural settings in which the text was produced. Its aim is the determination of the meaning(s) explicit and implicit in the text, meanings made possible and shaped by the social and cultural systems inhabited by both authors and intended audiences.

Social-scientific criticism, as a subdiscipline of exegesis, focuses primarily on biblical texts. Yet, like all interpretive efforts, it is also closely related to other disciplines with a broader focus not on specific texts but on ancient social and cultural systems in general as investigated by historians, sociologists, anthropologists, and archaeologists. The disciplines, like the materials investigated, obviously overlap and complement each other. The social-scientific analysis of texts is constantly carried out in conjunction with study of the social and cultural systems in which these texts were produced and which provided their frameworks of meaning. On the other hand, examination of the latter is constantly nourished by the research of the former. Accordingly, in the pages that follow, we shall consider not only the social-scientific criticism of texts but also the relation of this discipline of exegesis to the social-scientific study of the social and cultural contexts of the Bible, and specifically the New Testament. In order to avoid unnecessary redundancy, the label "social-scientific criticism" will be used to cover both related enterprises.

2
Why the Need for
Social-Scientific Criticism?

The development of the method of exegesis over time has been influenced by the conviction that the goal of biblical interpretation is the determination of the meaning of biblical texts in their original contexts through a comprehensive examination of all the features of that text (textual, literary, linguistic, historical, traditional, redactional, rhetorical, and theological) and all determinants of its potential meaning.

These texts, however, and the contexts within which they were produced always had a further *social dimension* as well. The New Testament, upon which we shall concentrate in this study, contains witnesses to a *social phenomenon,* the gathering of a community around Jesus of Nazareth conceived as Israel's Messiah and society's Savior. This event, in turn, is comprehensible only within a larger constellation of social, economic, political, and cultural currents.

Consider the Gospel of Luke, for example. Luke begins his story about Jesus and the Jesus movement by situating it within a specific social matrix involving not only Jesus' family but world and local events (Luke 1–3): reigning Roman emperors and their provincial governors (Caesar Augustus; Quirinius, governor of Syria; Tiberius Caesar; Pontius Pilate, governor of Judea); local rulers (Herod, tetrarch of Galilee; his brother Philip, tetrarch of Iturea and Trachonitis; Lysanias, tetrarch of Abilene); the Jewish high-priestly family of Annas and Caiaphas; imperial enrollment (census) for the sake of taxation and population census; Joseph of the lineage of David; Mary, his betrothed, related to Elizabeth and Zachariah; Jesus' birth witnessed by detested shepherds and heavenly messengers; and the parallel birth and prophetic activity of Jesus' relative, John the Baptizer. Luke makes explicit what is implicit throughout the New Testament: the lives, ministry and message, action and impact of Jesus and his followers are all rooted in a matrix of social and cultural forces. As these factors are essential to the narrating of this story and the concretizing of its implications, so the study of these factors is essential to a grasp of the story's meaning. The social historian Moses Finley makes a similar point in his study of the world of the Greek hero Odysseus (1979:74).

> The subject of heroic poetry is the hero, and the hero is a man who behaves in certain ways, pursuing specified goals by his personal courage and bravery. However, the hero lives in and is moulded by a social system and a culture, and his actions are intelligible only by reference to them. That is true even when the poet's narrative appears to ignore everything and everyone but the heroes.

The New Testament writings, however, are hardly devoid of social detail. Our texts regularly refer to social relations (Jews/Greeks, male/female, slave/free, and so on), social groups and organizations (Pharisees, Sadducees, disciples, the Twelve, the Herodian court, Pauline and Petrine circles), social institutions and events (taxation, census, temple and sacrificial system, family and kinship lineages, and such), political rule (Augustus, Tiberius, Herod, governors, chief priests, and others), and patterns and codes of social behavior (Torah observation, purity codes, honor and shame codes, familial and friendship relations, patron-client codes, and much else).

The contexts of these texts and the patterns of behavior they describe, likewise, are social contexts, environments involving pluralities of persons and groups, and shaped by economic and societal conditions, structures, and processes. In their language, content, structure, strategies, and meaning, then, these texts presuppose, encode, and communicate information about the social systems in which they were produced and to which they were a response.

Furthermore, texts, whether literary or oral, also were designed to serve as vehicles of social interaction.

These communications and their meanings, however, are not readily intelligible to modern readers today, who are far removed from these texts and their contexts in terms of historical, geographical, and cultural distance. These biblical writings are texts written in foreign languages (Greek, Hebrew, Aramaic) encoding elements of cultures and social systems alien to those of most modern readers. Further, the New Testament, like the Old Testament and other writings of antiquity, consists of documents written in what anthropologists call a "high context" society where the communicators presume a broadly shared acquaintance with and knowledge of the social context of matters referred to in conversation or writing. Accordingly, it is presumed in such societies that contemporary readers will be able to "fill in the gaps" and "read between the lines."

It is obvious that in order for the modern reader to understand such writings there must be clarity on what knowledge about the social system is presupposed in these ancient texts or what "reading scenarios" are appropriate for discerning the meaning communicated by these alien texts. This need for apposite reading scenarios is necessary so that modern readers avoid the twin errors of an anachronistic and ethnocentric reading of ancient Mediterranean texts, that is, reading into the text information from some present social context rather than comprehending the text in accord with its own contemporary social and cultural scripts (Malina 1990a, 1990b, 1991a). The acid test to be applied to all the conclusions of literary and historical critics of the Bible is to ask the questions, Did people really think and act that way and, if so, why? Do these exegetical conclusions square with ancient patterns of belief and behavior? Are the statements of the text as suggested by exegetes in fact coherent with the actual perceptions, values, worldviews, and social scripts of the communities in which these texts originated? Or, put more generally, does the Bible really mean what it is taken to say?

Accordingly, in order for us to grasp the meanings communicated in these ancient texts and to investigate the social dimensions of both these texts and their contexts, the conventional historical-critical method must be outfitted with a social-analytic capacity. Practitioners of the historical-critical method have generally shown an interest in the social features of the ancient world and in the references to these features contained in biblical texts and the numerous sources of additional information (classical texts, documents, inscriptions, papyri, coins, art, architecture, and the like). This information concerning the social "realia" of the ancient world is often presented, for example, in the commentaries on the biblical writings and discussed in the lexica and other reference works.

In addition, historical critics have also shown a keen interest in social history, in developments and changes over time in the social organization of the biblical communities, their varying relations to the larger society, and in developments of larger society itself of which the biblical communities were a small and generally vulnerable minority.

In the twentieth century, the development of the methods of source criticism, form criticism, and tradition criticism, in particular, promoted an intense interest in the social setting or *Sitz im Leben* of traditions and their tradents and the manner in which traditions undergo modification under changing social conditions. However, a refined social-scientific skill in conceptualizing and analyzing these various settings, such as Oscar Cullmann (1925) called for years ago, was remarkably slow in materializing. Redaction critics, likewise, have shown an interest in the social circumstances influencing authors and their compositional strategies. But here too the consideration of these circumstances seldom advanced beyond random hunches to a comprehensive analysis of the interrelation of texts and social contexts. In both instances these subdisciplines of the historical-critical method failed to fulfill their own promises.

Moreover, the general orientation of New Testament scholarship until late in this century has been shaped by an idealist tradition that assumes that "the determining factors of the historical process are ideas and nothing else, and that all developments, conflict and influences are at bottom developments of, and conflicts and influences between, ideas" (Holmberg 1980a:201). Scholars operating on the basis of this "idealist fallacy" (Holmberg) find little need or reason for considering the possible interrelation of ideas and material-social structures (as noted by Gager 1975; Holmberg 1980b, 1990a; Elliott 1981; Meeks 1983a). Thus theological issues and interests have tended to predominate in a manner that confuses theological ideas with historical realities and reduces social and cultural data to illustrative "background" information considered helpful but not essential to the interpretive task.

Furthermore, a typically modern assumption that it was *individual* geniuses (mostly male) who were the producers of texts and the motors of change has undermined consideration of the *circles and groups* responsible for the transmission of traditions and production of texts (Elliott 1981:4–5) and the several circles of *females* who figured prominently in the story of Jesus (Fiorenza 1983; Wire 1991). Until recently, this "big man" view of history has prompted more interest in the "chief figures of the New Testament" (Jesus, Paul, John) than in the communities they represented or on whose support they were dependent.

Moreover, historical criticism, given its preoccupation with specificity and detail, has been successful in identifying much of what can by termed "that" or "what" information but less insight into the questions concerning "how," "why," and "what for." Thus, in addition to details about specific individuals, events, or institutions, what might be known about how ancient society was organized and operated? How were attitudes, expectations, values, and beliefs shaped by the natural and social environment? How did shared social and cultural knowledge provide the basis for shared meanings and effective communication? How and why did conceptualizations of God and community vary over time according to changing circumstances? How were the religious beliefs and symbolizations of the followers of Jesus organized into coherent sets or "universes" of meaning? How were they employed to advocate and justify deliberate responses to specific and changing social situations? Why and under what conditions were they modified over time? What were the social as well as ideational features of Christianity that made it a viable, appealing, and ultimately enduring phenomenon? Finally, how and under what conditions might the self-understandings, strategies, and commitments of the early Christians in their social context provide models and motivation for believers today in their engagement in, and perhaps also confrontation of, the structures of the Leviathan of modern social life?

What was needed, therefore, beyond the collection of independent historical and social facts, was a way of envisioning, investigating, and understanding the interrelation of texts and social contexts, ideas and communal behavior, social realities and their religious symbolization, belief systems and cultural systems and ideologies as a whole, and the relation of such cultural systems to the natural and social environment, economic organization, social structures, and political power.

Such a perspective requires the cultivation of a "sociological imagination" (C. W. Mills) and a social-scientific methodology that has heretofore been a minimal element of the historical-critical enterprise with its limited focus on historical, literary, and ideational issues. Even the exegetical interest in "social history" has as yet failed to advance beyond the collection of social data and their "description" to a comprehensive set of methods for social-scientific interpretation. Nor has this interest in social description yet taken into account the distinctive social and cultural scripts characteristic of ancient Mediterranean and Near Eastern societies which differentiate the culture and perspectives of ancients from those of modern interpreters and Bible readers.

Thus it has gradually become apparent to a growing number of scholars across the globe that historical criticism has proved inadequate to the task of a comprehensive interpretation of the Bible and the biblical world. Many biblical interpreters now agree that a more sophisticated method is required for examining and understanding the biblical writings as products of and responses to their social and cultural environments. The time has arrived for moving beyond social description to social-scientific analysis.

Out of this realization, biblical scholars have turned to the social sciences with the intention of expanding and improving the historical-critical method as an adequate tool of interpretation. This has led to the development of what has been variously termed the "social-scientific study of the Bible and the biblical world," and, in relation to biblical texts, "sociological exegesis," "materialist reading," or, preferably, "social-scientific criticism."

Social-scientific criticism complements the conventional historical-critical analysis of the Bible by enabling it (historical criticism) to do what it is intended to do: to yield an understanding of what authors said and meant within the contours of their own environment. Social-scientific criticism does so with an orientation and method whose questions and objectives, modes of analysis and processes of explanation, are guided and informed by the theory, methods, and research outcomes of the social sciences.

The social sciences form that branch of modern science which specializes in the study of human societies, social systems and their component parts, social behavior, and social processes. It is the study of social relations (of two or more individuals), groups, institutions, organizations, patterns of recurrent social behavior and interaction, entire social systems and their interrelated parts, and social phenomena in general. A *social system* involves a group or groupings of persons who are engaged in some type of collective behavior and who are related to one another in various ways. *Social phenomena* are regularities of behavior imposed on individuals by a social system. The social sciences involve the study of those recurrent patterns of human behavior which enable and allow people in groups to live with one another in a meaningful and productive manner. Such socially shared patterns of behavior make living in a group tolerably predictable (hence somewhat unpredictable), tolerably secure (hence somewhat insecure), and tolerably sustainable (hence somewhat unsustainable). These routinized patterns of behavior are transmitted and internalized through the process of primary and secondary socialization. This process of socialization includes the providing of a comprehensive plausibility structure according to which patterns of society and sociality are invested with meaning and legitimacy.

In the social sciences, attention can range from a focus on the social roles and statuses of individuals in groups to wider issues of social relations, formations of groups, organizational structures, social stratification, to the social or societal system as a whole, the interrelation of its component sectors (economic, social, political, cultural [including belief systems and ideologies]), and its interaction with other social systems. That is, social-scientific study can range from micro-level to macro-level areas of analysis.

14

Moreover, social-scientific study can adopt either a synchronic or a diachronic point of view. That is, attention can be directed either to one constellation of social phenomena and their interrelationships at a given time and place. Or attention can be directed to features of social movement and change over the course of time. Cross-cultural analysis, moreover, can be undertaken with a comparison and contrast of the salient features and contours of societies either close or distant in terms of time, space, and material conditions.

Inasmuch as cultural anthropology (United States) and social anthropology (Great Britain) have developed a body of theory and methods for studying preindustrial societies and groups foreign to the cultures of the modern researchers, it is this branch of the social sciences that can contribute much to the development of a method useful for investigating the social features and formations of the biblical world. In addition, social-scientific criticism looks to and incorporates the research of other related disciplines, such as ethnology, history (economic, social, military, political, legal, and the like), economics (ancient economics, economic anthropology), classics, geography, archaeology, political science (and comparative politics), semiotics (perception and communication theory; sociolinguistics), sociology and its various orientations (structural functionalism, conflict theory, exchange theory, symbolic interactionalism, phenomenological and ethnomethodological theory) and subdisciplines (the sociologies of language and literature, of knowledge, of religion, of sectarianism, and the like), and finally theology and its subdisciplines.

Social-scientific criticism thus expands the historical-critical method by adding to its repertoire of foci and operations the perspectives, theory, models, and research of the social sciences in order to enable the reader of the Bible to understand and interpret more adequately the biblical texts and their contexts. It is not a method for creating or manufacturing new data but for viewing and understanding all the data available within a new and more comprehensive theoretical framework. It thus serves a "heuristic" function, that is, it aids discovery (heuristic, from the Greek *heuriskein*, "to discover") and thereby the stimulation of imagination and the expanding of conceptual horizons.

Faced with a plethora of already extant social information, the exegete and the historian of biblical antiquity, with the help of the social sciences, seek to construct appropriate questions for interrogating the sources in some systematic fashion so as to penetrate into the regularities of ancient social and cultural life and thereby to gain a clearer understanding of the whos, hows, whys, and wherefores of the related behaviors and beliefs of the biblical peoples, their relation to the world around them, and the perceptions, experiences, and hopes that so captured their contemporaries and eventually changed the course of history.

These "appropriate questions" involve inquiry into traces of repeated behavior and then the institutionalization of such behavior that provides evidence of pivotal values around which social life is organized; inquiry into the environmental and social conditions accompanying social diversification in first-century Palestine and the diaspora and the formation of multiple factions and coalitions; asking about the agents, causes, processes, and consequences of conflict; looking for the "bigger social picture" of the social system as a whole, the interrelations of Roman colonialism and native populations, the symbiotic relationship of cities and countrysides, the bearing of economic and political arrangements on Jewish and Christian group formations; or asking about the social and cultural scripts that establish the frameworks of meaning and the communication thereof, of plausibility structures (how and why words, beliefs, and actions "make sense"), and the universes of discourse reflected in the literary and artistic productions of the communities under investigation; or inquiring as to the various factors that conditioned the production and circulation of the biblical writings and their capacity as effective instruments of social interaction. In brief, this amounts to posing questions that enable us to grasp as concretely and comprehensively as possible the manifold social features of ancient life, the correlations of conceptuality and experience, and the intersections of biography and history.

3
The Recent Emergence of Social-Scientific Criticism

The systematic application of the research, concepts, and theory of the social sciences to biblical exegesis and the study of its social world emerged as a programmatic methodological enterprise in the 1970s. This effort at a self-conscious merger of exegesis and the social sciences was not without notable predecessors who had seen the value of the social sciences for biblical interpretation, let alone the generations of scholars vitally interested in the social context of the biblical documents.

Here particular mention might be made of the pioneering work of such scholars as sociologist Max Weber (1864–1920) and his study of ancient Judaism (1919); historian Ernst Troeltsch (1865–1923) and his work *The Social Teaching of the Christian Churches* (Ger. ed. 1911; first ET 1931); biblical scholar William Robertson Smith (1846–1894) and several of his successors in Old Testament interpretation; New Testament exegete and historian Adolf Deissmann (1866–1937) and his concern for the everyday world of ordinary people as illuminated by papyri and inscriptions; Shailer Matthews (1863–1941), Shirley Jackson Case (1872–1947), and Donald Riddle and the "sociohistorical" method typical of their American "Chicago School"; Karl Kautsky (1854–1938) and his classic Marxian analysis of the "foundations of Christianity" (1953 [1908]); and the work of social historian Edwin A. Judge (1960a, 1960b, 1972). The significance of these scholars and their work as precursors of, yet distinguishable from, current social-scientific critics in their perspectives and methods has been amply noted and assessed (Funk 1976; Rogerson 1978; Hynes 1981; Wilson 1984; Lang 1985; Schütz 1982:1–23; Morgan and Barton 1988; Osiek 1989:265–67; Rodd 1990).

In this period prior to the 1970s, the work of the biblical scholars among those just mentioned showed some awareness of the relevance of the social sciences then in vogue for the issues confronted by exegetes and ancient historians. But this awareness did not lead to any systematic attempt to lay out the principles and procedures of a specifically social-scientific analysis of the Bible and its environment. The full range of reasons for this has yet to be adequately examined, but certain possibilities come to mind. Exegetes in general remained preoccupied with the literary and formal features of texts, and with their ideational and theological content to the exclusion of their social dimension. A prevailing existential and individualistic "theology of the word" hermeneutic, furthermore, was on the whole inhospitable to social and societal concerns. Proponents of "new literary criticism" and textual structuralism, moreover, had begun to advocate an exclusive focus on the narrative world of the text in isolation from the actual world of its authors and audience. Accompanying these trends was also a debilitating isolation of the academic disciplines and the lack of training in and familiarity with the social sciences on the part of most biblical scholars, or, where there was familiarity, the fear of reductionism, that is, reducing religious matters to solely social phenomena, thereby ignoring the essentially theological character and content of the biblical writings. Finally, even within the social sciences a repudiation of the cross-cultural comparative method in the early part of this century (Murdock 1980:28–33) temporarily obscured a method that social-scientifically oriented exegetes and historians might have used to their advantage. Here, too, even within the social sciences themselves, balkanization, "provincialism, and mutual distrust reigned supreme" (Murdock 1980:32).

Whatever factors may have been operative, it is only since the 1970s that efforts were undertaken to engage the social sciences and to lay out the theoretical and methodological foundation for a specifically social-scientific study of the Bible and its environment.

By no means is every book or article with the term "social" or "sociological" in its title an exercise in social-scientific criticism as described here. Furthermore, as might be expected of any new method, there is as yet no universal consensus regarding presuppositions, procedures, or even nomenclature. However, studies concerned in any way with "social" matters can generally be classified into five main categories (expanding on Smith 1975):

1. First, there are investigations of *social realia* (groups, occupations, institutions, and the like), generally to illustrate some feature or features of ancient society but with no concern for analyzing, synthesizing, and explaining these social facts in social-scientific fashion. Joachim Jeremias,

Jerusalem at the Time of Jesus (1929/1968); Frederich C. Grant, *The Economic Background of the Gospels* (1926/1973); Stephen Benko and J. J. O'Rourke, eds., *The Catacombs and the Colosseum: The Roman Empire as the Setting of Primitive Christianity* (1971); Abraham J. Malherbe, *Social Aspects of Early Christianity* (1977); and John E. Stambaugh and David L. Balch, *The New Testament in Its Social Environment* (1986) exemplify this interest in social description.

2. Other studies take this interest in social issues a step further by integrating social with economic and political phenomena to construct a *social history* of a particular period or movement or group. Here, however, the conceptual framework is predominantly historical rather than social-scientific, generally with an eschewing of social theory and models. Typical examples of this social-historical approach include Martin Hengel, *Judaism and Hellenism* (1974); Robert M. Grant, *Early Christianity and Society* (1977); Luise Schottroff and Wolfgang Stegemann, *Jesus von Nazareth— Hoffung der Armen* (1978); Willy Schottroff and Wolfgang Stegemann, eds., *The God of the Lowly: Socio-Historical Interpretations of the Bible* (Ger. ed. 1979/ET 1984); Wolfgang Stegemann, *The Gospel and the Poor* (1984); and Helmut Koester, *Introduction to the New Testament* (1982).

3. The social organization of early Christianity in terms of both the social forces leading to its emergence and its social institutions has been the focus of yet another kind of study. The work of Gerd Theissen, John Gager, and Wayne Meeks, which will be discussed below, illustrates this approach, which includes *the deliberate use of social theory and models.* (Meeks describes his work as "a social description of early Christianity" [1983a:1], but in actuality he organizes and interprets his material with the help of social-scientific concepts and models.)

4. Still other studies interested in the social and cultural environment of the New Testament have concentrated on *the social and cultural scripts* influencing and constraining social interaction. This focus, illustrated in the work of Bruce Malina, Jerome Neyrey, and other members of the Context Group, as discussed below, is carried out with the deliberate use of explicit theory and models of the social sciences, particularly those of cultural anthropology.

5. Finally, the research, theory, and models of the social sciences have also been enlisted in the *analysis of biblical texts.* The work of Fernando Belo on Mark (French 1974/ET 1981), John H. Elliott on 1 Peter (1981/ 1990), Norman Petersen on Philemon (1985), Philip Esler on Luke-Acts (1987), Halvor Moxnes on Luke (1988a), and the recent collection of es-

says on Luke-Acts (Neyrey 1991a), as well as several other studies mentioned below, illustrates this aspect of social-scientific criticism.

These various approaches need not be considered antithetical or mutually exclusive but are best seen as complementary. It is clearly the case that analyses of a specifically social-scientific nature are enormously indebted to the extensive body of materials gathered by studies that are primarily descriptive in nature. However, when we consider the theoretical and methodological orientations of this diverse body of research, it is necessary to distinguish in general between approaches involving strictly "social description" with no attempt at social-scientific explanation and those employing social-scientific theory and models for the express purpose of social-scientific explanation so that we are clear about the aims of such research. This point has been aptly made by John Gager (1979:175), who notes that

> any *sociological* approach to early Christianity will be concerned with *explanations* of social facts, whereas a *social history* need not concern itself with anything more than a *description* of the relevant social data. The two approaches are certainly not antithetical. But neither are they identical. Each of these tasks is necessary *and* distinctive [emphases added].

Some scholars, moreover, exhibit an obvious sociological imagination in the execution of their work but little self-conscious reflection on the social theories guiding their analyses. Here the stimulating work of Edwin A. Judge comes to mind. This, however, is in contrast to other scholars who quite consciously discuss the social-science theory, models, and procedures that guide their research and inform their conclusions. When discussing below the presuppositions that inform the task of social-scientific criticism, I shall comment on the nature of such conceptual models and the importance of their clarification.

The current resurgence of interest in the social dimensions of the Bible and its environment has been abundantly chronicled.[1] In our discus-

---

1. Surveys of exegetical research along social-historical and social-scientific lines, some with critical discussion, as well as critical reviews of publications are variously offered by Gewalt 1971; Smith 1975; Gager 1979; Harrington 1980; Scroggs 1980; Rodd 1981; Gager 1982; Schütz 1982; Segalla 1982; Best 1983; Edwards 1983; Hollenbach 1983; Moxnes 1983, 1988c; Tidball 1983; Bassland 1984; Cahill 1984; Elliott 1984a, 1984b; Gallagher 1984; Osiek 1984a, 1984b; Richter 1984; Wire 1984; Aguirre 1985; Elliott 1985; Goell 1985; Kümmel

sion we shall restrict attention, where possible, to actual social-scientific studies. Although a significant body of research along social-scientific lines has been produced by Old Testament scholars (Gottwald 1983b), our attention will focus on their New Testament counterparts.

The story starts in the year 1973, when Gerd Theissen, at the time a German lecturer (*Privatdozent*) at the University of Bonn, published the first of several social-scientifically oriented studies, "Wanderradikalismus: Literatursoziologische Aspekte der Überlieferung von Worten Jesu im Urchristentum" (1973; ET: "Itinerant Radicalism: The Tradition of Jesus Sayings from the Perspective of the Sociology of Literature" [in Gottwald and Wire 1976:84–93]). In this essay the tradition of the Jesus sayings and their transmitters is analyzed for the first time from the perspective of a sociology of literature which "studies the relationships between texts and human behavior," behavior that is both socially "typical" and "socially conditioned." Theissen focuses on the *transmitters* of the Jesus tradition and the correlation between their social circumstances and behavior, on the one hand, and the content of their teaching, on the other. The startling conclusion is that the radical teaching of Jesus concerning homelessness, separation from family, and renunciation of wealth is a radical ethos that his followers themselves embodied and practiced. This ethos was not some unachievable ideal, as exegetes had often maintained, but rather a praxis of itinerant charismatics who as "outsiders" lived on the margins of Palestinian society.

This merging of exegesis and "sociology of literature" and this thesis burst upon the exegetical scene like a bombshell. No longer could the familiar but domesticated words of Jesus' radical ethic be treated in isolation from the material and social conditions of Jesus' time or from the

1985; Malina 1985c; Stowers 1985; Tidball 1985; Tiryakian 1985; Venetz 1985; Elliott 1986b, 1986c; Mosala 1986; Richter 1984; Scroggs 1986; Stenger 1986; Barbaglio 1988; Domeris 1988; Harrington 1988; Morgan and Barton 1988; Moxnes 1988d; Reis 1988; Alvarez-Valdes 1989; Botha 1989; Horsley 1989; Osiek 1989; Schmeller 1989a:7–49, 1989b; Schöllgen 1989; Taylor 1989, 1990; Holmberg 1990a; Nineham 1990; Rodd 1990; Van Staden 1991a, 1991b; Barton 1992; Duhaime and St.-Jacques 1992; Garrett 1992; Osiek 1992a, 1992b. Barbaglio (1988) presents a rich historical survey of relevant studies from 1900 to the 1980s. Morgan and Barton (1988) and Theissen (1992:1–29) situate the resurgence of exegetical interest in the social sciences within broader social and intellectual currents. Aguirre (1985), Holmberg (1990), Osiek (1992a, 1992b), and Theissen (1992:1–29) offer both overviews and perceptive assessments.

social circumstances and specific interests of Jesus' followers. This creative marriage of historical criticism and a more rigorous sociological perspective brought a new and refreshing perspective to bear on an old, dog-eared issue that was decisively to expand and improve the exegetical enterprise. Historical criticism was undergoing a promising transmogrification.

Theissen followed this groundbreaking study with a spate of further provocative articles and monographs, including *Soziologie der Jesusbewegung* (1977a; ET: *Sociology of Early Palestinian Christianity* [1978]), essays on Corinth and the social setting of Pauline Christianity (ET collection in 1982), and other essays both theoretical and analytical (collected in *Studien zur Soziologie des Urchristentums* [1979a; 2d. expanded ed. 1983] and *Social Reality and the Early Christians* [1992]).

In general, Theissen's research was provocative less for any social-scientific method introduced than for the sociologically motivated questions he addressed to the texts. His investigations have focused attention primarily on the social conditions, problems, and strategies of the Christian movement as it originated in Palestine and then spread throughout the Roman world. His study of the Jesus movement in Palestine from a structural-functional sociological perspective attempts to assess the "failure" of the Jesus movement there to overcome the causes of social tension and conflict as well as the conditions of its greater success beyond Palestine. In regard to Paul's mission at Corinth, fresh attention is given to the social issues and tensions at stake: conflict among the Corinthian Christians related to their differing social rank (1974b, 1975c), problems of social integration (1974a), and concern over apostolic legitimation and support (1975a, 1979b). In addition to reflections on social history and methodology (1974c, 1975b, 1979a, 1979b; 1982:175–200), Theissen has also proposed a mode of "psychological exegesis" (1983b) informed by theory on learning, psychodynamics, and cognition, and demonstrated its application to aspects of Pauline texts and thought. His recent work on "Lokalkoloritforschung" (1989b; ET: *The Gospels in Context: Social and Political History in the Synoptic Tradition*, 1991) examines the influence of local geo-cultural conditions and perspectives on the formulation of Gospel traditions and texts. Critiques of Theissen's work include Malina 1979; Stegemann 1979; Elliott 1986c:10–25; Horsley 1989; and Schmeller 1989a.

Theissen's studies range widely in their subject matter but in general demonstrate how fresh questions concerning the correlation of belief and behavior, ideas and material conditions, theological symbols and social relations can generate new perspectives on old texts and revisions of previously "assured results."

One year later, following Theissen's first essay along social-scientific lines, the Portuguese priest and New Testament scholar, Fernando Belo, in 1974 published his *Lecture matérialiste de l'évangile de Marc: Récit-pratique—idéologie* (2d ed., rev., 1975; ET 1981: *A Materialist Reading of the Gospel of Mark*). In this work Belo examined the social setting, narrative, and ideology of Mark from a Marxian perspective and laid the theoretical and methodological foundation for a "materialist reading" (as opposed to "idealist reading") of biblical texts in their social contexts. The characteristic concern of this "materialist reading" is the reciprocal relation of material conditions and ideological formulation, that is, the interplay between the social conditions prevailing in Palestine at the time of Jesus and the interpretation of the Jesus story as presented in the Gospel of Mark and as shaped by the author's political perspective.

Belo begins his "materialist reading" of Mark with an examination of the economic, social, and cultural circumstance of first-century Palestine and surrounds his study with theoretical discussions of the concept of the Asiatic mode of economic production and an essay on materialist ecclesiology. The methodological complexity of the work, combining features of structuralism (L. Althusser) with linguistic and social semiotics (F. de Saussure, R. Barthes, J. Derrida), makes for particularly dense reading and may account for its initial minimal impact (see the brief but insightful criticism of Myers 1988:468–69; for critical assessments, see also Poulat et al. 1975; Vanhoye 1977; Scroggs 1983). The subsequent publications of Belo's colleagues, Michel Clévenot (1976) and George Casalis (1978), were intended as popularizations of this approach for the general reader and as introductions to materialist approaches to the Bible in general. The German systematician Helmut Gollwitzer presents the fullest discussion to date on the theoretical underpinnings of this effort as a theological enterprise (1980; cf. also Füssel 1983). Kuno Füssel (1987) offers a concise and illuminating application of the method to an interpretation of Mark 11:7—13:2 and the social and ideological implications of Jesus' temple critique.

In the following year, 1975, an American professor at Princeton University, John Gager, published *Kingdom and Community*, an analysis of the social forces shaping Christianity and accompanying its growth from its millenarian beginnings to its triumph under Constantine. It was Gager's work that first brought the potential of the marriage of exegesis and the social sciences to the attention of the English-speaking world. Using

23

a variety of models from social-science research, he attempted to explain the nature and development of Christianity as a millenarian movement, the social function of its myths, Christian missionary activity as a response to the nonoccurrence of the anticipated end of the world, Christian means for legitimating power and controlling internal deviance, and the relatively rapid success of Christianity as a dominant religion in the pagan Roman world. Appreciative but also critical assessments of this work, more comprehensive in historical scope than those of Theissen and Belo, were quickly registered in the journal *Zygon* (13 [1978]) by D. L. Bartlett, J. Z. Smith, and D. Tracy; see also Malina 1986c.

In 1980 Howard Clark Kee of Boston University, stimulated by his experience of the work along social-scientific lines taking place in a graduate theological seminar in Berkeley, California (1975–76), published his *Christian Origins in Sociological Perspective*. Calling attention to the range of social-science research helpful for both historical reconstruction of Christian origins and the interpretation of its literature, Kee covered such issues as Christian self-definition, leadership and authority, cult and myth, and the social functions of the New Testament writings. While the study established its author as an advocate for the use of the social sciences, the precise nature and application of these methods remained for others to clarify.

Two works in progress in the mid-1970s eventually were published in 1981. One was the study by Bruce Malina of Creighton University, *The New Testament World: Insights from Cultural Anthropology*. The other was my analysis of 1 Peter under the title *A Home for the Homeless: A Sociological Exegesis of 1 Peter, Its Situation and Strategy* (reprinted with a new introduction and modified subtitle in 1990). As the subtitles of these works indicate, the former drew on the research of Mediterranean anthropology to understand the cultural scripts of New Testament society, while the latter turned to the sociological research on sectarian movements to decipher the situation and strategy of a particular New Testament writing. Malina, taking his cue from anthropological "culture area" study, locates the New Testament communities within the general culture area of the Circum-Mediterranean (for societies comprised, see Murdock 1980:46–47, and for analyses, the several studies cited in the Bibliography). Malina identifies and illustrates typical perceptions and "pivotal values" of ancient Circum-Mediterranean culture (such as honor and shame embedded in males and females, respectively, dyadic rather than individual personality, perception of "limited good," kinship and marriage structures, and the controlling codes of purity and pollution) and convincingly shows how these cultural patterns are implied and expressed in the biblical writings. The result of this study, the first of its kind, is a fascinating introduction to the alien yet coherent culture of the Bible and to the perceptions and values that governed the interactions of its characters. A truly seminal work, it has alerted exegetes to the valuable resources of Mediterranean anthropology and has spawned a host of subsequent studies of typical biblical cultural traits.

My study, on the other hand, built on the theory advanced by Robbin Scroggs (1975) that early Christianity constituted a messianic sect emerging within first-century Judaism. Finding in 1 Peter evidence of such a sectarian mentality, I employed the sociological model of the sect (as developed particularly by Bryan Wilson) to clarify the precarious situation of Asia Minor Christianity as portrayed in 1 Peter and the rhetorical strategy of the letter's response. In the opinion of one reviewer, "both in the method it outlines and defends, and in the substance of the interpretive results, this is a landmark in biblical studies" (Kee 1982:285). Later in this present volume (pp. 70–86) we will consider this approach to 1 Peter in greater detail when I use this text to illustrate the procedure for investigating a biblical text in social-scientific fashion.

Two years later, in 1983, Wayne Meeks of Yale University published his ambitious work, *The First Urban Christians: The Social World of the Apostle Paul.* Following upon a previous study of the sectarian contours of Johannine Christology (1972), a brief sketch of approaches to the social world of early Christianity (1975), and a study of social boundary marking in the Pauline communities (1979), Meeks's 1983 work offers a panoramic view of the Pauline churches, their social constituency, organization, governance, rituals, and correlated patterns of belief and behavior. Employing, like Theissen, the sociological perspective of structural functionalism, he explores such questions as the bearing of an urban environment on Christian social experience and theological reflection, social stratification within society and Christian communities, modes of Christian organization, self-identification, and governance; the social function of ritual; and the reciprocal relation between patterns of belief and patterns of behavior. Critical assessments hailed it as both a milestone in Pauline study and an example of the methodological issues yet to be sorted out in this nascent phase of social-scientific criticism (Elliott 1985a; Malina 1985c; Stowers 1985; Theissen 1985; Tiryakian 1985).

The works discussed thus far may be considered seminal for the many studies along social-scientific lines that have followed in their wake. Theissen, Belo, and Gager were the first to bring a self-consciously socio-

25

logical perspective to bear on the early church as well as a range of useful concepts for examining and ordering the material. Malina introduced the importance of cultural anthropology for analyzing the Mediterranean context of the biblical communities. My work on 1 Peter demonstrated the utility of the sectarian model for the analysis of a particular text and its strategy as well as the central importance of the household as social basis and symbol for early Christianity. Finally, Meeks showed how a variety of social-scientific concepts could be employed in reconstructing a more comprehensive picture of the social world of Paul and the chief issues involved in the formation of the Pauline communities.

These studies, however, also illustrate the wide diversity of methods, theoretical models, and foci of this initial phase of social-scientific research. The works of Theissen, Gager, and Meeks, for instance, focused generally on broad or narrower expanses of the Christian movement over time. Belo and I concentrated on particular New Testament writings, a focus also typical of the later instructive study of Norman Petersen on Philemon, *Rediscovering Paul* (1985), and other studies mentioned below.

Malina illustrates yet another focus, namely, attention to the typical Mediterranean cultural scripts encoded in the writings of the New Testament. A notable feature of his work is the clarification of all relevant models followed by their application and testing at the hand of the biblical evidence. His aim is the comparison of the social locations, modes of thought, and behavioral patterns differentiating the biblical communities, on the one hand, and their modern interpreters, on the other, so as to facilitate a culturally sensitive reading of the ancient biblical texts. Work in this vein includes Malina's studies on the social world implied in the letters of Ignatius of Antioch (1978b), on Paul and the law in social-scientific perspective (1981b), on Jesus as a "reputational" rather than "charismatic" figure (1984a), on the Gospel of John as product of a countercultural group (1985a), on poverty as the lack of social connections and not merely of material provisions (1986b), on religion as not an independent institution of ancient social life but embedded in the institutions of kinship and politics (1986b), a critique of Gager's theory of cognitive dissonance as incompatible with the perceptions and experience of Mediterranean society (1986c), and analyses of ancient codes of hospitality as implied in 3 John (1986d), of patron-client relations as a model for prayer (1980) and for portraying the God-human relationship (1988b), of Mark 7:1-22 as interpreted by a sociological conflict model (1988a), and of the differing ancient and modern perceptions of time with ramifications for contemporary notions of eschatology and apocalyptic (1989b).

In a second major study, in 1986, *Christian Origins and Cultural Anthropology*, Malina presented numerous models for discerning the social locations and strategies of biblical communities and authors, the cultural scripts governing social behavior, the social function of rituals, and the ideological perspectives of authors ancient and modern. The theory and methods presented here extend earlier discussions of why and how the social sciences are necessary for biblical interpretation (1982, 1983a, 1983b). In 1988 Malina coauthored with Jerome Neyrey a study of Matthew's presentation of Jesus and his interaction with disciples and opponents as investigated and illuminated by models derived from deviance and labeling theory. In the words of the authors, this is a study in Christology not "from above" or "from below" but "from the side," from the vantage point of Matthew's contemporary readers and modes of interaction typical of ancient Mediterraneans.

In the early 1980s two studies of Harold Remus (1982, 1983) explored the pagan-Christian conflict over miracle in the second century with attention to the manner in which the sociology of knowledge clarifies the contrasting perspectives and common strategies involved in this conflict. Norman Petersen's work on Philemon (1985) constituted yet another creative merging of disciplines, in this case new literary theory and the sociology of knowledge. In this work new perspectives are brought to bear on both the narrative and social worlds of the text and its author. Paul's Thessalonian correspondence, in turn, was analyzed by Robert Jewett (1986) through the combination of rhetorical and social-scientific criticism. He illumines both the situation and the strategy of the letters and the underlying problem in Thessalonica of "millenarian radicalism."

Meanwhile, on the other side of the Atlantic, social-scientific studies were also under way, even if their reception there generally was not as enthusiastic as such work in the United States. In 1977 Klaus Berger of the University of Heidelberg, in his *Exegese des Neuen Testaments,* called attention to "new impulses" from related disciplines that could enrich the conventional historical-critical method. One of these impulses concerned the social sciences and the "sociological questions" they could prompt (1977b:218–41). Unfortunately, this section of his interdisciplinary survey seems to have found little resonance among his German-speaking colleagues, and, equally unfortunately, the work was never translated into English. With few notable exceptions, most continental scholars remained in the more conventional track of "social history" (Schottroff and Stegemann 1979, 1980; Stegemann 1981/1984; Lampe 1987).

Nevertheless, here and there, the path forged by earlier scholars eventually attracted other explorers. Already in 1977, for instance, the German exegete Alfred Schreiber used sociological research on group dynamics to propose a hypothetical reconstruction of the social interaction between Paul and the Corinthians, its phases, features, and consequences. Bengt Holmberg of Sweden (1980) applied Weberian models of domination to analyze the levels of power in the Pauline churches and the process by which presumed "charismatic" authority was institutionalized and rationalized. A survey and analysis of the information on role and status in the Pauline literature enabled Aloys Funk of Austria (1981) to draw instructive conclusions regarding typical expectations and social scripts in the Pauline communities. In the Netherlands, Sjef van Tilborg (1986) examined the sayings of the Sermon on the Mount as "ideological interventions" in the context of prevailing and changing social actions, rites, and institutions of first-century Palestine.

In Great Britain, Stephen Barton explored the specifically social function of the symbols of the cross and resurrection in the writings of Paul (1982, 1984). Francis Watson (1986) applied a "sociological" perspective to the question of Paul's view of Judaism, the law, and the Gentiles in Galatians and Romans with particular focus on the social roots of the apostle's views and his efforts in these writings to legitimate a mission to gentile Christian communities not bound by the Mosaic law. Philip Esler (1987) similarly examined Luke-Acts and its theological program as an instance of ideological legitimation and cast many of the distinctive foci of this writing into a fresh and revealing light. Margaret MacDonald (1988), concentrating on the Pauline and deutero-Pauline literature, studied the strategies, process, and stages of early Christian institutionalization.

In Norway, Halvor Moxnes of the University of Oslo, following studies on the social role of meals in the Christian community (1987) and the significance of honor/shame values in Romans (1988b, 1988c), analyzed the Gospel of Luke in the light of ancient economic relations (1988a; cf. also 1991a, 1991b) and thereby brought a new perspective to bear on the Lukan portrait of the Pharisees as "lovers of mammon" and the social basis of Luke's "economy of the kingdom." Fellow Norwegian Torrey Seland (1987), stimulated by Malina's work on Jewish coalitions and factions, contested the sectarian character of earliest Christianity and argued instead for its identity as a Jewish faction.

One example of collaboration along social-scientific lines is *The Context Group,* an international team of scholars who have been working together since 1986. Formally organized in 1989 on the basis of previous associations in the professional societies of the Society of Biblical Literature and the Catholic Biblical Association of America, this group of scholars has been meeting annually to plan, mutually discuss, and evaluate their individual and collaborative work in social-scientific exegesis. The results have been numerous and wide-ranging. The correlation between the symbolizations of personal bodies and social bodies, in accord with the theory of anthropologist Mary Douglas, has been studied by John Pilch in regard to the problem of leprosy (1981) and by Jerome Neyrey in relation to the body symbolism of 1 Corinthians (1986a). Neyrey has also studied the social function of the Jewish purity codes and their critique in the Christian writings (1986a, 1986b, 1988d) as well as the manner in which witchcraft accusations in early Christianity served as mechanisms of social conflict (1986a, 1986b, 1988d). His 1988 work on the Gospel of John (1988b) addresses the crucial issue of the ideological dimension of the New Testament literature and exposes the "ideology of revolt" typical of the Fourth Gospel. His study *Paul, In Other Words: A Cultural Reading of His Letters* (1990b) gathers together ten essays along social-scientific lines. The contribution of the social sciences to Jesus studies has been reviewed by Paul Hollenbach (1983, 1986, 1989). The economic dimensions of the teaching of Jesus and the Jesus tradition have been analyzed by Douglas Oakman (1986; see also 1987, 1991). Leland White (1986b) used Douglas's model of grid and group to explain the righteousness/honor code underlying Matthew's Sermon on the Mount. Richard Rohrbaugh has discussed the theoretical issues concerning the concept of "class" in the study of early Christianity (1984), the use of models in social-scientific analysis (1987a), and the "social location of thought" as a heuristic device in New Testament interpretation (1987b). John Elliott, in addition to the work discussed above (1981, 1982, 1986a), presented extensive methodological critiques of the work of Meeks (1985b) and Theissen (1986c), a bibliographical introduction to the phenomenon of patronage and clientism in early Christian society (1987a), an examination of evil eye belief, practice, and its social dimensions from biblical to modern times (1988, 1990b, 1991a), and a study of the symbolical function of "household," "temple," and meals in Luke-Acts (1990, 1991c). Illness, healing, and the health care system in antiquity have been treated extensively by John Pilch (1985, 1986, 1988c; see also his lucid *Introducing*

29

the Cultural Context of the New Testament [1991]). K. C. Hanson has published a three-part study on the Herodians and Mediterranean kinship patterns (1989a, 1989b, 1990). A major collaborative effort of the Context Group, *The Social World of Luke-Acts: Models for Interpretation,* edited by Neyrey, was published in 1991. Its thirteen chapters comprise essays on the theory governing the reading of biblical texts, the pivotal values of honor and shame, first-century personality, labeling and deviance theory and models for interpreting conflict, the tensions of city and countryside, sickness and healing, temple and house as contrasting social and symbolical realities, patron-client relations, ritual of status transformation, dining ceremonies, the symbolic world of Luke-Acts, and the social location of its implied author. The text summarizes much social-scientific research relevant to biblical studies in general and is specifically designed for use of students and nonspecialists. The most recent product of such collaboration is the *Social-Scientific Commentary on the Synoptic Gospels* by Bruce J. Malina and Richard L. Rohrbaugh (1992), and *A Dictionary of Bible Values* under the coeditorship of John Pilch and Bruce Malina is in press.

Members of the Context Group publish regularly in the journal *Biblical Theology Bulletin,* which also includes occasional Readers Guides introducing the general reader to various aspects of early Christian society in social-scientific perspective (21/1 [1991]; 21/2 [1991]; see also the issue on Mediterranean gender classifications (20/2 [1990]).

Other works with a social-scientific orientation and with a broad societal and/or diachronic focus include the interdisciplinary studies of Dimitris Kyrtatas (1987), Anthony Blasi (1988), and Richard Horsley (1985, 1987, 1989) and several essays (Saldarini 1991; Stark 1991; White 1991; Wire 1991) contained in a volume on the Matthean community edited by David Balch (1991).

In the area of social studies of the New Testament from a feminist perspective, two monographs in particular call for mention: Elisabeth Schüssler Fiorenza's *In Memory of Her* (1983) and Antoinette Wire's 1990 study, *The Corinthian Women Prophets.* Both focus on neglected or ignored aspects of the role and status of women in the early church. Fiorenza, employing a social-historical approach, marshals a wealth of evidence for tracing the undulating and often contradictory fate of women in the early church from their central place in the proclamation of Jesus to their gradual resubordination and marginalization at the hands of the patriarchally ordered male establishment. A lack of clarity concerning the operative theory and models here (such as the confusion of inclusivity with "equality" or the implausible shifts assumed in the elimination and then reemergence of patriarchy) has raised doubts about the validity of her idyllic "Camelot" (Babcock 1984) view of Christian beginnings. But this is balanced by the new impulse she has given for a more critical assessment of male-produced texts and their ideological legitimations of male control (for critical assessments, see Babcock 1984; Elliott 1984; Malina 1984; Heine 1990; Stegemann 1991b). As of this writing, the verdict is not yet in on Wire's work. But it is clear that her merging of the disciplines of new rhetoric, exegesis, and models drawn from the social sciences has provided new windows for viewing the Christian women of Corinth, their self-understanding, values, behavior and function as prophets, tensions with Paul, and position in society.

These various studies are but a selective representation of the many recent publications with a social-scientific focus. Bengt Holmberg's *Sociology and the New Testament* (1990a) offers a competent, if overly cautious, recent overview and appraisal of exegetical studies with a social-historical or sociological (but not anthropological) orientation.

In this survey of research produced by exegetes and historians along social-scientific lines, mention should also be made of sociologists who have subjected social dimensions of early Christianity to social-scientific analysis. In 1983 a German sociologist with a self-admitted "love-hate" relationship to the Bible and the church, Anton Mayer, published a "sociology of the New Testament" with the title *The Censored Jesus,* which was intended as a broadside against the theological establishment and its manipulation of the New Testament. Its aim was an exposé and critique of the progressive "deproletarianization" of Jesus within the church beginning already in New Testament times. Through a comparison of lower-class (for example, Mark, Revelation, James) and upper-class (Paul, Luke) New Testament writings, and an examination of vocabulary, syntax, style, and thematic content as indicators of class interests, Mayer first attempts to establish the "proletarian" origins of Jesus. Then he traces the subsequent process of the "deproletarianization" of Jesus and his message in the Christologies within and beyond the New Testament. The social consequences of this trend, according to Mayer, are seen in the Christian programs and ideologies of sexism, anti-Semitism, and capitalism.

An American sociologist of sectarian and cult movements, Rodney Stark (1986), arrived at different conclusions concerning the class basis of early Christianity. He distinguished between sects and cults. Sects, according to Stark, are the result of schism within a conventional religious body and are aimed at increasing the tension between this otherworldly group and society. Cults, on the other hand, are characterized by Stark as thoroughly new movements with new beliefs violating prevailing religious norms. Cults, in contrast to sects, tend to attract the more educated and privileged strata of the general population skeptical of or disillusioned with conventional religions. Stark argued that early Christianity developed from a Jewish sect (before the death of Jesus) to a new cult after Jesus' death and his claimed resurrection and became a "new religion" with a new set of beliefs and culture. As a new cult it attracted its greatest number of recruits from "the middle and upper classes."

Another American sociologist, Anthony Blasi, holding degrees in both sociology and theology, applied a content analysis to the Q stratum of the Jesus tradition, its tradents, audience, and public beyond the Q communities, in order to provide a coherent picture of this community, its roles, status, and prescribed behaviors (1986; see also his 1988 and 1990 studies mentioned above).

In their methodologies, scope, foci, and degree of articulation of method and models, these studies along social-scientific lines illustrate the diversity that still characterizes this nascent method. Yet, on the whole, they signal a new methodological advance whose time has surely come. The growing number of such studies marks a significant modification and supplementation of the conventional historical-critical method which will no doubt shape a new generation of biblical scholarship.

This body of research illustrates two possible foci of the social-scientific study of the New Testament and its context. One focus of research with a social-scientific orientation has been the social and cultural conditions, features, and contours of early Christianity and its social environment. In this case, the social sciences are used to construct theories and models for collecting and analyzing data that illuminate salient features of ancient Mediterranean and early Christian society and culture: the structure and interrelated components of the imperial social system as a whole and the interdependency of ecological, economic, social, political, and cultural domains (or, more accurately, from an ancient Mediterranean perspective, the interrelation of public and private spheres, the areas governed by political [*polis*] and kinship [*oikos*] relations); the interrelated societal domains of a particular geo-cultural region such as Palestine or Asia Minor; the dynamics of the Roman colonialism of Palestine and its deleterious effect upon the Jewish population (military presence, taxation, land appropriation, and the like); prevalent forms of social organization at varying societal levels; dominant institutions and patterns of social behavior and interaction; patterns of faction formation and competition; occasions and processes of conflict; social roles, status, and societal stratification; cultural core values and their relation to group interests, goals, and norms of behavior, and their elaboration in cultural scripts; alternative belief systems, traditions, rituals, worldviews, and ideologies and their propagation by specific groups, classes, and factions of society; and the social conditions and consequences of conflict and change within Christianity and society over time.

While the evidence for such study remains fairly constant—though, of course, new material and literary evidence are always enthusiastically welcomed—it is the social theory and models determining the investigation that turn mere phenomena into social facts and provide the possibility for social-scientific examination and explanation.

A second dimension of social-scientific criticism is specifically exegetical in nature and directs primary attention to the interpretation of biblical texts. Here social-scientific criticism supplements the other methods of critical interpretation with the aim of elucidating the structure, content, strategy, and intended rhetorical effect of the text within its social context. The text is analyzed as a vehicle of communication whose genre, structure, content, themes, message, and aim are shaped by the cultural and social forces of the social system and the specific historical setting in which it is produced and to which it constitutes a specific response. Here the theory and methods of literary, semiotic, social, historical, theological, and ideological analysis are combined to understand the text as an encodement of information concerning the social system, as containing a message that is both ideational and pragmatic in nature, and as a medium of social interaction.

These two foci are not mutually exclusive but complement each other. Analysis of biblical texts requires attention to the research and conclusions regarding their social contexts. These contexts, in turn, are further clarified by the evidence supplied by the texts. As a social-scientific study of the biblical world provides the social and cultural maps for locating and interpreting the biblical documents, so a social-scientific criticism of the biblical documents provides the detail by which the broader delineations of social history are corroborated and critiqued (Elliott 1981/1990:7).

The progress that this approach to the New Testament represents is not simply an accumulation of more social data but a significant advance in its *explanation*. Analyses of Palestine in the first century, for instance, have shown how a constellation of ecological, economic, social, political, and cultural factors resulted in tensions that favored the rise of a reformist movement such as that spearheaded by Jesus of Nazareth. Studies of the

Jerusalem temple as the economic, social, political, and cultural nerve center of Jewish life and of its discriminating purity regulations have explained why this institution and its controlling aristocracy are the focus of the unrelenting critique of Jesus and his followers. Comparative analysis of this temple on the one hand and the private household on the other and the differing modes of social and economic relations they embody has demonstrated why the household and its familial relations rather than the temple and its stratifications along purity lines were favored by Jesus and his followers as the most apt image for spelling out the nature of social relations in the kingdom of God. Consideration of typical modes of authority (traditional, charismatic, legal-rational) has explained why in early Christianity charismatic leaders emerge but are eventually replaced with "officeholders" in the process of social institutionalization.

Sectarian models have accounted for the stress found in the New Testament on such features as communal identity, cohesion, and ideological commitment. They have helped to explain the apparent tension between a Christian emphasis and even exaggeration of differences that distinguish Christians and "outsiders," on the one hand, and a concerted quest for recruits among these outsiders, on the other. Sectarian models have also proved useful in explaining the simultaneous stress on Christianity's *continuity* with Israel as the heir of its promises, on the one hand, and its social and ideological *disengagement* from its Jewish parent body, on the other. Tensions within Christian groups have also been clarified as not simply contentions over ideas but as disagreements over the more mundane and practical issues of cultural and class differences as well. The writings of Paul and Luke have been shown to focus on the issue of legitimacy not simply to assert the validity of the Christian message but also to secure the status of the Christian community and the authority of its individual leaders.

Consideration of the paramount value placed on honor and shame and its symbolization in males and females, respectively, has helped to explain the various values, roles, tasks, and even places associated with males and females in the New Testament, the "macho" character of male behavior, and the dread of gender confusion. The prevalent notion of "limited good" (according to which all the resources of life are considered in scarce and limited supply) has helped to explain the antagonistic character of Mediterranean society, the dread of envy and the evil eye mentioned by Jesus and Paul, and the further perception of the wealthy as inherently thieves and robbers. Study of this evil eye belief has shown what Jesus and Paul implied with their evil eye accusations and how these accusations were used to affirm communal values, discredit opponents, and draw social boundaries. Analysis of patronage and clientism has demonstrated how this institution shaped the web of social relations and obligations among Jews, Gentiles, and Christians and how it provided an experiential model for the conception of God as ultimate patron and benefactor, Jesus as mediating broker, and Christian prayer and worship as the expressions of grateful clients. Studies of ceremonies such as meals and rituals (including baptism and eucharist) have demonstrated the social function of these activities in delineating group identity, articulating group values and loyalties, and demarcating group boundaries.

Through research on these and other aspects of ancient social life we have made important strides toward the understanding of early Christianity as an all-encompassing social, cultural, and religious phenomenon. By including within the historical-critical method a sociological perspective and methodology, we have made significant advances in exposing and interpreting the social conditions, constraints, capacities, and consequences of the biblical writings and the social forces that shaped the societies and communities within which these writings were produced. Such study has thus achieved a more comprehensive contextualization of the biblical writings and a more accurate understanding of the correlation of religious thought and belief with the realities of ancient everyday life. Finally, by clarifying the difference between the historical conditions, social institutions, and cultural scripts proper to the biblical writings and those proper to the modern interpreter, social-scientific criticism provides a clearer framework for the reading and use of the Bible and biblical history by the contemporary student.

4
The Method in Operation: Presuppositions

Clarity regarding theories, models, and methods is a characteristic concern of social-scientific criticism. It will therefore be appropriate to precede a description of its method with an initial clarification of the major presuppositions informing and guiding its procedures. The following discussion of key presuppositions will also touch on more general issues concerning method and models.

More than four decades ago, Rudolf Bultmann enunciated what has since come to be regarded as a fundamental methodological axiom of biblical interpretation: exegesis without presuppositions is impossible. Positively put, exegesis, as science in general, is informed and guided by the presuppositions and research paradigms of the investigator and his or her social group (Kuhn 1970). Presuppositions are not to be denied but to be clarified and then tested on the basis of the data examined. Bultmann, to be sure, was speaking of *theological* presuppositions. But the axiom holds for all forms of presuppositions, including sociological and anthropological presuppositions. Social-scientific criticism is particularly concerned with adding these latter presuppositions to those which require clarification, preferably at the outset of an investigation.

Social-scientific presuppositions, like theological presuppositions, pertain to three aspects of the interpretive enterprise: the interpreters, the objects to be interpreted, and the method of interpretation. The following constitute some of the chief presuppositions of the social-scientific critical endeavor, though not all may be shared by all practitioners. For earlier discussion, see Elliott 1981/1990:9–13; Malina 1983a; and Rohrbaugh 1987b.

1. First, social-scientific critics presuppose that all knowledge is socially conditioned and perspectival in nature. This is in continuity with

the conclusions of Karl Mannheim (1936) and subsequent sociologists of knowledge (for example, Berger and Luckmann 1967). This applies to both the knowledge of the *interpreter* and that of the *authors and groups* under examination. Acknowledgment of this fact in no way eliminates a concern for relative objectivity on the part of the investigator or efforts to restrain freewheeling subjectivity. But it does reject the possibility of complete objectivity as an unsustainable "myth of objective consciousness." Total objectivity is illusory. There is no such thing as "immaculate perception" (Carney 1975:1). Both interpreters and authors of ancient texts have specific temporal, psychological, social, and cultural locations that affect general perceptions and constructions of reality (Rohrbaugh 1987b). "Reality" itself, in fact, as the sociology of knowledge has taught us, is a social construction (Mannheim 1936; Berger and Luckmann 1967). This also does not mean that such conditioning eliminates the possibility of creative thought and expression on the part of the ancient authors whose work we study. But it does imply that such expression is always shaped by the "constraints of history," the constraints of personal and social experience and of frameworks of plausibility that communicators share with their contemporaries. Without this sharing of social and cultural patterns of thought and behavior, no *communication* would even be possible. Nor does this presupposition dispute or eliminate the claims to truth (assertions about the nature and destiny of all things) made by either ancient authors or modern interpreters as totally relativized and compromised in their persuasive power. But it is to recognize that even such truth claims are entertained and expressed in a language, conceptual frame of reference, and social context that determines their plausibility and persuasiveness.

Accordingly, the social-scientific critic at the outset of an investigation considers *her or his own personal and social location* and its influence on the interests, presuppositions, preunderstandings, theories, methods, and goals of the analysis. On the sociology of knowledge and its relevance to the study of early Christianity, see K. Berger 1977b:240–41; Remus 1982; and Petersen 1985.

2. This implies that the method of analysis must include means for *distinguishing and clarifying the differences between the social location of the interpreter and the social location of the authors and objects to be interpreted.* "Social location" here is an encompassing category involving all the factors that influence one person or group, their socialization, experiences, perceptions, frameworks of rationality, and views of reality. This would include such factors as gender, age, ethnic roots, class, roles and

status, education, occupation, nationality, group memberships, political and religious affiliations, language and cultural traditions, and location in place and time.

Awareness of such influencing factors on knowledge and perception sensitizes readers of the Bible to the fact that things can look different and assume different significance to persons of different genders, ethnic origins, and classes, let alone to persons of different cultures. There may be a great difference, for instance, between the manner in which Jesus' blessing of the poor (Luke 6:22-23; cf. Matt 5:3-9) is understood by a crowd of destitutes, on the one hand, and a modern middle- or upper-class Western congregation, on the other. One's social location generally makes one sensitive or insensitive to nuances in the text that are not fully spelled out. This essential point is justifiably stressed by proponents of various liberation theologies.

Being mindful of such social and cultural differences, modern readers may become more like "respectful visitors" to a foreign culture and avoid the posture of "ugly Americans" forcing their language, patterns of thought, and values on the "primitive" natives. Moreover, it alerts readers who wish to understand "what's really going on here" to familiarize themselves with the encompassing social and cultural scripts according to which these "natives" communicate meaning. Accuracy in translation and interpretation of the information provided by "foreigners" is determined by the extent to which interpreters can put themselves in the alien's sandals and imaginatively relate to his or her total situation. Through such effort the student of the Bible will be aided in avoiding those twin pitfalls of an anachronistic and ethnocentric reading of ancient texts and environments.

One of several means available for distinguishing ancient biblical and modern conceptual points of view is the conventional distinction in anthropology between "emic" and "etic" information and perspectives. This distinction is analogous to the linguist's distinction between "phonemic" (pertaining to speech sounds) and "phonetics" (the science of speech sounds considered as elements of language). In anthropological field study, the term *emic* identifies information provided by the "natives," accounts of phenomena as perceived, narrated, and explained according to the experience, folk knowledge, conceptual categories, ratiocinations, and rationalizations of the indigenous narrators in their historical, social, and cultural locations.

The term *etic*, on the other hand, identifies the perspective of the external investigator or interpreter as determined by his or her different social, historical, and cultural location, experience, and available knowledge and the conceptual categories used for analyzing these same phenomena (M. Harris 1976; R. Feleppa 1986).

Emic descriptions and explanations are those given by the natives themselves from their experience and point of view. They describe *what* and *how* the natives thought but not *why* they thought so rather than otherwise. *Etic* constructs, by employing cross-cultural comparison and by taking into account a full range of factors not mentioned or considered in native reports, attempt to explain how native concepts and perceptions correlate with and are influenced by a full range of material, social, and cognitive factors. They seek to explain *why* the native thought and behaved so and not otherwise.

When this is applied to the study of the Bible and its social setting, it means that the biblical writings, along with ancient texts and artifacts in general, provide the modern student with sources of emic data. The modern investigator or commentator, on the other hand, categorizes and interprets this data according to etic concepts, theories, models, knowledge, and canons of contemporary science. Thus the ancient "native" speaks of rulers such as "kings" and "ethnarchs," whereas the modern investigator classifies both within the more comprehensive and abstract category of "government." The former is concerned with "fathers," "mothers," "sons," and "daughters"; the latter considers these as instances of "roles," "statuses," and the "kinship system." All commentaries and scientific studies of the Bible and the ancient world work with emic data but necessarily shift to etic categories when they seek to explain evidence from one culture with social and cultural constructs drawn from their own time.

Such a distinction between emic and etic perspectives acknowledges the fact that different cultures may have different ways of construing, describing, and explaining "reality" as they experience it. At the same time, it recognizes the integrity of differing perceptions and descriptions of reality as each is shaped by specific bodies of shared knowledge and social location and, accordingly, the limits of all translations.

Thus in the biblical world the cause of illness is often traced to demon possession or disrupted social relations (an emic account), whereas moderns would regard illness as "disease" possibly attributable to bacterial inflection and/or poor sanitation or the like (an etic view). Sensitivity to this emic view of the biblical "natives" provides the interpreter with a different set of questions to consider in analyzing ancient stories of illness: What personal agent (human or demonic) may be thought responsible for the illness? What accusations are being made and against whom?

What efforts toward social discrimination or social reconciliation are being made? Who has the power to heal (that is, repair social as well as physical disorder) and how is this effected? See, for example, the illness and healing stories of Matt 12:22-30/Mark 3:22-27/Luke 11:14-23 or John 9.

In the distinguishing of emic and etic perspectives, interest shifts from decrying the "primitive" (and "uninformed") views of the native to the questions of how and why the natives found this explanation plausible and cogent. What differing frameworks of knowledge and construals of reality make both emic and etic explanations viable?

Such a distinction also allows the modern interpreter the freedom to employ different schemes of classification and more inclusive categories of analysis. This facilitates cross-cultural comparison, generalization, and abstraction through the use of a consistent set of terminology and an inclusive range of empirical categories. Thus the investigator might examine the ancient materials for evidence of such things as "institutions," "roles," "faction groups," or "social stratification," even though these terms and concepts are foreign to the language and conceptual world of the ancient "natives" and their writings. The use of these etic concepts will allow the interpreter to put data into a larger social perspective and to discern connections that may not have been so readily apparent or of interest to the "native" informer.

Useful comparisons and contrasts of aspects of ancient and modern cultural systems in general are offered by Malina 1986e, 1989a, 1989b, 1992a; Malina and Neyrey 1988:145–51; Hanson 1989a, 1989b, 1990; Pilch 1991a, 1991b, 1992a, 1992b; and Rohrbaugh 1991a, 1991b.

3. For the clarification of the differences between the contexts of ancient texts and of modern readers, and for the further clarification of the properties and relations of ancient social and cultural systems, *theory and models* likewise have always played an essential role, whether or not this is actually acknowledged (Carney 1975; Malina 1981a:16–23; Meeks 1983a:2–7; Elliott 1986c). As Meeks explains (1983a:5), theory and models are essential tools of interpretation and "without interpretation there are no facts. The pure empiricist would drown in meaningless impressions. . . . To collect facts without any theory too often means to substitute for theory our putative common sense. . . . The advantage of an explicitly stated theory is that it can be falsified."

Theories and models, in fact, even dictate which competing sets of materials are to be examined and regarded as "relevant data" for an investigation in the first place. Thus, to study Pauline Christianity as an urban phenomenon, for instance, involves a theory that Paul operated primarily in urban locales and a conceptual model of what constituted a city in antiquity and hence what materials are relevant for investigation (Sjoberg 1960; Rohrbaugh 1991a, 1991b). Since theory, conceptual frameworks, and models determine both the materials to be examined and the process of interpretation, it is imperative that they be stated at the outset of an investigation so that both researcher and reader are clear about precisely what is being investigated, which data are relevant, and what criteria of evaluation of the investigation are applicable.

Since conceptual models are thus crucial tools in the interpretive task, it is essential that we be as clear as possible about their nature and function. In the comments that follow, I draw upon an earlier discussion of models and method in my volume *Social-Scientific Criticism of the New Testament and Its Social World* (1986b:3–9). For further reflection on models, see M. Black 1962; W. Buckley 1967; E. Laszlo 1969; T. F. Carney 1975; I. G. Barbour 1974; and J. Richardson 1984.

In *Myths, Models, and Paradigms*, Ian Barbour (1974:6) defines a "model" as "a symbolic representation of selected aspects of the behaviour of a complex system for particular purposes." In more comprehensive terms, Bruce Malina (1983b:231) adds that a model is "an abstract simplified representation of some real world object, event, or interaction constructed for the purpose of understanding, control, or prediction." As conceptual instruments of analysis, models are used in all the sciences and can vary in size and complexity and degree of abstraction from concrete scale models to highly abstract theoretical models. As Thomas F. Carney notes (1975:8),

> a model is something less than a theory and something more than an analogy. . . .A theory is based on axiomatic laws and states general principles. It is a basic proposition through which a variety of observations or statements become explicable. A model, by way of contrast, acts as a link between theories and observations. A model will employ one or more theories to provide a simplified (or an experimental or a generalized or an explanatory) framework which can be brought to bear on some pertinent data.

The difference between a model and an analogy or metaphor lies in the fact that the model is consciously structured and systematically arranged in order to serve as a speculative instrument for the purpose of organizing, profiling, and interpreting a complex welter of raw material.

41

Models are variously classified (Inkeles 1964:28–46; Buckley 1967:7–40; Richardson 1984:1–18). Carney (1975:9–11) distinguishes between isomorphic and homomorphic models. The former are built to scale, such as globes or model trains. The latter are cast in abstract terms and reproduce only selected salient features of an object, which itself may even be an abstraction such as a social system, a bureaucratic form of government, or a kin group.

Conceptual models are a major subset of such homomorphic models and are those generally employed in the social sciences. Here they are used to analyze and interpret the properties of social behavior, social structures, and social processes. From observation and then generalization about the regularities perceived in human behavior, concepts and theories are formed to account for such regularities and patterns of interrelated properties. Models are used explicitly to articulate these theories and test their validity.

Models are part of the human process of perception and understanding. All perception, as we have already noted, is selective and constrained psychologically and socially. Models are the cognitive maps or lenses through which we perceive, filter, and organize the mass of raw material available to our senses. Thus there is no choice as to whether or not we use models. "Our choice," notes Carney, "rather lies in deciding to use them consciously or unconsciously." For scientific analysis which presumes standards of accountability and evaluation, including exegesis and historical criticism, this point is of crucial importance. Although the use of models in other sciences is self-understood, we still find many exegetes and historians reluctant to "fess up" to the implicit theory and models guiding their research. As a result, "conclusions" arrived at by intuition and "educated guesses" remain inaccessible to testing and verification.

On the other hand, social-scientific critics seek to expose at the outset those models according to which they view and attempt to understand the social material under investigation. The sociologist Matilda White Riley (1963:14–15, 26–29, and 33–77) offers an extensive discussion of the use of models in social-scientific analysis and their role in the research process. She notes that, on the whole, models may serve two main types of research objectives, one that is exploratory in nature and one that aims at testing certain hypotheses. Exploration is undertaken when additional information is required for constructing an adequate model. This she calls the "descriptive approach." This approach is most familiar to exegetes and historians who engage in what they call "social description." For many, this seems to imply a procedure that is more "objective" and less theory-laden than one that aims at testing hypotheses set out in advance. In actuality, however, the difference is one of degree, not of kind. Both objectives are generated by conceptual models that embody theories. Hypothesis testing simply operates with more highly defined theories, whereas in exploration and description the model remains skeletal and the theory it embodies, less articulated.

"Exploratory studies," Riley advises (1963:68), "are not to be confused with raw empiricism, with fact-gathering that is unrelated to sociological theory," for, even in this process, researchers are already selecting from the universe of phenomena, and "this selection tends to reflect the theory he has in mind, the kinds of assumptions which are implicit, if not explicit, in the original conceptual model." Thus "social description" is no safe haven for exegetes and historians leary of theory or murky about models. Even exploration cannot proceed without models as guides. It would be an inconclusive expedition indeed in which the explorers could not or would not say why they went, why they chose the routes they followed, why they collected what they did, and what the trophies tell us of the culture of the world they explored.

In everyday life, models come in an assortment of shapes and sizes, from the maps in our glove compartments and the globes in our studies, to scale models of trains or mannequins in department stores, to blueprints of houses or shopping centers, to patterns of husband-wife or parent-child relations, to the experimental and analytical models employed in the various fields of science. These models have no ontological status but are only cognitive maps. A map is not the territory itself but a simulated pattern of selected and prominent features of the terrain (hills, valleys, lakes, roads, sites) to provide the traveler with an overview of a territory and thus to acquaint him or her with the lay of the land.

Social models are "maps" that organize selected prominent features of social terrain such as patterns of typical social behavior (for instance, at work, at meals, in law courts), social groupings (kin and fictive kin groups, factions, coalitions, patrons and clients, and such), processes of social interaction (for example, buying and selling, oral and written communication, feuding, making contracts), and the like. Such models alert the social traveler to typical and recurrent patterns of everyday social life in given times and places.

Models do not create material evidence; rather, they provide the means for envisioning relationships and patterns among the evidence.

Moreover, because they are abstract theoretical constructs, they can be altered as the terrain (geographical or social) shifts in level of abstraction or as more information comes into view.

Conceptual models, in addition to their cognitive value, have an important *heuristic* function. They can serve as vehicles for discovery, trying out new points of view, asking new sets of questions. More specifically, they prompt the search for patterns, correlations, and coherency among masses of material. With an abstract model of a symphony or fugue in mind, a listener will be better prepared to appreciate a coherent and structured piece of music amid the myriad of notes. With a model of ancient dining etiquette in mind, a reader of the New Testament will be more sensitive to the complex social dramas involved in the biblical dining scenes.

Besides serving as tools of exploration of new territory, models have an essentially explanatory function. Exploration is undertaken when an area of study is perceived as vague or incomplete so that more information is required first to articulate a working model. At this early stage of investigation, a provisional model is used to gather and describe data. Once a satisfactorily complete model is developed and tested, it can then serve as a means for testing broader theories or hypotheses and their explanatory power. Thus a well-tested model of ancient urban organization and settlement can be used to test a theory of the spatial location of certain classes or occupational groups within the city and explain patterns of association and interaction. A model of ancient kinship structures and of the reciprocal relations typical of families, for example, can help explain the reason why the family rather than the temple figured so prominently in Jesus' teaching on the familial character of the kingdom of God and his stress on the values of generosity, mutuality, and giving without counting the price (Elliott 1991b, 1991c).

In the case of social phenomena, models serve as "cognitive maps" for observing, categorizing, comparing, and synthesizing elements of social data and drawing generalizations and conclusions about their salient, recurrent social features. They provide the means for seeking, analyzing, and explaining repeated behaviors, social roles, institutions, patterns of stratification, modes of social interaction and conflict, and correlations between beliefs and behavior, social organization, and worldviews.

As in the case of methodological presuppositions, furthermore, the choice is not whether to use conceptual models, as we have already noted, but whether or not we use them consciously. Every imagining or reconstructing of "how it actually was back then" necessarily involves the use of some conceptual model. "If we use them unconsciously," Carney warns (1975:5), "they control us, we do not control them."

The selection of models is determined by the types of social phenomena to be analyzed and explained and by the theories that the researcher wishes to explore. Appropriate and adequate models are models that have been constructed on the basis of empirical evidence and that are coherent with both the theory and the material under examination (Malina 1983a:130–31). Thus, to examine the social dynamics involved in the biblical accusations of Jesus as an agent of Beelzebul or of Paul as an evil eye possessor, some larger conception of that society as what anthropologists call a "witchcraft society" is useful. Familiarity with the salient features of such societies will help in clarifying the conditions, premises, procedures, and consequences that these accusations of social deviance involve (Malina and Neyrey 1988; Neyrey 1990b:181–217; Elliott 1988, 1990b, 1991a, 1992). Analyses of biblical comments concerning poverty and wealth, on the other hand, will be aided by models of traditional, peasant societies and their perception of "limited good" and their related evaluation of all wealthy persons as "thieves" who have benefited at the expense of the poor (Malina 1981a:71–93, 1987; Hollenbach 1987). On the whole, models useful for analysis of the Bible and its environment, Malina (1982) suggests, should have the following six features: (a) A model should facilitate cross-cultural comparison of the social situations of the interpreter and the object interpreted; (b) its level of abstraction should be general enough to display similarities that allow comparison; (c) it should fit a larger sociolinguistic framework for interpreting texts; (d) it should be designed from experiences that match as closely as possible empirical evidence from the biblical world; (e) the meanings it exposes should be culture-specific and thus possibly irrelevant yet comprehensible to modern Westerners; and (f) the quality of the model should conform to social-scientific standards.

The utility of particular social models, in turn, is evaluated both by the degree to which they articulate the theory and the hypotheses of the researcher and by the degree of their interpretive and explanatory power. This means that what counts is their capacity for revealing and explaining the relations among social phenomena and the regularities and peculiarities of social behavior.

Thus, for an analysis of the social (and not simply ideational) dimensions of the disputes between Jesus and his opponents as recorded in the Gospels, a model of a typical disputing process in Mediterranean society will be useful for exposing and explaining the salient aspects of the social

interaction taking place: the issues at stake (including the status and reputation [honor] of the conflicting partners), the process of the dispute
(challenges to honor and their response), and its outcomes (Jesus' successful defense of his honor) (Malina and Neyrey 1988, 1991d:97–122).
Likewise a study of the healing stories at the hand of a model of illness/
wellness as understood in traditional agrarian societies will focus attention
on the issue not of disease (modern Western model) but on that of illness
as rupture of community (ancient model). It will help explain why, when
Jesus engages a paralytic (Mark 2:1-12) or a hemorrhaging woman (Mark
5:25-34), his healing action involves a pronouncement of the forgiveness
of sin or the blessing, "Go in peace"—both restorations of physical and
social wholeness (Pilch 1981, 1985, 1986, 1989, 1991c). Similarly, a study
of many of the New Testament writings as products of sectarian consciousness will prompt the investigator, at the hand of a sect model, to
consider issues previously unexamined (strategies employed for promoting group consciousness, enhancing group esteem, group cohesion, and
group commitment). It will provide a means of explaining previous interpretive problems such as why Christian groups engage in recruitment of
outsiders while simultaneously urging distinction from outsiders or claim-
ing continuity with Israel while also distinction from Judaizers (Elliott
1981/1990).

Models vary in scope and complexity according to the phenomena to
be interpreted. A map of the entire Mediterranean region is a macro-
level model in contrast to a micro-level map or model of, say, the city
of Jerusalem, Antioch, Ephesus, or Rome. As one map might model the
topographical features of a region, other maps might model the region's
natural resources, its cities, or its system of roads and transportation.

In the social sciences, models are used to analyze and explain various
aspects of social phenomena at varying levels of abstraction or scope, from
person-to-person relations to entire social systems. As tools in cross-
cultural study, they facilitate macro-level comparisons and contrasts of
salient features of one culture with another, such as that of the ancient
Circum-Mediterranean with modern Western society, or modern Middle-
Eastern cultures, or preindustrial and postindustrial societies, and so
forth.

Other models at a lower level of abstraction can be used to conceptualize and explain the social scenarios and cultural scripts that govern the
economic and social interactions (including literary communications) of
particular groups in particular geo-cultural locations of the Circum-
Mediterranean, its cities and countrysides. At a still lower level of abstrac-

tion, models are used to conceptualize and interpret patterns of group formation, organization, and governance; rituals and ceremonies; schemes and hierarchies of values; processes of economic and social exchange; family and kinship structures; structures of personality; and the like.

Where certain phenomena are not manifest or explicit but are conceivably latent or implied in a text or a social scene, a well-tested model embodying a hypothetical construct of a total or "ideal" set of properties and relations allows inferences to be drawn concerning the unexpressed elements. Such use of theoretical models is basic, for instance, to the procedure of text critics attempting reconstructions of fragmentary texts on the basis of intact documents or archaeologists seeking to imagine the entirety of a building or settlement when only partial material evidence is at hand. From comparative evidence gathered elsewhere, models of complete texts or settlements are assembled that enable text critics or archaeologists to hypothesize the location and extent of fragments of data. When technology becomes available, these hypotheses can then be tested and verified or falsified, as with the aid of infrared lighting in the case of texts or aerial photography in the case of settlements. In the latter instance, layout patterns of ancient settlements invisible to the eye at ground level become apparent from an airplane at a higher elevation, as in the case of aerial archaeology (Rieche 1978).

The situation is similar in the case of social and cultural models. For example, what is invisible to the reader of a single text or even corpus of texts in regard to social institutions or pivotal cultural values (for example, patron-client relations, dining conventions, or values of honor/shame or hospitality) becomes apparent at a higher level of abstraction when an entire cultural area and its literary and artistic products are taken into consideration or when cross-cultural comparisons are undertaken.

Social-scientific criticism uses such theoretical constructs to hypothesize the relation of social properties and the patterns of culture in the material under investigation. These models are means by which the interpreter makes explicit the scenarios presumed in texts under study and the social codes embedded but not explicitly mentioned in these texts. They provide the means of generating insight. Such insight is concerned not with supposed "laws" of social relations but with *repeated patterns* of belief and behavior and their accompanying social conditions, scripts, and consequences.

All interpreters (including exegetes, historians, and social scientists) can only imagine the social constellations of ancient or alien societies with

47

the help of such models. Only by clarifying, explaining, and justifying one's imaginings or conceptual constructions of social reality can the interpreter expose them to verification and/or critique by others and thereby contribute to an actual advance in understanding.

An explicit presentation of theory and models is necessary and valuable on three scores. First, explicit presentation of the theory and models that guide the analysis makes it possible for the reader to follow an investigation and to evaluate its conclusions. Second, when theory and models are set out clearly at the outset, the fit of the data to the models can be more easily ascertained and the model's interpretive capacity more easily assessed. Third, clearly exposed theory, models, and research design make it possible for other researchers to employ and experiment with the method and the models for themselves rather than submit to the impressive but inimitable inspirations of the "great teacher." Studies that are actually social-scientific in nature explicate social theory and models and thereby gain in clarity, testability, persuasiveness, and the possibility of emulation. For a list of models that have proved useful in the study of the New Testament and its environment, see Appendix 4.

4. Social-scientific criticism involves a process of logic that is neither exclusively deductive (from model to material) nor inductive (from material to hypothesis) but inclusive of both in a procedure characterized as "abduction."

Abduction (also called "retroduction") "is a process in logic of the discovery procedure of working from evidence to hypothesis, involving a back-and-forth movement of suggestion checking. In this process two pieces of data could be explained by a hypothesis, the validity of which could be corroborated by the finding of another piece of data" (Woodson 1979:1).

C. S. Peirce, who first gave the name to this logical process, emphasized that our knowledge is not derived from experience alone. In fact, "every item of science came originally from conjecture, which has only been pruned down by experience. . . .The entire matter of our works of solid science consists of conjectures checked by experience" (Peirce 1958:320). The scientific explanation suggested by abduction, as Malina (1991a:259–60) notes, entails an explanatory hypothesis that renders the observed facts necessary or highly probable. This requires consideration of realities that are not explicit in the material under analysis and that frequently are not capable of direct observation, such as conventional ancient beliefs regarding spirits or the evil eye as the cause of illness or the values and scripts according to which Mediterranean male and female role behaviors and relations are governed and evaluated (Peristiany 1965;

Schneider 1971; Pitt-Rivers 1977; Malina 1981a:25–50; Abu-Lughod 1987).

This process of abduction, in general, lies behind the focus on the culture of the traditional peoples of the Circum-Mediterranean as the source of scenarios for New Testament interpretation rather than on the cultures of the Circum-Baltic or the imagination of the modern historian of ideas. This mode of reasoning and hypothesis construction enables the construction of reading scenarios that in turn facilitate a historically sensitive reading of texts produced in this Circum-Mediterranean environment.

5. The social and cultural models most appropriate for the analysis of the Bible and its environment, it is presumed, are those constructed on the basis of research and data pertaining to the geographical, social, and cultural region inhabited by the biblical communities, that is, the area of the Circum-Mediterranean and ancient Near East. Just as historical criticism insists on situating the biblical documents within their respective time frames, so social-scientific criticism insists on situating them within their appropriate geographical, social, and cultural contexts. Thus social-scientific critics read the biblical writings as products of the preindustrial, advanced agrarian society of the Circum-Mediterranean region, the features of which are conveniently summarized by Gerhard and Jean Lenski (1987) and Gideon Sjoberg (1965).

Social-scientific critics likewise read the biblical writings as encodements of the cultural values and scripts typical of the Circum-Mediterranean and Near Eastern culture regions as summarized by David Gilmore (1982, 1987) and other Mediterranean anthropologists (see also the pre-Renaissance "pattern of life" outlined by J. M. Romein [1958]). Its practitioners presuppose that along with historical and archaeological studies of these regions, it is historical, sociological, and anthropological research on these social systems and culture areas that will provide more apposite data and models for reconstructing the "world of the Bible" than models constructed from analysis of Western, postindustrial societies. The pertinent social-scientific research is generally cited in the publications of social-scientific critics, and a sampling is listed in the second of the appended Bibliographies.

6. In regard to the analysis of texts in particular, social-scientific criticism presumes the following understanding of texts, their features, functions, situations, and strategies.

Texts are units of meaningful social discourse in either oral or written form. Meaningful social discourse presumes a shared system of significa-

49

tion. Both the capacity of a text to serve as a medium of communication and the meanings communicated are determined by the conventions and constraints of the social and cultural systems in which the text and the communicators (senders and receivers) are based. Communicative conventions (including possibilities of variation, improvisation, and innovation) and constraints on expression and meaning are determined by social and cultural scripts that vary according to time and place. Therefore the expression (form and content) and the meaning of a text are relative to its historical and social location. A text encodes elements of, information about, and comment upon, the social system of which it is a part (Halliday 1978).

Biblical texts, like all texts oral or written, presuppose and encode information regarding the social and cultural systems in which they were produced and in which they made sense. Both the meanings communicated by the author(s) of these texts to their intended hearers or readers and the texts' persuasive power are determined by the social and cultural systems that author(s) and audiences inhabited and that enabled meaningful communication in the first place.

To ascertain what texts originally meant or could be taken to mean in their original contexts requires knowledge of these social and cultural systems. It is this fact that requires a social-scientific component of the exegetical enterprise.

When new readers inhabiting a different social system attempt to read these ancient texts, that original situation of shared meaning between authors and audiences vanishes, because social and cultural systems are no longer shared. Unless appropriate reading scenarios are employed to discover the range of meaning possible within the original social context, other, alien scenarios will be imagined for making sense of the text in a different context (Malina 1991b). The result may bear little if any resemblance to what an original text said or implied and what its intended audience conceivably could have heard. For example, Paul's stress on the *unity* of Jew and Greek, slave and free, male and female in Christ (Gal 3:28) is often mistaken as a statement of their *equality* in Christ by moderns inspired by the much later values of the American and French revolutions ("All men [sic] are created equal"; *Liberté, égalité, fraternité*). Or the comment, "If any will not work, let him not eat" (2 Thess 3:12) will be misread as an expression of Christian "capitalistic" principles and individual enterprise. Commentaries seeking to make the New Testament "relevant" to modern readers are unfortunately replete with such anachronisms.

50

Adequate reading scenarios, on the other hand, enable modern readers to "get in sync" with the social and cultural scripts embedded in ancient texts and thus facilitate a merging of conceptual "horizons" (in H. G. Gadamer's terminology) necessary for the sharing of meaning.

A further feature of all texts, whether written or oral, is that their content and intended effect have been shaped by the socially rooted self-interests of their producers. Texts, in other words, have not only a cognitive and affective dimension but also an ideological dimension. Social-scientific criticism is vitally concerned with ideas, cognitive perspectives, beliefs, belief systems, and worldviews as these are evident in the texts and culture under investigation. However, in contrast to a conventional theological or exegetical approach in which ideas and beliefs are often treated in isolation from the material and social forces of everyday life, social-scientific critics examine the correlation of beliefs and social behavior, of world and worldview, of experience, ideas, interests, and ideology (Gewalt 1971; Holmberg 1980a; Elliott 1981:11–12, 267–95; Meeks 1983a:164–92). Here it is assumed that ideas and beliefs have social as well as personal origins and affinities and serve, among other things, to articulate and advance specific social interests and agendas.

Ideas and beliefs generally serve a variety of social purposes. They can express cultural perceptions, values, and worldviews and articulate the relation of persons to the other more abstract dimensions of human experience: other persons and society, time, space, nature, the universe, God. They can describe social relations, behavior, and institutions and explain how and why they work. They can serve to motivate and direct social behavior. They can conceptualize for groups faced with present deprivation a compensation for current suffering later. They can legitimate social institutions by tracing them to ancient sacred or divine origins. They can situate and integrate social phenomena cosmologically within the social, cultural, and physical cosmos and invest this cosmic order with coherence, plausibility, and ultimate meaning. Thus the communication of ideas has a pragmatic as well as expressive, emotive, and aesthetic capacity. Social-scientific criticism, therefore, investigates the social capacity of ideas and beliefs as well as their relation to the material and social circumstances of those who hold and promote them.

This method presumes, moreover, that the ideas, values, and perceptions of reality that texts and other cultural artifacts communicate are related to and are expressions of the specific self-interests, perspectives, and goals of the persons and groups from which the texts emerge. The self-interests of the early Christians as members of the Christian brotherhood are clearly manifold and diverse. In general, however, they include concern for the group's continued viability and growth as a means of protection and support of its members, concern for its cohesion and member loyalty, interest in its clear and attractive social identity and its strong, nonporous social boundaries, and maintenance of a shared consciousness of its favored status with God and its assurance of salvation as motivation for continued commitment to the values, goals, and programs of the group.

The ideas, concepts, beliefs, and traditions espoused and promoted by the group are those which are most compatible with the self-interests of its members and/or their leaders. Self-interests, ideas, and ideology are interrelated and interdependent in the following way: self-interests generate and are articulated in ideas that, when organized and employed to explain and justify these self-interests, constitute an ideology. Ideology is understood here not in the reductionist (Marxian) sense of "false consciousness" or "the dominant ideas of (only) the dominant class" but as a cognitive and strategic feature of all self-conscious groups and classes and their textual productions. Thus ideology is understood as

> an integrated system of beliefs, assumptions and values, not necessarily true or false, which reflects the needs and interests of a group or class at a particular time in history. Because ideologies are modes of consciousness, containing the criteria for interpreting social reality, they help to define as well as to legitimate collective needs and interests. Hence there is a continuous interaction between ideology and material forces of history. (D. B. Davis, 1975:14, quoted in Elliott 1981/1990:12)

Theological formulations, like all other cultural, social, and material expressions of human consciousness, are ideological in nature, since they express in symbolic form the self-understandings and interests of the persons and groups by whom they are formulated and transmitted under specific sets of social circumstances. Moreover, not only the investigated texts (and all other material, social, and cultural productions) but also their investigators are themselves likewise influenced in their selection, reading, and interpretation of these texts by their own constellation of experience, ideas, and ideology.

A further important concern of social-scientific criticism, therefore, is the investigation and assessment of the ideological perspectives of both the interpreters and the objects of their investigation. In regard to the former, this ideology critique will involve a consideration of the identity of the interpreter, the interpreter's social location and the self-interests involved in the choice of texts and topics for study, the presuppositions, theories, and methods employed, and the conclusions reached. In regard to the latter, this will involve an analysis of (*a*) a text's dominant ideas, symbols, and perspective; (*b*) their coherence with an overall worldview or "symbolic universe" of meaning; (*c*) their correlation with specific group self-understandings, needs, and interests; and (*d*) the manner in which these ideas articulate and advance these specific group interests. In this process, theological formulations and writings are studied as products of social experience as well as of religious imagination and are seen as expressions of social interests and goals and as vehicles of social interaction.

The features of a text as an instrument of communication include (*a*) its expression of reflections on experience and implicit encodements of, as well as possibly explicit comments on, the natural and social orders external to the text; its expression of perceptions, ideas, beliefs, opinions, logical relations, self-interests, and ideology; and its expression of feelings, attitudes, expectations, wishes, and judgments; (*b*) an implied or explicated relationship of author and targeted audience/readers; and (*c*) a specifically textual mode of organizing the preceding elements (syntactically, semantically, and pragmatically) as a coherent, aesthetic, and persuasive discourse related to a particular situation and designed to have a specific effect (cognitive, affective, and behavioral) upon its intended readers.

The possible functions or capacities of a text (as an instance of language, expanding on Halliday 1978:19–20) include

- an instrumental function ("I want")
- a regulatory function ("Do/not do X")
- an interactional function ("You and I")
- a personal function ("Here I come!")
- a heuristic function ("Tell me why")
- an imaginative function ("Let's pretend")
- an informative function ("It is thus")
- a group-identifying function ("We are X")
- a persuasive function ("I want you to do X")
- a critical function ("X is/is not good")
- mixed functions

While written texts are not as extensive in length as oral texts, those such as the writings of the New Testament obviously combine several of these enumerated functions, although one or the other may predominate.

It is these functions and the forms by which they are communicated which determine a writing's *genre*. Genre is a social category of communication defined by the community to which one belongs. Social convention, for instance, determines the difference between "history" and "fiction," "comedy" and "tragedy," "gospel" and "prophecy," and the "appropriate" situations in which each is employed.

The critic, keeping in mind this constellation of textual features, situations, and potential functions, directs particular attention to the correlation of the text's social situation and compositional-rhetorical strategy. This entails an examination of the manner and means by which the text in its totality (its genre, content, literary organization, and rhetorical argument) is designed to address the envisioned situation and motivate to action in a plausible and persuasive fashion.

The concepts of "situation" and "strategy" and their correlation were used by the present author as foci for examining the letter of 1 Peter in *A Home for the Homeless*. As noted there (Elliott 1981:19), I subsequently learned that precisely these concepts and their correlation were proposed earlier by the rhetorician Kenneth Burke (1967:ix, 293–304) for the purpose of what he called "sociological criticism." Thus here we find an important intersection of the interests of rhetoricians and social-scientific critics. See also, for instance, the important article on "The Rhetorical Situation" by rhetorician Lloyd Bitzer (1968) and the overlap of rhetorical and social-scientific criticisms noted by both Vernon Robbins (1992) and the present author (Elliott 1991a:xxxi).

In place of the conventional exegetical concern with "occasion" and "purpose" of a writing (generally conceived in ideational or theological terms [ideas needing reinforcement or misunderstandings requiring correction]), "situation" refers to the social circumstances and interactions that motivated the writing of a text (social disorder or conflict, threats to group cohesion and commitment, problems with group boundaries, conflicts over legitimate authority, events to be celebrated, communities to be galvanized to action, and the like).

"Strategy," on the other hand, rather than "purpose" or "intention," better communicates the fact that the text is specifically designed by its producer not simply to communicate ideas but to move a specific audience to some form of concerted action. Social-scientific criticism thus aims at discovering how a given document was designed as an author's motivated response to a specific situation and how it was composed to elicit a specific social response on the part of its audience.

The situation of a text involves various levels and phases. The *macrosocial level* of a text's situation concerns the total social and cultural system

54

of which the text is a product. The *microsocial level* of a text concerns the more specific social conditions and features of its specific sender(s) and receiver(s). The situation of a text also can be viewed (*a*) *synchronically* (with attention to the social relation and locations of author(s) and addressees, the prevailing social and cultural patterns of behavior, institutions, structures, processes, and their relations at a given point or period in time), or (*b*) *diachronically* (with attention to where the text stands temporally and socially in relation to other texts and traditions alluded to in the document or how it relates to other texts and groups with which this text has some affinity; for example, the relation of the Synoptic Gospels and their communities to one another, the Pauline and deutero-Pauline writings, 2 Peter to 1 Peter and Jude, and so forth. In the latter case the social location of a text is important for tracing the history of texts, traditions, and communities and then subsequently for charting the history and nature of the reception of the text by later generations characterized by different social circumstances. Sources of information concerning the synchronic situation of a text will be discussed in chapter 5.

The strategy of a text concerns its pragmatic and rhetorical dimension, that is, the manner in which the text in its totality of form and content (syntactic and semantic dimensions) and embodiment of the aims, self-interests, and ideology of its author(s) is designed to have a specific effect upon the receiver(s) and thereby serve as a persuasive communication and effective medium of social interaction (pragmatic dimension). The means for discerning a text's strategy, including the self-interests and ideology of its author(s), are also discussed in chapter 5.

7. Practitioners of social-scientific criticism presume that this method is different from but complementary to a historical orientation. The latter tends to focus on individual or exceptional actors, extraordinary or unusual actions, independent or distinctive properties, personal rather than societal relationships, and diachronic movement and change. These are always important foci of investigation, but such distinctive properties can be perceived only when common and regular features of social life are first known. This latter concern is the focus of social-scientific inquiry. Such research tends to focus on social groupings and collectivities; regular, recurrent, routinized behavior; common and typical properties; social and systemic relations; institutionalized and structured patterns of behavior and relationships; and synchronic structures and process. Historical critics concentrate on discrete detail with an interest in concrete description and a skepticism toward overgeneralization. Social-scientific critics are concerned with commonalities and connections with an interest in

generalization, abstraction, theory building, and a skepticism toward claims of complete objectivity.

Social-scientific criticism is concerned, as is historical criticism, with the differences between modern and ancient conditions and their causes. But this criticism, in continuity with a fundamental thrust of Max Weber's work (1978 1:xxxix), also recognizes the need for comparative research, the establishing of analogies, the use of generalization, and attentiveness to typicalities in order to establish and explain differences and distinctiveness. "Sociologists live, and suffer, from their dual task: to develop generalizations and to explain particular cases," Guenther Roth has noted in commenting on Max Weber's oeuvre and program (1978 1:xxxvii). "The sociology of [Weber's] *Economy and Society* is 'Clio's handmaiden'; the purpose of comparative study is the explanation of a given historical problem" (ibid.). As Weber himself observes in commenting on agrarian conditions in antiquity (Weber 1924:257, 288), distinctiveness can be ascertained only on the basis of established similarities.

Social scientists approach their sources with specific questions in mind with the purpose of locating the information generated by these questions within some theoretical framework of concepts and hypotheses so as to render the data intelligible and open to interpretation and explanation. Social historians proceed in similar fashion, but in practice there are two main differences, as the historian Geoffrey Barraclough has observed (1979:49–50, 58):

> The first is that the historian's conceptualization tends to be implicit, arbitrary and unsystematic, whereas the social scientist's is explicit and systematic. The second is the historian's tendency, because his sources usually provide him with some sort of loose narrative pattern to which the facts can be related, to evade so far as possible the theoretical issues, and also to deal for preference less with the underlying structure than with events and personalities, which are usually far more sharply delineated in historical records than in the material anthropologists and sociologists commonly use. . . .One of the main practical contributions of sociology is to provide them with tools and techniques by which this lack of precision can be corrected; it enables the historian to replace inspired guesses by exact and rigorously constructed hypotheses.

(Barraclough's entire comment [1979:45–94] on "the impact of the social sciences" on new historiography is apropos here.) This means that the foci and the methods of both disciplines are necessary for an adequate interpretation of ancient texts and their social contexts. Both offer complementary and mutually corrective approaches to the subject matter. For to discern the unusual, we first need to establish the usual. To grasp the uncommon and startling interaction of Jesus with the Samaritan women in John 4 or the shocking force of the parable of the Good Samaritan, it is essential first to know the common and expected patterns of Palestinian social behavior that these stories "violate." Thus, as Norman Gottwald (1979:17) in his discussion of the complementarity of humanistic and sociological perspectives has observed (1979:8–17), paraphrasing Kant, "sociology without history is empty; history without sociology is blind" (1979:17). Appendix 1 offers a comparative summary of the dominant foci of the social sciences and historical criticism.

8. A further presupposition of social-scientific criticism is that the study of "religion" in the Bible and its environment requires a study of social structures and relations. The reason for this is that in biblical antiquity there was no freestanding, independent institution of "religion" as in modern society with its five major institutions of kinship, economics, politics, education, and religion. Instead, religion, like economics (Polanyi 1957; Finley 1973) and education, was embedded in the two dominant institutions of kinship and politics (Malina 1986e; Garnsey and Saller 1987:163), those basic institutions according to which the total constellation of social and economic relations, public and private, was organized. "Just as there was domestic economy and political economy in the first-century Mediterranean, but no economy pure and simple, so also there was domestic religion and political religion, but no religion pure and simple" (Malina 1986e:93). The several features and processes conventionally associated with religion, such as prayers to God or the gods, rites, worship, calendar, cultic personnel, and expressions of piety, ethics, and worldview, were, in the biblical world, determined by the institutions of kinship and politics.

Social-scientific critics, therefore, seek to avoid imposing modern conceptions of "religion" and "religious" phenomena upon ancient texts and thereby isolating religion from its public and domestic matrices. Rather, they seek ways and means to detect and analyze the characteristic features and social capacities of domestic and political religion as determined by the social and cultural scripts of the ancient world. This involves examining relations of power, areas of conflict, mechanisms of social constraint, details of status and stratification, competing values and beliefs, expressions of allegiance, social networks, appeals to transcendent authorization, and vehicles of propaganda as these are interwoven in the total social fabric.

9. It is further presupposed that the practitioner of this method may draw on the full range of social-science theory, methods, and research. At the same time, the researcher will have to be aware of the theoretical, methodological, and developmental differences among the various disciplines and orientations within the social sciences. As the discipline of theology involves numerous schools of thought with differing sets of philosophical convictions, religious and confessional allegiances, traditions and histories, and methods of theological analysis, the same is true of the social sciences. Each particular sociological orientation (structural functionalism, conflict theory, symbolic interaction, ethnomethodology, and others; see J. Turner 1978 for full discussion) has its specific history and agenda, strengths and limits. Accordingly, social-scientific critics will require more than superficial knowledge of social-scientific research. A critical awareness of the strengths and limits of the various schools of social-scientific thought, their presuppositions, theory, models, and conclusions is also essential.

10. Social-scientific criticism is concerned not only with the original meanings of the biblical documents but also with the aggregations of meanings down through the centuries. It also asks how and under what conditions the Bible continues to be meaningful for modern readers. As an operation of exegesis and theological understanding, it seeks to link present Bible readers with a distant but sacred heritage of the past and to explore as precisely as possible where different horizons of perception, experience, and meaning might eventually merge. This type of analysis sensitizes exegetes, theologians, and modern readers to those aspects of society and culture which both distinguish and unite ancient authors and audiences and modern readers. It presupposes that awareness of such differences is essential in order to avoid an anachronistic and ethnocentric misreading and misappropriation of the Bible. Thus it aims at clarifying the constellation of social and cultural features that determine any and all contexts of meaning in which the biblical texts have been composed and received down to the present. It seeks to discover how and why texts of the Bible were understood as they were, why certain texts "spoke" with power to particular generations, why and how they were appropriated in the liturgy, hymnody, prayer, creeds, theology, and piety of the church, and especially how the biblical texts may continue to inspire and animate believers faced by the urgencies of a new day.

The foregoing represents a list of some of the typical presuppositions that guide the work of many if not most social-scientific critics today. Methodological presuppositions, of course, are by nature open to challenge and in fact invite critique. The progress of this method will be measured in great part by the degree to which these premises are substantiated, refined, and modified by future research. Many of these presuppositions relate to one fundamental concern of the method: to clarify as clearly and comprehensively as possible the social and cultural differences that separate ancient and modern worlds and to discover adequate bridges for facilitating conversation between these worlds. As a conclusion to this part of our discussion, therefore, it seems appropriate to quote from a recent publication produced by an agency involved in intercultural communication.

The Center for Responsible Tourism, based in San Anselmo, California, has drawn up the following Code of Ethics for Travelers visiting foreign countries. It seems worth citing in this context, for, anachronisms aside, it captures the spirit with which practitioners of social-scientific criticism seek to equip visitors approaching the unfamiliar turf of the Bible with the means to be respectful and intelligent listeners and with the tools to be perceptive readers.

Code of Ethics for Travelers

Travel in a spirit of humility and with a genuine desire to meet and talk with the local people.

Be aware of the feelings of the local people; prevent what might be offensive behavior. Photography, particularly, must respect persons.

Cultivate the habit of listening and observing rather than merely hearing and seeing or knowing all the answers.

Realize that other people may have concepts of time and thought patterns that are different from yours—not inferior, only different.

Instead of only seeing the exotic, discover the richness of another culture and way of life.

Get acquainted with local customs; respect them.

Remember that you are only one among many visitors; do not expect special privileges.

When shopping through bargaining, remember that the poorest merchant will give up a profit rather than give up his or her personal dignity.

Do not make promises to local people or to new friends that you cannot keep.

Spend time each day reflecting on your experiences in order to deepen your understanding. What enriches you may be robbing others.

You want a home away from home? Why travel?

5
The Method in Operation: Procedures

The specific procedures followed in a social-scientific study of a text or dimensions of its social context will vary according to the object to be studied. For instance, the analysis of a single text or document will differ in scope and method from the study of a specific social institution (such as marriage) or general value object (such as personality) or an entire social system (such as that of the Circum-Mediterranean). Each analysis will involve different sets of questions, theoretical models, operations, and levels of abstraction.

In general, however, we may speak of two distinct, though related phases of the research process, whether the focus is on a text or a feature of the social context. The one is an initial empirical phase of research and the other is a subsequent interpretive phase of research.

The first phase is that of *data gathering and data organization and classification* according to a specified research design. In this empirical phase the design of the research is shaped by a hypothesis concerning certain social properties of the material to be explored, the interrelation of these properties, and the significance of these relations. This hypothesis which is formed on the basis of previous empirical research and verified theory is articulated through the use of a conceptual model that displays salient properties of the social phenomenon to be studied and its relation to other social phenomena and properties. Here the salient features of the model are clarified and definitions of the operative concepts and terms are presented. The research design then translates the model into specific methodological operations and identifies the source and scope of items to be studied, their context, the basis and criteria for their selection, and the method of their collection and classification. The empirical phase concludes with a report of research findings, an ordering of the facts and their empirical regularities and relations.

This empirical, analytical phase of the investigation is then followed by a *synthetic, interpretive phase* in which the method of interpretation is stated and the findings regarding the data are analyzed in relation to the initial model. At this point the aim shifts from the description of social properties and relations to the explanation of social properties and relations. In this hypothesis-testing phase of the study, an examination is made of the fit or coherence between what the hypothesis proposed and what the data demonstrate. If the findings fit the model, the hypothesis is confirmed and the study is added to the body of confirmed social-science theory. If the findings do not accord with the model, the hypothesis is disconfirmed or falsified, and it is made clear that the model requires modification or rejection. Among the numerous studies that clearly illustrate this procedure we might mention Bruce Malina's discussion of pivotal Mediterranean values (1981a); Malina and Neyrey's study of ancient labeling (1988); and the essays in Elliott (1986b) and Neyrey (1991a), as well as many of the works given in Appendix 4.

In general and abstract terms, this procedure is followed in examining either the social features and functions of a text or the social features, structures, or processes of the social system. A more extensive description and discussion of this general research process, as employed in the social sciences, is presented in Matilda White Riley, *Sociological Research*, vol. 1: *A Case Approach* (1963), and is summarized in the following diagram (Figure 1).

SOCIAL-SCIENTIFIC STUDY OF THE SOCIAL ENVIRONMENT

In the study of the social environment of the biblical documents and their communities, attention can be directed to either features of the social system (institutions such as kinship relations or subsets such as patronage) or features of the cultural system (values and value objects such as honor/shame, generosity, reputational leaders). Investigation can range from the macro-level to the mid-range to the micro-level of social relations or cultural features. *Systemic* analyses are interested in the structure of the social system as a whole and the interrelation of its constituent sectors (natural environment, resources, knowledge, and technology; economic and social system and processes of organization and socialization; political-military-legal system; personality structures; cultural system in-

61

Figure 1: Diagram of the Research Process

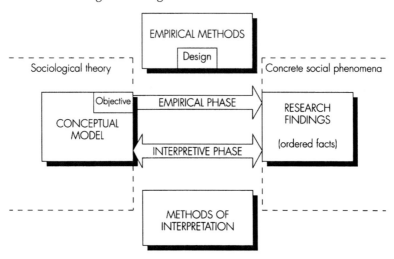

cluding belief systems and ideologies; and the relation of the social system to external factors and forces [natural and social]). The following diagram, for example, offers a model for a systemic analysis of the Roman Empire in the first century C.E. and its interlocking sectors (Figure 2, pages 64–65).

A variety of such models for analyzing ancient social systems at differing levels of complexity is offered by T. F. Carney's highly informative study, *The Shape of the Past: Models and Antiquity* (1975). Salient features of preindustrial agrarian societies (typical of the first-century Mediterranean) are succinctly outlined in Gerhard and Jean Lenski (1987). Gideon Sjoberg (1965) offers much valuable information on the preindustrial city and its contrast to modern urban societies (for a summary of developments since Sjoberg, see Rohrbaugh 1991a, 1991b). For more restricted analyses of social stratification and class relations in particular in agrarian and imperial Roman societies we have the useful models of Gerhard Lenski (1966:284) and Géza Alföldy (1984:125), respectively. The importance of such systemic studies lies in their providing a coherent picture of society as a whole in which Christianity emerged and in their alerting students of this movement to the interconnection of natural, economic, social, political, and cultural forces that influenced Christianity's birth, development, and viability (as discussed by Rohrbaugh 1991a, 1991b).

Studies still more limited in scope may examine specific institutions of Greco-Roman or Jewish society involving such regularized activities as the production, distribution, and consumption of goods and resources; land tenure and economic occupations; commerce, trade, and banking; socialization, education, and the dissemination of information; social organization, faction formation, and processes of cooperation, competition, and conflict; political, military, and legal control; and the cultural maintenance and dissemination of traditions, rituals, values, and norms. See again the models contained in Carney (1975) and, for instance, those of Douglas Oakman (1986) concerning economic exchange and land tenure in first-century Palestine, the study of Herodian Palestine by David Fiensy (1991), and several of the models given in Appendix 4.

Attention may focus still more narrowly on specific groups, coalitions, factions, or sects and the social conditions of their formation, continuation, and modification over time; their geographical location, constituency, and organization; their interests, traditions, beliefs, values, goals, and ideology; the symbols and strategies used for the establishment of group identity, member replacement, the maintenance of internal commitment and cohesion, and the legitimation of values and norms; and the nature of their interraction with other groups and agencies of the social system as a whole. Figure 3 (page 66) presents a model for collecting data and comparing features of several competing interest groups in first-century Palestine.

Appendices 2 and 3 offer further models of the constellation of issues that might be examined and the data that might be sought in attempting either a synchronic or a diachronic study of Christian groups in their environment and their changes over time.

In general, the method employed in the analysis of such topics involves the following six steps: (1) determination of the topic to be investigated, (2) determination and justification of the research design and the relevant theory and model to be employed, (3) gathering and classification of data, and (4) the explanation of the evidence at the hand of the theoretical model. Two final steps concern the model itself. Step 5 involves an evaluation of the model, its fit with the data and its explanatory power (does it actually explain the data or merely restate the obvious?). Step 6, finally, involves either a confirmation of the model as a useful heuristic tool or its modification as prompted by the data or its rejection and the search for a more apposite theory and model.

The studies employing a social-scientific approach that were discussed earlier generally follow this procedure implicitly if not explicitly. The most

A Model for Synchronic Analysis

POLITICAL (Legal & Military) SYSTEM
Systems Characteristics & Functions

1. Political institutions — Adaptation
2. Political process — Maintenance
3. Political culture — Integration

EXTERNAL ENVIRONMENT

1) Adaptation via:
   - Organization & administration
   - Security (military)
   - Allocation (goods & services)
2) Maintenance & Control via:
   - Extraction of surplus (goods & services): tribute, taxation, booty, robbery, exploitation
   - Monopolized control of production, distribution, consumption
   - Regulation & enforcement of law
   - Patronage-clientism; parasitism
   - Information dissemination

3) Integration via manipulation of:
   - Information: propaganda, dominant ideas, assumptions, expectations
   - Cultural beliefs, values, norms, symbols, myths
   - Cultural history & heritage

INTERNATIONAL RELATIONS

SOCIO-ECONOMIC SYSTEM
Social Organization

Institutions (Familial & Civil), Patronage & Clientism
Roles, Status, Stratification, Classes, Social Relations,
Activities, Mobility,
Consumption, Standard of Living

Distribution and Exchange
- Media of exchange, exchange centers
- Trade, transportation
- Prices, wages, banking systems
- Communications

TECHNOLOGICAL INNOVATIONS

Land Tenure
- Agriculture
- Subsistence sector
- Taxation

Household (*oikos*) management   Crafts   Industries

Commerce
- Expenditures
- Investments
- Levels of money and credit
- Taxation

TECHNOLOGY
- Labor force (human & animal)
- Scientific knowledge
- Tools, processes
- Sanitation, hygiene, medicine

MOVEMENTS OF THOUGHT

NATURAL ENVIRONMENT AND RESOURCES

Geography, topography, climate, water, food supply, flora and fauna

PREVIOUS EVENTS

of the Roman Empire *following T.F. Carney*

BELIEF SYSTEM & IDEOLOGIES

- Group myths & traditions
  - conservative
  - anti-innovative
  - anti-empirical
  - anti-technological
- Expansionist & syncretistic
- Commitment, loyalty
- Interdependence

- Ascriptive roles & status
- Nonequality
- Noncompetition
- Law & order
- Past-orientation
- Public good (vs. private)
- Sociality (vs. individuality)

CULTURE

Cultural hegemony (relative autonomy yet role in domination process)

- Knowledge, beliefs, worldviews
- Language, art, drama, music
- Folklore, folkways, traditions, customs
- Ethos
- Values, goals, norms, sanctions
- Life-Styles & Life Chances (structural immobility)

1) **Socialization**
   - Instrumentalities
   - Processes
     - information, communication
     - education
     - enculturation

2) **Personality Structure**
   - Dyadic
   - Authoritarian, coercive
   - Aggressive
   - Apathetic
   - conservative

POPULATION STRUCTURE

- Size
- Density
- Morbidity, mortality
- Population movement

Figure 3: A Multivariate Matrix Model for Comparing
Palestine Interest Groups

GROUP PROPERTIES	REBEL GROUPS	QUMRAN-ESSENES	JESUS GROUP	BAPTIST GROUP(S) John B.	PHARISEES	SADDUCEES	HERODIAN RULE	ROMAN RULE
A. SOCIOECONOMIC FACTORS 1. Group constituency + size 2. Geographic location 3. Economic base and occupations 4. Class, status 5. Organization 6. Roles, institutions								
B. POLITICAL-LEGAL FACTORS 1. Position and role in Roman and Jewish government 2. Basis and exercise of power/authority 3. Domestic relations 4. Foreign relations								
C. CULTURE, BELIEF SYSTEM 1. Pivotal values 2. Accentuated beliefs + their symbolization 3. Norms and sanctions 4. Socialization and personality structure								
D. STRATEGY AND IDEOLOGY 1. Group interests, goals 2. Tactics and foci of attention 3. Oppositions 4. Alliances, affinities 5. Ideology								

trenchant critiques of these works focus on the manner in which these procedures are executed as well as on the cogency of their conclusions.

Aspects of the cultural traits and scripts encoded in the New Testament can be another focus of research. Here attention is given to features of Mediterranean and Near Eastern culture ranging from the cultural system as a coherent whole to such issues as dominant or pivotal values (such as honor and shame, loyalty, and generosity), typical perceptions (such as "limited good"), kinship relations, contests of challenge and riposte, feuding, personality structures (such as dyadic personality), notions of illness and healing, or the coherence of specific beliefs with dominant worldviews and distinctive symbolic universes.

The aim of the study of such issues is to understand how and why people thought, behaved, and spoke the way they did as this is recorded in the pages of the New Testament, how and why these modes of action and communication made sense within the cultural parameters of the ancient Mediterranean, and how the cultural scripts of these peoples were related to and symbolizations of the material and social realities they experienced. Clarity about these issues enables the reader of the New Testament to discover the integrity of this strange but coherent world and thus better understand the New Testament within its own particular cultural framework. The models devised for this effort clarify the differences between ancient Mediterranean values and cultural scripts and those of the modern reader and thereby facilitate a more accurate contextualization of the New Testament and the avoidance of interpretive distortion.

The methodological procedure for analyzing these cultural features is the same as that outlined above with respect to aspects of the social system. Here too the most incisive critiques of these works evaluate the appositeness of the models employed, their fit with the data, and the ability of the investigation to explain features of the material otherwise opaque to other forms of analysis.

This procedure for examining a typical cultural phenomenon of Circum-Mediterranean and biblical antiquity is illustrated in my publications on the evil eye (Elliott 1988, 1990b, 1991a, 1992). The biblical writings contain a remarkable number of references to the "evil eye" (*ayin hara; baskanos,* etc.; *ophthalmos ponēros; oculus malus, fascinatio,* etc.; *invidere, invidia:* Deut 15:7-9; 28:54-57; Prov 23:6-8; 28:22; Sir 14:3-10; 18:18; 31:12-13; 37:7-12; Tob 4:15-17; 4 Macc 1:16; 2:15; Matt 6:22-23; 20:1-15; Mark 7:22; Luke 11:33-36; Gal 3:1). A survey of ancient literature, inscriptions and papyri, art, artifacts (amulets) and architecture, moreover, reveals that this dread of the evil eye and its deadly effects was a major preoccupation of the ancient Mediterraneans in general.

On the basis of this information, a model or "ideal type" is formed of the salient and recurrent features of evil eye belief and practice, typical evil eye possessors and victims, the cultural and geographical distribution of the phenomenon, the environmental and social conditions fostering this belief and the worldview making it plausible, the values associated with this concept, and its social capacities for regulating social interaction, enforcing cultural values and norms, controlling social deviance, and marking group boundaries.

This model is then used to examine the various biblical writings referring to the evil eye and to consider the conditions and concerns with which it is associated. This analysis would take into account a variety of interrelated social and cultural factors such as the high valuation of the eye as prime access to the truth, as emitter of rays, channel of internal disposition, and as instrument of aggression; the economic conditions of unequal distribution of property and wealth; social stratification and the competition over scarce resources; the prevalent envy of the "haves" by the "have-nots" and the association of envy with the evil eye; the high value placed on generosity and the serious condemnation of envy and miserliness; the concern over social boundaries; the absence of formal rules and agencies for adjudicating conflict; the informal labeling and discrediting of social deviants through their accusation as evil eye possessors; a prevailing sense of human vulnerability to hostile forces both natural and supernatural; and conventional attribution of sudden and otherwise inexplicable illness and misfortune to evil eye affliction.

These traits of evil eye belief and the conditions under which it flourishes then serve to explain aspects of the social interactions described in texts (warnings against or accusations of injuring with the evil eye, public discreditation of the accused, affirmation of generosity and censure of envy, maintenance of community boundaries and norms, explanations of aggression or misfortune).

Such a study reveals the pervasiveness of evil eye belief in the ancient Circum-Mediterranean (including the biblical communities), the logic of this belief and its accompanying practices, the conditions under which this belief thrives, and its use in clarifying values, enforcing norms, discrediting opponents, and assigning cause to otherwise puzzling manifestations of evil.

The adequacy of this model, as of any other, is determined by its fit with the data (biblical and extrabiblical). Its utility is demonstrated by its capacity for explaining cultural cues and social processes that are present or implicit in the texts but that are frequently overlooked by translators and modern interpreters.

SOCIAL-SCIENTIFIC CRITICISM OF BIBLICAL TEXTS

Social-scientific criticism of a biblical text, in turn, has as its goal the understanding of a text, its genre, content, structure, meaning, and rhetorical strategy as a vehicle of meaningful persuasive discourse in its original historical, social, and cultural context and as a medium of social interaction.

As a vehicle of social communication and interaction, a biblical text might be analyzed from a variety of theoretical perspectives. These might include semiotics, communication theory, or rhetorical criticism. Semiotics is the study of signs (including language) and the sign system (including language) within the context of their production, performance, and reception (U. Eco 1976). Here the focus is on the semiotic features and functions of the text, with particular attention to its pragmatic dimension. The relation of semiotic theory to text theory has been treated masterfully by H. F. Plett in *Textwissenschaft und Textanalyse: Semiotik, Linguistik, Rhetorik* (1975).

The value of this theory of text analysis lies in its appreciation of the interrelation of the literary, semiotic, linguistic, and rhetorical dimensions of the text. As a consequence it sets the stage for examining the text as a medium of social interaction, particularly through its attention to the semiotic features of the text (semantic, syntactic, pragmatic) and the relation of the "worlds" within and outside the text. Norman Petersen's study of Philemon (1985), as noted earlier, is a creative and instructive example of the application of this approach to a New Testament text.

But, as Petersen also indicates, this theory in the end remains one of literary, rather than social, analysis. To examine the social issues raised it must be supplemented by a method designed for analyzing such matters, particularly the methodological means for examining the social and cultural system outside the text that shaped the features of the text itself and its semiotic functions. It is at this point that social-scientific criticism makes a decided contribution.

Another approach to the biblical text as medium of social interaction might examine it in the light of communication theory. The South African exegete Jacques Rousseau in his analysis of 1 Peter (1986), for instance, seeks to integrate Plett's text theory within a broader model of the communication process (1986:35–74). Here the focus is on the five basic components of communication: the communicators or authors of a text; the message; the medium of communication; the receptors or addressees; and the context or social and cultural system within which the communication takes place along with the specific occasion of the communication. (See the work of Everett Rogers 1983 on the communication of innovations for actual data sets and field study.)

The value of this approach to biblical texts likewise lies in its consideration of the text as an instrument of social communication and interaction and in its identification of the specific elements of the communication process that require analysis. However, communication theory also needs to be supplemented with means for analyzing the communication's social dimensions. In particular, this theory may leave undefined the precise nature of the variables influencing the relationship of communicators and receptors, their social context and shared frames of reference, and the "noise" that may possibly hamper the communication. Here once again social-scientific criticism provides the needed supplementation.

Thus, while students of the biblical text must attend to the semiotic, linguistic, literary, and rhetorical features of the text and its function as a medium of communication and interaction, it is also evident that means must still be devised for exposing, examining, and explaining the specifically social features and dimensions of the text, its author(s), recipients, and their relations, its social context, and its intended impact.

This is the specific aim of social-scientific criticism, as a dimension of the exegetical enterprise. Its general objective is the analysis, synthesis, and interpretation of the social as well as literary and ideological (theological) dimensions of a text, the correlation of these textual features, and the manner in which it was designed as a persuasive vehicle of communication and social interaction, and thus an instrument of social as well as literary and theological consequence (Elliott 1981/1990:8–9; see also Gottwald 1985:595–609 in regard to Old Testament texts).

SOCIAL-SCIENTIFIC CRITICISM OF A BIBLICAL TEXT: 1 PETER AS AN EXAMPLE

To illustrate the process of such a textual investigation it will be useful to focus on one particular text, which we can then discuss in greater detail. Inasmuch as New Testament texts vary in the amount of explicit social information they contain regarding authors and audiences and their social situations, it is advisable to begin with a document that contains a maximum, or at least sufficient, amount of relevant data. Examination of such a text can then serve as a methodological model for interrogating other texts where such detail is more implicit than explicit. For our purposes, then, let us examine the letter of 1 Peter.

At least three reasons prompt this choice. First, as a letter, 1 Peter contains more explicit information about its situation than do, say, the Gospels or other writings where information must be inferred from implicit details. Second, 1 Peter offers one of the most sustained statements of the New Testament on the relation of the community of believers to their social environment. Thus this text provides not only a ready amount of explicit data but also a systematic statement that allows us to study in detail its correlation of situation and strategy. A final motive for this choice is to acquaint readers with the resources that this document offers to those interested in the social-scientific criticism while simultaneously introducing readers to one of the more neglected but fascinating "stepchildren" of the New Testament canon.

In the outline of method that follows I shall presume that the conventional exegetical operations have already taken place, namely, text criticism, literary criticism, historical criticism, source/form/tradition criticism, and redaction criticism. On the basis of these analyses it is clear that 1 Peter is a genuine letter sent in the name of the apostle Peter by a circle of Petrine associates in Rome to fellow Christians of Asia Minor in order to console and exhort the brotherhood there to remain steadfast in loyalty and hope despite their suffering at the hands of hostile neighbors. For my more extensive discussions of these details the reader may consult Elliott 1979, 1981, 1982a, 1982b, 1983, 1985, 1986a, 1990a, and 1992. Conclusions drawn from these analyses will also be used in the discussion that follows.

With regard to 1 Peter, as with all biblical writings, two sequential fields or arenas of social interaction might be analyzed: (*a*) an original and narrower field of interaction and (*b*) a subsequent and wider field of interaction. The immediate field of social interaction in which a text serves as a vehicle of social exchange concerns the original historical and social setting of the communication: its author(s) and addressees (actual and implied), and their respective geographical and social locations, the nature of their relationship, the circumstances that precipitated the writing, and the manner in which the text is designed to serve as a vehicle of their interaction.

A wider field of interaction that could be investigated subsequent to the text's composition, delivery, and reading/hearing would involve the circumstances of its actual reception and effect upon, first, its targeted audience and then upon subsequent audiences in varying times and places. This would involve a tracing and examination of the text's so-called history of reception and impact (*Wirkungsgeschichte*), its canonical history, and its role in later theological, liturgical, and spiritual tradition. Such an extended investigation is of crucial importance for ascertaining the knowledge and attitudes that inform current readers of a text such as 1 Peter and their theological as well as social perceptions. We are all shaped in our reading and understanding of biblical texts by the history that precedes us. An excellent example of the contribution such an investigation can make to the study of a New Testament writing is the multivolume commentary of Ulrich Luz on the Gospel of Matthew (1989–). For the limited purposes of this present study, however, we shall restrict our attention to a treatment of only the immediate field of interaction, that of the original author(s) of 1 Peter and its original addressees.

In regard to this immediate field of interaction, our aim is to determine the text's situation and strategy and their correlation, that is, the social situation as perceived and portrayed by its author, the author's strategy in portraying and speaking to this situation, and the nature of the relationship of situation and strategy.

To explore these issues, we pursue a series of questions that might be addressed to any biblical document (see Elliott 1990a:xxv-xxvi).

1. Who are the explicitly mentioned (or implied) *readers-hearers* of this document? What is their geographical location? What is their social composition? What is their relationship to the author(s)? To what social networks might they belong, and what is their social location in general? What are the social and cultural scripts, plausibility structures, and particular traditions and beliefs that readers are presumed to share with the author(s)? Can this information be supplemented by further historical and social data external to the writing and organized by social-scientific and cross-cultural models appropriate to the data at hand? Can a social profile of the audience be constructed?

2. Who is the explicitly mentioned or implied *author-sender* of the text? If the document is anonymous, what can be inferred about the author's identity and on what basis? If the document is ascribed to one or more authors or senders (as, for example, 1–2 Thessalonians), what information on these persons is available outside the text? If the text is pseudonymous (ascribed to someone other than its actual author), how is this determined and what was the motive? What is the relationship of intended audience and author-sender(s)?

3. How is the *social situation* described in the text? What information is explicitly provided or implied? What information is stressed through repetition, reformulation, or emphatic placement? Can further information on the situation be supplied from external sources? Does external information confirm or contradict internal information?

4. How does the author(s) *diagnose and evaluate* the situation? What phenomena are singled out for approval, commendation, disapproval, condemnation, or necessary change? What ideas, beliefs, values, norms, and sanctions are invoked or involved in this evaluation?

5. How is the *strategy* of the text evident in its genre, content (stressed ideas, dominant terms and semantic fields, comparison and contrasts, traditions employed and modified, semantic relations), and organization (syntax and arrangement, line of thought and argumentation, integrating themes, root metaphors, ideological point of view, and in narrative, the mode of emplotment of the story [romance, satire, comedy, tragedy])?

6. What *response* does the author(s) seek from the targeted audience (as perhaps indicated in explicit statements of reasons and goals for writing and response expected)? What part does this play in the author's overall strategy?

7. How does the author attempt to *motivate and persuade* the audience? To what shared goals, values, norms, sanctions, and traditions is appeal made? What are the modes and means of rhetorical argument employed? Are any dominant symbols or "root metaphors" used to characterize and express the collective identity and action of the audience and the author(s)? How do these features figure in the author's overall strategy?

8. What is the nature of the situation and strategy of this text as seen from a social-scientific *etic perspective* with the aid of historical and comparative social-scientific research? What social system constitutes the larger context of this writing? What are its dominant institutions and the Christian group's relations to these institutions? Are there comparable groups in comparable situations (Qumran, apocalyptic groups, coalitions and factions; cross-culturally comparable groups and movements [sectarian, millenarian, or brotherhoods and fictive kin groups]; and such)? What are the prevailing social and cultural scripts? What social issues and problems are at stake—Conflicting groups with competing interests and ideologies? Problems concerning group identity, organization, order, and cohesion? Issues regarding roles and statuses, internal and external social interaction? Tensions regarding norms, values, goals, worldviews, and plausibility structures? How does the document conceptualize, symbolize, and articulate the relation of patterns of belief and patterns of behav-

73

ior? How does the text explain, justify, and legitimate emphasized social relations and behavior, thereby providing a plausible and persuasive rationale for the integration of experience and aspiration, hope, and lived reality? How is the document constituted to be an effective instrument of rhetorical persuasion and social interaction? To what social model(s) does the strategy of the text conform (for example, strategies of coalitions, factions, sects, reform movements)?

9. What are the *self-interests and/or group interests* that motivated the author(s) in the production and publication of this document? How are they expressed or able to be inferred? What *ideology* is discernible in this document, and how is it related to the interests of the author and the group the author represents? How does this ideology compare and contrast with ideologies of other contemporary groups or social entities, and what are its distinguishing characteristics? How do interests and ideology reckon in the writing's overall strategy?

Such questions guided the investigation of 1 Peter in *A Home for the Homeless;* they might profitably inform a social-scientific exegetical analysis of any biblical document. For further types of guiding questions, see Berger 1977b:234–39 and Kee 1989:65–69.

Let us turn now to 1 Peter in particular, its immediate field of interaction, and its situation and strategy.

The *strategy* of this text, we recall, concerns its pragmatic dimension. How did its author or authors design this communication as a specific response to a specific situation? How was it constructed to have a specific and persuasive effect upon its intended recipients? Because it is the situation as known or presupposed by an author which determines the strategy of his or her response, our first phase of inquiry involves a determination of the situation presupposed by 1 Peter.

Here we might consider what Lloyd Bitzer (1968) has stated regarding the situational nature of all rhetoric (efforts at persuasion), since it applies to the biblical texts as well. Rhetorical discourse comes into existence, he notes (1968:5–6), as a response to a situation in the same sense that an answer comes into existence as a response to questions or as solutions to problems. Second, a text (oral or written) is given rhetorical significance by the situation in the same manner as are answers to questions or solutions to problems. Third, a rhetorical situation must exist as a necessary condition of rhetorical discourse. Fourth, a situation is rhetorical insofar as it needs and invites discourse capable of participating in a situation and altering its reality. Fifth, discourse is rhetorical insofar as it functions (or seeks to function) as a fitting response to a situation that invites it. Sixth, the situation controls the rhetorical response in the same sense that questions control answers and problems control solutions.

A "rhetorical situation," Bitzer thus summarizes, involves three constituents: "[1] a complex of persons, events, objects and relations presenting [2] an actual or potential exigency which can be completely or partially removed [or altered] if [under prevailing social and natural constraints] [3] discourse, introduced into the situation, can constrain human decision or action so as to bring about the significant modification of the exigency" (Bitzer 1968:6).

This concept of rhetorical situation provides a useful model for examining New Testament writings such as 1 Peter as instances of rhetorical discourse. It suggests as determinative features of a text's situation not only a specific "exigency" or "occasion" but also the social relation of author(s) and audience, and the constellation of factors not only constraining an author's response (author's capabilities, creativity, and communicational conventions) but also conditioning the circumstances of author and audience on the whole (general geographical, economic, social, cultural setting). Furthermore, Bitzer's stress on the fitness of the response (1968:10–11) suggests attention to what we refer to as the correlation of situation and strategy. In examining these features of a text, social-scientific criticism complements rhetorical criticism in its capacity to clarify the social dimensions of these features and their correlation.

To analyze the *situation* of the Petrine text, then, its intended audience and their geographical and social location, the circumstances of the audience, and the authors-senders of the document, we examine the following:

1. The Audience Addressed

a. Geographical location of addressees: Pontus, Galatia, Cappadocia, Asia, and Bithynia (1 Pet 1:1). These are Roman provinces of Asia Minor comprising about 129,000 square miles of territory. Much of the rural interior of this area was sparsely populated and only lightly urbanized. This address presupposes the wide spread of Christianity throughout Asia Minor and beyond the mission activity of Paul (none in Pontus, Cappadocia, and Bithynia), a rural setting (in contrast to Paul's urban communities), and a date of composition allowing for such expansion.

b. Identity and social location of addressees

■ members of a worldwide suffering Christian "brotherhood" (2:17; 5:9).

■ a mix of free persons (2:16) and slaves (2:18-20), with status and roles established by conventional civic (2:13-17) and domestic (2:18-20) norms, but behavior motivated by appeal to the "Lord" (2:13), God's will (2:15) and the Lord's example (2:21-25).

- a mix of males and females (wives directly addressed in 3:1-6; husbands, in 3:7), with status and roles established by conventional social norms but behavior motivated by appeal to the example of the holy matriarchs of Israel (3:5-6), the hope of recruitment (3:1), and the notion of husbands and wives as "coheirs of the grace of life" (3:7).

- a mix of older and younger persons (in perhaps both biological age and years as Christians, 5:1-5a), with status and roles established by conventional social norms but behavior motivated by appeal to fidelity to the will of God (5:2-3), hope of divine reward (5:4), and mutual humility (5:5b-6; cf. 3:8).

- a mix of converts of both gentile (1:14, 17; 4:1-4) and Jewish origin, the latter indicated by the frequent appeal to Scripture (1:16, 24; 2:4-10; 3:10-12; etc.), biblical persons as models (matriarchs, Sarah, 3:5-6; Noah and family, 3:20), and abundant Jewish tradition that would have had its greatest effect upon those directly familiar with this tradition (see 1:1, 13, 14-16, 17-19, 23-25; 2:2-3, 4-10, 22-25; 3:5-6, 10-12, 14-15; 4:14, 17-18; 5:5, 8-9, 13).

- economic and social status: "strangers and resident aliens" (1:1, 17; 2:11) whose social and legal rights were curtailed and who were frequently the object of suspicion, slander, and abuse from the natives, who were endemically hostile to strangers and suspicious of their commitments to local standards of obligation and morality. (On the conditions and status of resident aliens in Asia Minor; expropriation of land and reduction of agrarian natives to "resident aliens"; Christian mobility as traders and missionaries; prevailing suspicion toward strangers, and so on, see Elliott 1981/1990:21–58.)

2. The Author-Senders

"Peter, apostle of Jesus Christ" (1:1) is cited as the chief person in whose name and under whose authority this letter was written. In 5:1 he is portrayed as a "fellow-elder, witness of the sufferings of the Christ, and also sharer in the glory about to be revealed." Simon Peter was a leading figure of the early church who, according to tradition, died in Rome (ca. 65–67 C.E.) after a substantive ministry there. Because the circumstances of the letter presume a date after the apostle's death (wide dissemination of Christianity in Asia Minor; "Babylon" as surrogate for Rome only after 70 C.E.; sectarian disengagement of "Christians" [4:16] from Judaism), with high probability "Peter" represents the authoritative figure in whose name and authority the letter was written.

76

The conclusion of the letter, however, also indicates other persons and factors associated with the composition and dispatch of the letter:

- Silvanus, "a faithful brother" (5:12), is identified and endorsed as the person "through" whom the letter was delivered. He is probably identical with the Silas mentioned in Acts 15, who was a colleague of Peter in the Jerusalem church and co-deliverer of the letter from Jerusalem to Antioch.

- Personal greetings are sent from "Mark, my son" (5:13), a further colleague and possibly protégé of Peter earlier on in Jerusalem (Acts 12:1-17; cf. 15:37-39) and later, according to tradition (Papias), also in Rome, and from

- "the co-elect" [brotherhood]. ("Church" or "wife" [of Peter] has been suggested as implied here, but "brotherhood," which is used in 2:17 and 5:9, is the more likely implied term.)

- "Babylon" (5:13), used as a biblically flavored term for the capital of world empire, and after 70 C.E. as a designation for Rome as the destroyer of Jerusalem, implies Rome as the location of the senders of the letter and its place of composition. The terms "diaspora" (1:1) and "Babylon" (5:13) signal the similar vulnerable social situation of both addressees and senders living as strangers and aliens in foreign and hostile regions.

Thus, 1 Peter is a letter composed by a circle of Christians in Rome associated with the apostle Peter (core in-group). This letter was sent in his name (and under his legitimating authority) to members of the Christian brotherhood living as strangers and resident aliens in the provinces of Asia Minor.

3. The Social Situation as Described and Diagnosed in 1 Peter

The problem most explicit in 1 Peter and most directly addressed is that of adverse social relations between the Christians of Asia Minor and their neighbors. Hostility on the part of the latter had led to the innocent suffering of the former. Ignorance on the part of the natives concerning the addressees (2:16; 3:15) prompted slander, reviling, reproach, and abuse of the Christians as "evildoers" and social deviants (2:12, 16; 3:9, 13, 15, 16; 4:14, 16; cf. 5:9). Such abuse, in turn, led to fear (3:6, 14) and unjust suffering (1:6; 2:19, 20; 3:14, 17; 4:15, 19; 5:10) on the part of the believers. This picture of strained social relations between the Christian movement throughout the Mediterranean basin and its neighbors can be corroborated and supplemented by evidence from other contemporary Christian writings (Mark 13 and par.; Acts; letters of Paul; Hebrews; James; 1–2 John; and Revelation). Greco-Roman sources on this period are far fewer and are restricted to events at Rome under Nero (ca. 64–65 C.E.) (Tacitus, *Annals* 15.44; Suetonius, *Life of Nero* 16) and Bithynia-

Pontus under Trajan (ca. 111–112 C.E.) (Pliny, *Epistles* 10.96–97). These external sources, however, do corroborate in general the unorganized sporadic outbreak of local hostility against Christians, as the Christian writings illustrate the debilitating effects of such opposition on internal Christian cohesion and commitment.

In response to this situation, the letter declares that the addressees through faith in Jesus Christ, the elect and holy one of God (2:4; 1:19), have become the elect and holy people of God (2:4-10). The rejection and suffering they experience unite them with their rejected and suffering Lord (2:18-25; 3:13—4:6; 4:12-16). Nevertheless, they can live with hope, for as Christ was raised from death and exalted by God, so they too can anticipate a certain salvation. They are God's reborn children, his household and family(1:3—2:10; 4:17), and form a distinctive brotherhood in the world (2:17; 5:9). Their divine calling requires a separation from a formerly ignorant way of life and the responsibility of living as holy nonconformists (1:14-16) who renounce all Gentile vices (2:1, 11; 4:2-4). Such resistance to evil, endurance in doing good, and fidelity to Christ will, with God's help, enable them to "stand firm in the grace of God" (5:12) and even lead their detractors to "glorify God on the day of visitation" (2:12, RSV).

4. The Situation (and Strategy) of 1 Peter from an Etic Perspective

The response offered in 1 Peter is theologically eloquent and moving. But what of its power to persuade and move to social action? What are the social dynamics that are presupposed in this overtly religious communication? Why might the recipients find this a persuasive piece of communication? If they act in accord with what the letter says and urges, what will be the social consequences? With these questions we shift from a consideration of so-called *emic* data and begin to look at the bigger social picture from an *etic* perspective.

What social aim lies behind the heavy stress on the collective identity of the addressees, their depiction as an "elect race," "royal residence," priestly community," God's special people (2:9), gathered flock (2:25; 5:2),and a "brotherhood" of the reborn (2:17; 5:9)? What does the application of these traditional epithets for Israel to the messianic community imply about its social relation to Judaism? What does their distinctive label as "Christians" (4:16) and the stress on their superiority over Judaism (1:4, 10-12) also imply about this relationship? What social circumstances are reflected in the lumping together of all nonbelievers as "Gentiles" (2:12; 4:3), including even Jews? For what social reasons is such emphasis laid on the distinction of believers versus nonbelievers (1:14-16; 2:7-10; 3:1-6, 13-17; 4:1-6, 12-19), union with God and Jesus Christ (1:3-5, 10-12; 2:4-10, 18-25; 3:13—4:6; 4:12-19; 5:1-5, 6-11) versus resistance to the Gentiles (1:14-17; 2:11; 4:2-4) and the devil (5:9)? What social reasons may have prompted the exhortation to "brotherly love," mutual service, respect, and material support (1:22; 3:9; 4:7-10; 5:1-5)? What sense is there to urging distinctiveness and resistance, on the one hand, while, on the other, hoping for a conversion of unbelievers (2:12; 3:2)? What might be the social implications of their paradoxical identification as both "strangers and resident aliens" (*paroikoi*) (2:11; cf. 1:1, 17) and yet "household of God" (*oikos tou theou*) (2:5; 4:17)? What might happen to the social integration and emotional commitment of the community if faith and hope, in the face of suffering, give way to disillusionment and despair? In sum, what are the social circumstances presupposed in this writing, and how might the letter's strategy be understood as outlining an effective response to this situation?

A more complete analysis than can be demonstrated here would also examine further social and cultural features of the environment that are encoded in the text. This would include the general inimical relations of strangers and natives; the institution of kinship and household and its significance in the ancient world; the use of familial and household metaphors in imperial programs and propaganda and the political ramifications of its contrary use in 1 Peter (see Elliott 1981/1990:174–80); the social conditions of Jews and Christians in the diaspora and in Asia Minor in particular; conventional concerns regarding social order, status and roles; the social scripts regulating relations in the civic, public sphere (strangers vs. natives; in-groups and out-groups) and in the private, domestic sphere (kinship systems; owners-slaves; husbands-wives; elders-younger persons); modes of social interaction (ranging from assimilation to conflict); processes of status degradation and status elevation; modes of internal group governance; the institutions of slavery, hospitality; and encoded aspects of the culture, including the values and scripts concerning honor and shame, male-female relations, prayer and patronage; personality structures (group-oriented rather than individualistic); and attitudes toward suffering and physical discipline as occasions for demonstrating courage and fortitude.

The specific social situation and strategy of 1 Peter can be more fully construed with the aid of an etic model. The picture of the Christian movement presented in the letter is that of an in-group of believers loyal to Jesus as the Messiah who are living as strangers and aliens among the provincials of Asia Minor. While originally a faction within Judaism, this messianic movement to which these believers belong is now at a stage of social and ideological dissociation from mainstream Judaism. The community is distinguished from Jews of the region in terms of its faith in Jesus as Messiah (1:2, 3-12, 18-21; 2:4-10, 21-25; 3:15; 3:18—4:6; 4:12-16; 5:4), its inclusion of non-Jews (1:14-17; 4:2-4), its heavenly rather than territorial inheritance (1:4), and its superiority to Israelite prophets because of its reception of the word of the good news (1:10-12, 22-25). Nonbelieving Jews are associated with nonbelieving pagans as "Gentiles" (2:12; 4:3), an out-group hostile to the brotherhood and responsible for Jesus' death.

Thus the form of Christianity depicted in 1 Peter is that of a messianic *sect.* Once a faction within Judaism, it is now dissociated from its parent body socially and ideologically and is known by the distinctive label "Christian" (4:16). The honors, divine favor, and tradition once associated exclusively with Israel are now appropriated by the followers of Jesus Christ and are applied exclusively to the Christian believers as God's fictive kin group (children of God, household of God, brotherhood).

Features typical of sectarian communities, as indicated by social-science research, include their emergence under conditions of social tension and conflict; their initial stage as a protest group within a larger corporate entity; their gradual marginalization and then dissociation from their original parent body because of "deviant" stances taken toward central issues of corporate identity, exercise of power, and moral behavior; their experience of social disapproval, harassment, and pressures urging conformity; their conception of themselves as an elect and elite community favored with special grace and revelation; a rigorous moral code and demand for exclusive allegiance; a separatist response toward all "outsiders"; and further related strategies for asserting their collective identity, assuring internal social cohesion, and maintaining ideological commitment.

Virtually all of these characteristics of sectarian groups are evident in the portrait painted of the Christian movement in 1 Peter. In fact, this holds true for many of the New Testament writings and thus suggests that the model of the sect provides a useful heuristic concept for analyzing early Christianity as a social movement. For 1 Peter in particular, this model offers a conceptual framework for envisioning the dilemma facing the Christians and the strategy shaping the address of this situation. (For the relevant sociological literature on the typical conditions and features of sectarian formation, examinations of early Christianity as a Jewish sect, and the application of this model to 1 Peter, see Scroggs 1975; Wilde 1978; Elliott 1981/1990 [using the work of Bryan Wilson on sects].

In regard to the dilemma described in 1 Peter, the Christians were, in the minds of their neighbors, no longer mainstream Jews but "messianists," "Christ-lackeys" (*Christianoi*, 4:16). Therefore they no longer enjoyed the political and legal privileges of ethnic Jews. Ignorance and suspicion of the new movement led to slander of "evildoing" and the pressure to conform to pagan standards of morality. Increased hostility resulted in innocent suffering. Continued unjust suffering could lead to despair, loss of hope, uncertainty over the surety of salvation and divine protection, and eventually defection. Pressures from outside the group could also lead to internal disorder, the breakdown of roles and properly ordered relations, and conflict over differing ways to remedy the situation. Wholesale defection from the community, in turn, would diminish its already small numbers and seriously endanger the very viability of the movement, let alone its missionary success. The situation, in other words, had serious implications for the continued survival of Christianity in Asia Minor as a missionary movement.

The Petrine author seems to have viewed the predicament as severe, for this communication tackles these problems head on. This brings us to a consideration of the letter's strategy as viewed in the light of sectarian strategies in general.

5. The Sectarian Strategy of 1 Peter

The strategy of 1 Peter is to empower and motivate its addressees to meet the challenge posed by their abuse in society and their unjust suffering. In more comprehensive (etic) terms, its strategy is threefold.

First, it affirms the *distinctive collective identity* of the believers, their union with God, Jesus Christ, and one another as the reborn children of God, the elect and holy people of God, the family of the faithful (1:2; 1:3—2:10), and asserts their holy distinction from and moral superiority over the outsider Gentiles (2:11—4:19). The Christian community, it is asserted, constitutes a privileged in-group favored by God and distinct from and superior to all out-groups.

Second, it encourages *internal solidarity and cohesion* through a binding obedience of, and subordination to, the divine Father's will (1:14, 17, 21; 2:13, 15, 18-20, 21; 3:17; 4:19; 5:6), loyalty to Jesus Christ (1:8; 2:7, 13;

81

3:15; 4:14, 16), and constant love (emotional attachment), mutual respect, humility (status acceptance), hospitality (generosity), and service toward one another (1:22; 3:8; 4:8-11; 5:1–5).

Third, it promotes a *steadfast commitment* to God, Jesus Christ, and community (1) by providing a plausible rationale for innocent suffering (solidarity with the sufferings of Jesus Christ [2:21-25; 3:13—4:6; 4:12-16], suffering as a "test" of loyalty [1:6; 4:12] and as a sign of the Spirit's presence [4:14]); (2) by stressing the hope of vindication and salvation through union with the vindicated and exalted Christ (1:3-12, 18-21; 2:2-10, 24-25; 3:18—4:6, 12-19; 5:10-11); and (3) by depicting the Christian community as a "brotherhood" (2:17; 5:9), a "household of the Spirit/of God" (2:5; 4:17), a family of God in which "reborn" converts (1:3, 23; 2:2) are "obedient children" (1:14) of a heavenly "Father" (1:2, 3, 17) bound with God the Father in holiness (1:14-16; 2:5, 9) and with each other in "brotherly and sisterly love" (1:22-23; 3:8; 4:8; cf. 5:12-13). Christians, in other words, form a fictive kin group, a community bound by the loyalties and reciprocal roles of the natural family—a potent notion of community in a culture where religion is embedded in kinship!

Acting in the fashion, the addressees will be able to resist (2:11) the pressures of a "devilish" society (5:8-9) urging conformity to out-group modes of conduct once renounced (1:14-16; 4:1-4), to stand firm in the grace of God (5:12), and even to win erstwhile detractors to the faith (2:12; 3:2). Subordination to civic and domestic authority for the sake of good order and the "doing of good" may allay opponents' suspicions. But such submission and conduct are ultimately not a sign of compromise but a testimony to the believers' fidelity to the will of God and solidarity with Jesus Christ (2:11—5:11).

The letter does not ignore or downplay the precarious predicament of the believers as objects of abuse and reproach in society. Rather, it acknowledges the reality of this situation but balances it with the assurance that believers who are strangers and aliens in society (*paroikoi*) have a secure home and place of identity and belonging in the household of God (*oikos tou theou*). Thus the terms *paroikoi* and *oikos tou theou* function as social as well as theological correlates to describe the paradoxical condition of the addressees as identical to that of their crucified and exalted Lord—rejected by humans but elevated by God as the elect and holy family of God.

In this communication of consolation and exhortation, the reality of fictive kinship serves as powerful means for affirming and promoting the distinctive communal identity, social cohesion, and moral responsibilities of the believers in the civic and domestic realms. The process of salvation and conversion is pictured as a "rebirth" (1:3, 23; cf. 2:2) initiated by God the "Father" (1:2, 3, 17). Those who have been reborn have become God's "children" (1:14) and heirs (1:4; 3:7, 9), sharing in his holiness and subject to his will (1:14-16; 2:13—3:9; 5:1-5) and protected by his power and care (1:5; 4:19; 5:6-7, 10). As "brothers and sisters" through faith, they are bound to one another by familial loyalty and love (1:22-23; 3:8; 4:8). As "household stewards" of God's grace (4:10), they emulate household servants (2:18-20) and Jesus the servant of God (2:21-25) in their subordination to the will of God. As "elders" and "youth" of the family, they owe one another mutual respect (5:1-5). As a community, the reborn believers constitute a family on the way from rebirth to growth to consolidation (1:3—2:10), a "household" of God (2:5; 4:17), a "brotherhood" of faith in a hostile environment (2:17; 5:9).

This declaration of the Christian community as the household of God builds on the traditional conception of household and family as the fundamental unit of society and on house and home as that chief place of identity, security, acceptance, and belonging. This is, moreover, an appropriate symbol for the early Christian movement in which Christian households formed the basis, focus, and locus of Christian mission. Finally, in 1 Peter it serves not only as a comprehensive symbol for integrating various metaphors for salvation, God, believers, and community but also for addressing the specific situation of its intended recipients.

Their situation is one of social estrangement and alienation as *paroikoi* in society. But this condition, 1 Peter asserts, need not be deplored as a bane; to the contrary, it can be embraced as a blessing in disguise. Strangers they are and holy, set apart strangers they are to remain. Their vocation is to resist the pressures and encroachments of a hostile society (2:11-12; 5:8-9) and to stand firm in the grace of God (5:12). Such a life of holy nonconformity is possible because in the community of the faithful the strangers in society (*paroikoi*) have found a home (*oikos*) with God. On a similar depiction of the Christian community as the "household of God" in the Pastorals, see Verner 1983; on familial symbolism in Paul, see Von Allmen 1981; and on the Christian household churches, see Klauck 1981.

Thus the factors of alienation in society versus "at-homeness" with God play a central and decisive role in the correlation of the situation and strategy of 1 Peter. The letter represents a typically sectarian "response to the world" (B. Wilson) and more specifically that of a "conversionist sect" which urges conversion as a realignment of loyalties, ethical transformation, and involvement in a community of the "reborn" as the most effective means for personal and social survival and access to salvation. In such a response to the world, an ethic of resistance and nonconformity based on a claim of special divine favor and moral superiority is combined with an insistence upon group solidarity, ideological commitment, and attractive conduct which can win others to the cause.

6. Interests and Ideology

The self-interests or group interests that motivate the composition and dispatch of this letter are, as typical of all biblical writings, difficult to ascertain. Self-interests, in contrast to altruistic interests, are generally concealed from view and thus from critique. In many cases they can only be inferred from the content and strategy of a text and from what is known about its producers. In the case of 1 Peter, we are dealing with a communication between a Petrine group in Rome and a segment of the Christian brotherhood in Asia Minor. The sole overt expression of purpose occurs at the conclusion of the letter: "I have written briefly to you, exhorting and witnessing fully that this is the grace of God; stand fast in it!" (5:12). It is clear, however, from the very genre of the communication— a personal letter from a group of Petrine colleagues at Rome (including Silvanus, Mark, and the co-elect brotherhood there) to a segment of the brotherhood in Asia Minor—that the senders are interested in affirming and maintaining personal ties with their fellow believers in Asia Minor. They are likewise interested in assuring their cohorts in the faith that they share not only the same traditions but also the same experience of alienation and suffering (5:1) that is common to all believers (4:12-13; 5:9). Such commonalities of belief and experience strengthen the "ties that bind" and build bridges that can be traveled in both directions. The letter and the personal presence of their representative, Silvanus, would forge a bond upon which the Roman Christians could count if and when it was required in the future. This letter, moreover, extended the sphere of influence of the Roman group abroad in a manner similar to that of 1 Clement addressing the Christians of Corinth. Such influence abroad, in turn, would enhance the prominence and stability of the Christians at Rome. The advantageous position of the Roman Christians, located as they were at the hub of political and cultural power, would make this community an ideal center for the congregation of the "faithful from everywhere" (Irenaeus, Adv. Haer. 3.3.2), the coalescence of traditions, the convergence and distribution of information, and eventually the exercise of powerful influence throughout the Mediterranean region.

84

In terms of ideology, it is clear that the senders of the letter are concerned with strengthening their suffering fellow believers in Asia Minor through a theological conception of the privileged status and distinctive communal identity and responsibility which is theirs as God's favored people, the elect and holy family of God. This ideology of the Christian community as the household of God served as a means for promoting internal sectarian cohesion and commitment while at the same time distinguishing and insulating the Christian in-group from other social groups, including Jews, other cults, and voluntary associations, as well as from the pretensions of imperial propaganda celebrating the emperor as "father of the fatherland" (*pater patriae*) (see Elliott 1981/1990:174–80). It offers a powerful contrast to the imperial ideology of the Roman emperor whose goal was to legitimate himself as "caring father" over a worldwide region of vanquished peoples now proclaimed to be his *patria*. By contrast, the authors of 1 Peter assert that God alone is the father of the Christian household and that, while the emperor deserves respect, as do all persons, God alone is the object of their awe and reverence (2:17). It is God's will that is the ultimate criterion of good conduct and it is Jesus Christ alone who serves as the enabler and example of obedience. Thus the household ideology serves as a plausible social as well as religious rationale for the encouragement of Christian resistance to alien pressures urging conformity and as a veiled critique of imperial paternalistic pretensions.

First Peter, we can thus conclude, was composed and dispatched by a Petrine group in Rome writing in the name and after the death of its leading figure, the apostle Peter. Reflecting in its content the confluence of diverse Christian traditions typical of the communities at Rome, this letter bearing the authority of the apostle Peter stresses the solidarity of believers at Rome with suffering co-believers in Asia Minor and throughout the world. Within the worldwide Christian movement this demonstration of solidarity and support would soon result, as undoubtably hoped, in the prestige and renown of the church at Rome. Over against the ideologies of other contemporary groups competing for membership and allegiance, the household ideology of 1 Peter, with its roots in the family structures of the region as well as in the history of ancient Israel, and its concretization in fraternal support and solidarity, provided Christians with a powerful means for gaining new members and maintaining commitment. Over against an imperial ideology proclaiming the emperor as "father of the fatherland" (with the rights and powers of a *paterfamilias*), 1

Peter and its household ideology assured Christians in Asia Minor that God alone is father and judge and that it is this God alone to whom God's family owes fear and reverence (1 Pet 2:17). Finally, the ideology of the Christian community as the household of God provides a persuasive rationale for suffering Christians to "stand firm" (5:12) and "resist" (5:8), for while in society they were strangers and aliens (*paroikoi*), in union with God and the Christ they constituted the reborn household (*oikos*) of God.

On the whole, analyzing 1 Peter in terms of a sectarian model has provided a heuristic means for surfacing the underlying social dynamics implicit in this writing and clarifying the manner in which the various content, themes, and organizing metaphors have been integrated to form a coherent and persuasive communication able to motivate its audience to an effective form of social action.

Examination of other New Testament writings as expressions of sectarian consciousness is a promising endeavor that has already yielded some fruitful results (Meeks 1972, 1985, 1986a; Scroggs 1975; Wilde 1978; Stanley 1986; Rensberger 1988; White 1989). The success of such study will be measured by the degree to which the sectarian model, like all models, provides a means for surfacing latent social dynamics hitherto unconsidered and for clarifying the social as well as theological correlation of a document's situation and strategy.

6
Critical Assessments

Social-scientific criticism, as a component of the historical-critical method, is still narrowed to a relative handful of practitioners. They have launched the ship that is now presently completing its maiden voyage. Maiden voyages involve shakedown activities. The ship is put through its paces to see whether and how it works, whether and how it sustains expectations of performance, what its limits are. However, the marked increase of exegetical studies along social-scientific lines, the growing use of and dialogue with the social-scientific literature, and the growing sophistication in the use and testing of social-scientific models all indicate the positive response this approach has encountered, particularly among younger scholars.

In 1986 I summarized some of the initial advances and payoffs of social-scientific criticism (Elliott 1986b:2–3). This merging of exegesis with the social sciences, I noted,

> has stretched our personal and scientific horizons, alerted us to the limitations of our received exegetical wisdom, sharpened our perception and deepened our understanding of early Christian texts as media of social interaction. It has developed our awareness of behavioral patterns, pivotal values, social structures, cultural scripts, and social processes of the biblical world, the world within which and from which our sacred traditions draw their vitality and meaning.

In this way the social dimensions and implications of a wide range of New Testament texts have been brought to light. Dominant social and cultural scripts of ancient Mediterranean life have been identified and used to clarify New Testament texts. Models for analyzing first-century social systems have been developed, and the intersection of text and con-

87

texts, of social milieu and conceptual worldviews, have been profitably explored. This progress, accompanied by the reciprocal conversation and critique among scholars employing and refining this approach, has established social-scientific criticism as an indispensable feature of the total exegetical and historical enterprise.

Because refinement of any method, however, calls for sympathetic attention to substantive criticism, we would do well to consider some representative responses that have been forthcoming from the exegetical community. This discussion in turn sets the stage for a fuller account of the method's "payoffs."

Critical response thus far has varied from rather knee-jerk reaction, on the one hand, to substantive critique, on the other. In fact, it is interesting to note that the most substantive criticism has come from practitioners themselves of one another's models. For numerous assessments of work along social-scientific lines, see the literature listed above in the account of the emergence of social-scientific criticism in recent times (p. 20, n.1).

One early response has been the cry "Caution, caution." Exegetes dallying with the social sciences have been compared by one reviewer, Derek Tidball (1985), to "wooing a crocodile." Tidball adopts this analogy from Winston Churchill, who first used it with reference to maintaining good relations with the Communists, stating, "You do not know whether to tickle it under the chin or beat it over the head. When it opens its mouth you cannot tell whether it is trying to smile or preparing to eat you up" (Tidball 1985:106). This is a curious and wary analogy indeed, especially in view of the fact that sociologists themselves are fond of citing Thomas Hobbes's description of the raging beast of societal chaos, "Leviathan," as that daunting phenomenon upon which the science of sociology seeks to gain some handle. Tidball's comparison takes us from sociology as animal tamer to the danger of the enterprise itself, and the uneasiness of innocent exegetes courting the menacing crocodile. Is there cause for caution and wariness? If the lion is invited to lie down with the lamb, is it likely, as philosopher Woody Allen has observed, that "the lamb won't get much sleep"? Some wary critics of the exegetical–social-science merger seem to think so. Consider but a sample of the "dangers" cited by the caveatmongers which echo early twentieth-century fears about the discipline of sociology in general.

Exegetes using the social sciences will allow everything, especially theological beliefs, to be reduced, in Durkheimian fashion, to social phenomena.

In using the social sciences, exegetes, like sociologists, of necessity must bracket out and exclude "the God hypothesis." The exegetical task will then become agnostic if not atheistic.

Exegetes showing any interest in Marxist theory or conflict theory will inevitably succumb to the Marxist dogma of economic and historical determinism and end up regarding religion as an opium of the people.

In response it must be said that while these represent directions that were taken by earlier nineteenth- and twentieth-century philosophers, they are hardly inevitable features or consequences of the method as such or typical of the contemporary social sciences at large. Such concerns, rather, relate to the hermeneutical presuppositions that each interpreter brings to the interpretive task. A study of social phenomena does not involve in its methodology judgments about the possibility of revelation or the validity of theological beliefs concerning the existence and nature of God, demons, miracles, and the like. In exegetical social-scientific criticism, attention focuses on the social conditions, capacities, and consequences of such beliefs whether "valid" or "invalid." That is, the social sciences regard beliefs as real in their social consequences, and it is this which they are interested in understanding and explaining.

There is nothing inherent in the method itself that makes it "reductionistic," although this has been a constant worry of its critics. Robin Scroggs (1986:140) has put the matter accurately:

> No "scientific" approach need be reductionistic. *Every* "scientific" approach—including the historical—*can* be reductionistic. That is, reductionism does not lie in the methodology itself, but in the theological [or philosophical] presuppositions which one brings to sociological or any other methodology. Statements informed by social pressures *can* be apprehended as revelation. That is as legitimate a faith as the contrary.

As Scroggs goes on to note, however, a social-scientific method does imply

> one limitation to any view of the New Testament as revelatory for all times and situations. Along with every other scientific approach to Scripture, it increases the awareness of the *contextualism* of the New Testament statements. We come to see more and more clearly what the New Testament *said*, what it *meant* in its own social context. Sociological analysis thus makes it more obviously problematic to claim those statements as directly revelatory for other social contexts. This

does not mean that no transfer of revelatory value from New Testament times to our own is possible. But this problem belongs to the area of hermeneutics and is not in and of itself an issue debatable by sociology of the New Testament.

The same applies to judgments concerning theological beliefs or the manner in which specific sociological orientations are employed. It is the hermeneutical presuppositions that the investigator brings to the method and the critical, selective use of the theory and method that are determinative. Methods as such do not obligate to dogmas. Social scientists are not all atheists. Even exegetes include atheists among their number. As Theissen found it necessary to remind his readers in a remarkable final footnote to his *Sociology of Early Palestinian Christianity* (1978:125), not everyone who learns from Marxism is necessarily a Marxist and not everyone who writes about the radicalism of early Christianity is a radical.

Here it is important to distinguish between "reduction" as concentration and "reduction" as identification. Every method of analysis concentrates/reduces attention to specific phenomena and their relationships. Historical criticism concentrates on events. Literary criticism concentrates on literary texts. Social-scientific criticism concentrates on social structures, processes, and interactions. Theological criticism concentrates on religious and dogmatic belief and practice.

Reduction in the second case is not concentration of focus but identification of all phenomena as exclusively historical (singular or related events) or literary (aesthetic text) or social (social product) or theological (doctrinal) phenomena. Such an identification is not implicit in or required by these respective methods but derives from certain hermeneutical presuppositions accepted by their practitioners. Exegesis of an idealist bent has reduced attention to theological ideas in a kind of "methodological docetism" (Scroggs) presupposing that ideas alone matter and can be examined apart from their historical and social context. Historical, literary, and social-scientific critics likewise are not immune from the danger of identifying their respective foci of attention as the only possible or valid object of analysis. This type of reductionism is naive, if not pernicious, and must be challenged. For that which we are attempting to understand is a reality involving several interrelated dimensions, none of which can be comprehended apart from the other dimensions.

A decision to accept or dismiss the validity of religious beliefs is made, not on the basis of sociological, but on philosophical and theological grounds. The social sciences treat, not the "essence" of religion, but indeed the social conditions and consequences of its social expression. The reason for this is that the latter phenomena are empirical and available to scientific scrutiny as the former is not. Both factors, however, can be fruitfully studied through the complementary, and not necessarily antagonistic, perspectives of both theology and the social sciences.

Social-scientific criticism is not a "sociology or anthropology of the Bible." Rather, it merges the social sciences with exegesis as a composite theological as well as literary, historical, and social-scientific operation. It is concerned with determining what an author said and meant to say to his or her contemporaries. Meaning is controlled by the social system—in the past as in the present. In reading texts of the past, one either considers the social system in which they were produced or imposes a contemporary one. Without social-scientific criticism, only the latter choice is possible.

Social-scientific criticism does not reduce the focus of attention; rather, it expands it. It does not eliminate at the outset the validity of claims concerning the existence of God, the resurrection of Jesus, or the action of the Spirit as irrelevant to exegetical and historical investigation. It rather asks under which conditions such beliefs are plausible and persuasive, which persons and groups hold which beliefs, and what were the social consequences of such beliefs. This method in no way denies or ignores the validity of religious ideas but asks what they meant in their own context. It examines their correlation and affinity with specific forms of social behavior, relations, and interactions under specific sets of material and social conditions.

Another objection holds that social-scientific criticism is too "pretentiously scientific." Exegesis, like history, it is claimed, must allow room for the haphazard and serendipitous. Effort at clarity and rigor of method, however, should not be confused with scientific pretense. Critics speak in terms of relative probabilities, not absolute certainties. The operative question is how these probabilities are best envisioned and assessed. Social-scientific criticism aids the historical critic in more adequately assessing the contours and degrees of the probable by attending to the regularities and typicalities of ancient Mediterranean life.

A further objection claims that a historical sociology of the past is *tout court* impossible. Cyril Rodd (1981:95–106) has critiqued John Gager (1975) and Robert Carroll (1979), both of whom employ the theory of cognitive dissonance to explain developments in formative Christianity and among the ancient prophets, respectively. Rodd maintains that when one is dealing with events and texts of the past, "experiment and participant observation are impossible" (p. 98). This absence of the possibility of hypothesis testing, he claims, creates "a world of difference" between sociology of contemporary societies and historical sociology (p. 105). This critique concludes with a sweeping dismissal of recent work along with that of Max Weber's entire program: "Indeed, the weaknesses of sociological studies of historical movements from Max Weber onwards suggests that historical sociology is impossible" (p. 105).

This obvious difference between social analysis of current phenomena and ancient cases, however, does not preclude the possibility of retrospective hypothesis testing altogether, as most of the studies reviewed above demonstrate. In these cases, the testing consists of measuring the degree to which the evidence (1) fits the model and (2) is explainable retrospectively on the basis of the model. Moreover, Rodd himself concedes that the historian also "is never a mere collector of 'facts' but in his selecting, ordering, interpreting and explaining of those facts he works with theories about the use of evidence and the interaction of human beings" (p. 105). It is precisely these theories which social-scientific criticism seeks to clarify and test.

These objections do not require extensive comment. They all operate with theories of inevitable contamination through association and fail to allow for the possibility of critical adaptation, on the one hand, and critical rejection of unwarranted assumptions, on the other. Attempting to dismiss recent social-scientifically oriented exegesis as recrudescences of Weber's work can hardly impress those convinced of the epoch-making character of Weber's program. Such anxieties themselves belie an unwarranted mistrust and lack of confidence in the critical capacities of exegetes to accept what is useful and ignore what is not. So let us turn to more serious concerns regarding the limits and potentialities of the wedding of exegesis and the social sciences.

First, there are certain limiting factors that must be acknowledged. In part, these are similar to limits relating to the historical-critical method in general.

A first limiting factor concerns the amount and fragmentary nature of the material available for analysis. In the case of the biblical texts themselves, they presume far more than they explicitly state concerning the social world in which they were produced. While such a limit of social information is evident, it is not crippling, for generations of research have made available a vast reservoir of evidence concerning the social world of the Bible. This evidence from literature, inscriptions, papyri, coins, artifacts, architecture, art, and the like, has long been a focus of historical-critical attention and now may be interrogated from a social-scientific perspective as well. This perspective entails the posing of a new set of questions that in turn can yield yet new data. Data, as we recall, are always "givens" (from *dare*, "to give") of some hypothesis. New hypotheses raise questions about unexplored relations of phenomena and possible patterns of behavior and interaction previously unconsidered. Moreover, the introduction of cross-cultural comparisons also further expands the potential data base by identifying sets of relations present in one culture that may also be hypothetically present but not explicated in another.

This relates to a second limitation: the restricted availability of contemporary and contiguous analogies to Christian social formations (for example, other Jewish factions [Pharisees, Sadducees, Essenes, baptizing groups; synagogal communities]; Greco-Roman groups, such as philosophic schools, voluntary associations [*koina, collegia*], the military) as well as limited analogies from societies and cultures similar in situation (ecological, economic, social) but removed from early Christianity in terms of time and space. In the search for such analogues, it is clear that critical attention will have to be given to differences as well as resemblances and that caution must be exercised against superficial overgeneralization.

A third limitation concerns the adequacy of the models employed to gather and analyze the social phenomena. Here the investigator must exercise sound critical judgment concerning the fit between the features and dimensions of the model and the phenomena being examined. This is in contrast to numerous social historians who keep their models concealed and hence beyond criticism.

In addition to pointing out these obvious limitations, scholars have also registered some further concerns. For one thing, is there not a problem of excessive focus on external social causes of events without sufficient attention to human intention (Stowers 1985)? A purely Durkheimian application of social analysis that identified God or the gods solely as symbols of society, that ignored human intentionality as a causal factor, and that focused only on the function of religion as "social glue" would indeed be vulnerable to this criticism. But it is difficult to see, as yet, any exegetical work along social-scientific lines that assumes this position. As Stowers correctly indicates, while such an approach is conceivable and in fact historically attested in the case of Durkheim himself and his followers, it hardly is equipped, theologically or methodologically, to interpret the documents of the New Testament community of faith.

Social-scientific criticism, however, does not ignore human values or intentions but inquires as to the relation of this feature of motivation to ancient beliefs about motivation in general, and to the conditions that give these beliefs and intentions plausibility. Of course, finding some of the theories of Durkheim, or any other social scientist, useful does not automatically transform one into a fanatical Durkheimian. Similarly, the use of Marxian theory does not turn one into a Marxist, as Theissen felt compelled to point out (1978:125).

Then there is the dread of the procrustean bed: forcing material to fit the theory. Procrustes, Greek myth tells us, would overpower strangers and then force them to lie down on one of his two beds. If those on the longer bed were too short to fit, he hammered or stretched them out until they matched the bed's length. Those unfortunates who were too long for his short bed he relieved of their extremities. Filling the beds mattered more than accommodating the sizes of the guests.

Procrustean procedures are by no means absent in the world of science. Here too the bed of a precious theory often can count more than the variant shapes and sizes of the material to be interpreted. In the field of exegesis, the two-source or four-source theory of Gospel origins or the documentary hypothesis in Old Testament studies, or the theory of theological as well as biological evolution (from polytheism to henotheism to monotheism), serve as graphic and contested illustrations. History too is replete with examples, such as the doctrinally based history of the biblical communities in fundamentalism or versions of United States history with limited or distorted treatments of Native Americans, Afro-Americans, women, the labor movement, and their roles in the story of this country.

As a criticism directed against biblical social-scientific analysis, therefore, several things need to be said. First, all exegetes and historians are potentially vulnerable to this charge and must be vigilant against a forcing of material into "cookie-cutter molds." Second, this is a universal danger, because, as noted early in this study, all investigators work with theories, whether or not acknowledged and whether or not explicated. Only through hypotheses and theories is random raw material transformed into data, that is, "givens." Data are raw material that is identified, selected, organized, and interrogated according to a specific theory, "givens" of a specific hypothesis. "Evidence" is data that make a theory evident and probative.

Thus the similarity and the differences of the three Gospel accounts of Jesus' baptism (Matt 3:13-17//Mark 1:9-11//Luke 3:21-22) are regarded by many exegetes as data of the two-source hypothesis regarding the literary relations of Matthew, Mark, and Luke, the so-called Synoptics (another exegetical theory that distinguishes them from the Gospel of John).

94

This theory, which postulates that Mark (along with a second sayings source, Q) was the source used by both Matthew and Luke and therefore accounts for or explains the similarities of all three Gospels, does not enjoy universal acceptance, for it cannot adequately explain all the similar and divergent features of all three writings. Therefore Gospel scholars insist on indicating at the outset which theory of Gospel relations they prefer and for which reasons, before they proceed to their gathering and explanation of evidence. In brief, the theory espoused will determine which raw material will be examined as "data" (of the theory) and eventually used as "proof" substantiating the initial theory. Those scholars who hold a different view of synoptic relations than that proposed by the two-source hypothesis and Markan priority direct their primary criticism not at the raw material but at the theory and introduce other raw material which is then used as data and proof of another possible or preferable theory.

The same procedure is used to confirm or to challenge other theories regarding the putative "family relation" of textual manuscripts, the now contested theoretical distinction of "Palestinian Judaism" and "Hellenistic Judaism," the distinguishing features of "apocalyptic" literature, the now contested distinction between "epistle" and "letter," the dubious theoretical distinction of "Greek" versus "Semitic" modes of thought, and innumerable other theories according to which raw material has been classified, analyzed, and explained.

Specific theories likewise determine scholarly notions of how ancient society was organized and functioned, how control was exercised and by whom, what institutions were in place, where and why and how conflict emerged, what values and norms governed social conduct and determining social scripts, how the ancients perceived the world and their place in it, and how they sought to make sense of their everyday experience.

These theories concerning the nature and structure and processes of social reality, social-scientific criticism insists, also need to be made explicit at the outset of an investigation. Only when all theories and models are made explicit can they be submitted to evaluation, critique, modification, or rejection as implausible or unpersuasive. This is not tantamount to "trimming" the material to fit a procrustean bed any more than clarifying one's theory of Gospel relations is proceeding in "cookie cutter" fashion. It is, rather, an essential step in a sound exegetical or analytic procedure. Such explication allows for adequate evaluation by others and thus for genuine advances in understanding. Above all, such a procedure is intellectually honest.

Exegetes trained in historical criticism and therefore oriented to historical particularities have objected that social-science models as intrinsic generalizations tend to blur the contours of particular historical situations. This objection has been discussed and addressed by Richard Rohrbaugh (1987a), who has noted that the issue is less one of generalization per se, since all science, including historical criticism, involves generalizations. At issue are, rather, the *levels of abstraction* at which models work. The higher the level of abstraction of a model (for example, patterns of Mediterranean culture as a whole), the more the specific details of a particular historical situation (Syria-Palestine, Egypt, Asia Minor, Rome) are blurred but the more general patterns of behavior become evident. On the other hand, the lower the level of abstraction (the Jewish temple-Torah-purity system as ideational construct), the more the particularities become evident but the vaguer become its similarities as centralized storehouse economy with other ancient redistributive, storehouse economies and hence the less the possibility of comparative analysis (see Moxnes 1988a; Elliott 1991c).

The solution lies not in eliminating abstraction and generalization altogether—an impossible as well as unnecessary option—but in clarifying the specific social phenomena to be analyzed and employing a model appropriate to that level of particularity. In this way we will avoid what Carney (1975:35-36) terms the "strategic mischoice" of models and its confusing consequences. Thus a model concerning the dynamics of the Jesus faction during his lifetime will not be an appropriate instrument for analyzing the dynamics of the spread of Christianity in the Mediterranean basin, just as a model of the Roman imperial bureaucracy will not serve an analysis of the organization of the Christian communities in Asia Minor. Here also the fundamental issue is one of fit and compatibility—in this case between the model and the scope of the topic under investigation.

Moreover, in recognition of the influencing factor of changing conditions, it must be kept in mind that models that explained one social phenomenon at one point in time (for example, the Roman execution of Jesus) are not likely to fit or explain occurrences in other times and places (such as the execution of Christians in Rome by Nero or their treatment in Asia Minor under Trajan).

Here again it must be acknowledged that generalization—that is, abstraction—is a feature of all the sciences, history included. The issue is not whether generalization as such is valid but how generalizations are generated and validated and what ends they serve. To speak of "unusual" or "unique" phenomena implies some sense of assumed generality. The identification of the former, in fact, is impossible without the identification of the latter. The tasks of the social sciences and historiography, as noted earlier, are not mutually exclusive but complementary.

Another point raised concerning social-scientific criticism is its supposed inversion of procedures: putting the theoretical cart before the factual horse. Edwin A. Judge (1980:210), in criticizing Bengt Holmberg's study of Paul (1980a) and its use of Weberian theory, asserts that before any sociological theories are entertained, the social facts must first be gathered: "Until the painstaking field work is better done, the importation of social models that have been defined in terms of other cultures is methodologically no improvement on the 'idealistic fallacy' [which Holmberg criticizes]. We may fairly call it the 'sociological fallacy.'"

The merit of this observation is that it recognizes the great divide between current societies and ancient societies and the precariousness of using models derived from analysis of only contemporary social structures for the study of ancient social patterns. Its fatal flaw, however, is an erroneous assumption, discussed earlier in this volume: namely, that investigations of social phenomena can be carried out free of theory. In reality, it is specifically theory that determines what is a social fact and what makes certain social facts "characteristic" of an entity and others not. Again, there is no such thing as "immaculate perception."

A further question has been raised concerning the commensurability or incommensurability of ancient and modern societies and of the models constructed on the basis of the social and cultural structures of the latter to analyze social and cultural patterns of the former (Stowers 1985). Here the investigator must be particularly sensitive to the dangers of anachronism and ethnocentrism. Certain models proposed by social-scientific critics of the New Testament are open to serious critique because they derive from modern social experience with no ancient counterpart.

This would include such models as those of "cognitive dissonance" (presupposing an undocumentable consonance of ancient popular opinion and expectation); "middle class" (contrary to the sole two-class division of ancient society and presupposing economic conditions favoring a middle class which emerged only centuries later); "charismatic" authority (presupposing an individualistic concept of personality in contrast to the dyadic personality structure and "reputational authority" of antiquity); and "office" (presupposing a bureaucratic structure undocumentable for the early church, instead of leadership "role"); and so forth.

In the case of these objections, it has been practicing social-scientific critics themselves who have pointed out the inappropriateness of these models—a good example of healthy self-critique (for instance, Malina

[1986c, 1986d] regarding Gager and Malherbe; Malina [1984a] of charism; Seland [1987] of sect; Elliott [1986c] and Horsley [1989] regarding Theissen's "functional" model). Historical sense urges that we strip models for examining biblical texts and culture of any details that are only attestable for later times and conditions. Once polished by such elimination, the lenses and models can work.

Historical and social differences, however, do not eliminate any possibility of comparison whatsoever; rather, they call for precision in the mode of comparison and the complexity of factors (variable and invariable) taken into account. Because models are merely constructs and therefore flexible, they can be modified and shaped to fit the circumstances more closely.

This is the case, for instance, in regard to the sect model. In contrast to the initial definition of sect proposed by Troeltsch (a social grouping emerging from and opposing the official church), the concept of sect can be modified, as Bryan Wilson has done, to denote social movements in preindustrial societies that emerge and organize over against social parent bodies and that adopt varying "responses to the world" (and not the church). Thus the redefined construct "sect" becomes a more apposite means for analyzing a specific stage of early Christianity in its development from Jewish faction to dissociating and "deviant" Jewish sect.

Models, it has been noted, can also be falsely "reified." That is, a hypothetical construct (such as the efficient operation of a social system) can be erroneously assumed to have actual ontological status. Thus, for example, a social system might be compared with an organic entity like a human body or an ecosystem where all components of that organism are conceived as having a "function" or role to play in maintaining the society's equilibrium and contributing to its efficient operation. Such a model is useful for conceptualizing society as an integrated system of interdependent sectors. However, when it is further presupposed that the society (as abstract entity) has certain "needs" to be fulfilled if its equilibrium is not to be endangered, "society" and its alleged "needs" have been reified and erroneously used to explain the behavior of individuals. Gerd Theissen (1978), as I have noted (1986c), makes this mistake in assessing the "failure" of the Jesus movement in Palestine to contain the violence threatening the well-being of Palestinian society. The verdict of failure hinges on the supposition that social equilibrium was an actual reality "needing" to be maintained. An alternative theory that regards conflict as typical of competing groups in unstable environments and productive of

98

positive as well as negative change would have enabled a different and possibly more positive assessment of the impact of the Jesus movement in first-century Palestine.

A further real danger of "wooing crocodiles" is a superficial acquaintance with "crocodile culture." Uncritical acceptance of social theory or unfamiliarity with competing schools of social thought can seriously weaken an exegetical analysis. This is as true of the appropriation of social-scientific theory and research as it is of the use of the theory of competing theological schools of thought (neoorthodoxy on the one hand and existential demythologization on the other). The only realistic solution is what initially seems to be a rather daunting one: adequate familiarization with the social sciences as well as with the disciplines of theology and exegesis. For the latter, however, this means adding yet one more discipline to the many already embraced under the label "exegetical method." Personal conversation and collaboration with social scientists can be a great help toward this process of familiarization. Teamwork with others engaged in this method has also proved immensely profitable, as in the case of the Context Group and other collaborative efforts in the professional societies. Ideally, social-scientific critics should seek to establish and maximize opportunities for cross-disciplinary collaboration and critique. This emergence from islands of splendid isolation would benefit all parties concerned.

Another concern regarding social-scientific criticism involves the use to which this method might be put, its ideological component and praxis orientation. This point has been raised by the South African scholar Itumeleng Mosala (1986). Mosala adopts the viewpoint of British theorist Terry Eagleton, who maintains that "unless modern criticism is now defined as a struggle against the bourgeois state, it might have no future at all" (Mosala 1986:16). On this premise Mosala finds the results of social-scientific studies that lack this aim as unproductive and as inconsequential as other "new criticisms" in general. Its practitioners, he claims, are captives of their own capitalist and class agendas. They are judged woefully deficient in "taking seriously issues of class, ideology, and political economy not only of the societies of the Bible but of the societies of the biblical sociologists themselves" (Mosala 1986:30). Thus biblical social critics are found wanting in self-critique and deficient in providing a method that could lead to genuine social liberation in the present hour.

This objection is itself ideologically motivated and pertains more to the ideological stances and contemporary political agendas of the practitioners than to the method itself. This would be the subject of another

99

and much-needed study in and for itself. It may suffice to say in this regard that the method's concern with the examination of the ideologies of both ancient authors and modern readers/researchers is consistent with Mosala's interests, though such critique is not transformed into critical praxis on the part of all practitioners. Nor would there be agreement on the direction that such critical praxis might take. But then this is hardly a problem restricted to exegetes or social scientists alone. The issue is obviously one for the future agenda of social-scientific criticism, for it raises, as Elisabeth Schüssler Fiorenza has also stressed, the question of the partisan character of all biblical appropriation, whether acknowledged or not. For a review and critique of various "socio-political readings of the Jesus story," see Ched Myers (1988:459–72); on liberation theology, the essays edited by Norman Gottwald (1983b); and on feminist theology, Fiorenza (1979, 1983).

Finally, it has been suggested that ways must be found for discovering the points of intersection between social-scientific criticism and other recent methods within biblical interpretation (new literary criticism, narratology, structural criticism, and sociorhetorical criticism). What are evident points of convergence? How do these methods complement each other? How might these new methodologies be integrated so as to further mutual critique and more effective interpretation? This is less a critique than a desideratum and a call for necessary conversation and methodological bridge-building between several of the "new" currents in exegesis. In the case of rhetorical criticism and social-scientific criticism in particular, Vernon Robbins (1992:xxx–xxxi) and I (1990a:xxxi, 10–11, 19) have both recently noted obvious features of convergence that deserve further exploration. With the gradual maturation of these newer criticisms, it now seems an appropriate time to pursue this issue of methodological integration.

7
Achievements and Contributions

What may be said of the provisional achievements and contributions of this recent expansion of the exegetical tool kit?

The past two decades have seen a rapid growth of international interest on the part of scholars, book publishers, and lay readers in this amplification of the historical-critical paradigm. Its proponents have succeeded in convincing a new generation of scholars and nonspecialists of its necessity and utility. Among its several contributions thus far, the following deserve particular mention.

1. In an often used and abused expression, the Bible "has come alive" as never before. Its people become purposeful actors thinking, feeling, behaving, and communicating as real people in a real world. Narrated stories take on rhyme and reason as characters are seen to be acting out roles and scripts of their own culture. By informing themselves of the prevailing cultural perspectives, patterns, and values of ancient Mediterranean life, Bible readers have become more sensitive to the cultural scripts presumed in the biblical writings. The cultural nuances of these communications and the plausibility structures they presume are becoming accessible as never before to modern Western readers.

These writings assume fresh meaning as persuasive communications specifically designed to move targeted audiences to concerted social action. Greater clarity has been gained concerning the contours of such concerted action and their possibilities and limitations as determined by an interlocking network of ecological, economic, social, and cultural conditions. A more profound sense has been gained of the interrelation of mundane experience and formulations of faith. The ideas and beliefs of the biblical communities have taken on new plausibility and meaning insofar as they are shown to be rooted in and responses to specific material and social conditions. These ideas and beliefs have been linked not only with specific conditions but with particular groups and social programs, particular propagators and their self-interests. They have been shown to be socially concretized in specific social arrangements and patterns of behavior and to be coherent with encompassing symbolic universes.

Such attention to the social conditions, correlations, concretizations, and consequences of ideas and beliefs has assisted exegetes and readers to minimize the danger of methodological docetism. The belief systems and worldviews, projects and communications of the biblical communities, thereby gain in plausibility and persuasive power insofar as they are understood as reflections of and responses to the conditions and constraints of actual social experience. Thus the work of social-scientific critics has helped to show the meaningfulness of ancient biblical discourse and the whys and wherefores of ancient human behavior.

Furthermore, we are now provided with a new set of appropriate questions to ask and new nets and lenses for gathering data, viewing total realities, and comprehending Christian and other groups as integrally related to and interwoven in the fabric of ancient society. We have come to see more clearly how ideas and ideals, hopes and goals, are both reflections of and creative responses to the conditions under which the early believers "lived, and moved, and had their being."

We are gaining a more adequate comprehension of early Christianity as a social phenomenon, the conditions under which it emerged and expanded, the problems it confronted, and the strategies it employed in this confrontation for advancing its cause.

Work along social-scientific lines has convinced biblical scholars and readers alike of the need for a sociological imagination and for a method that can examine the interstices of biography and history, the reciprocal relations between economy, ecology, and society, the correlations between patterns of belief and patterns of behavior. As the atomic age information explosion continues and modern communication technology indeed turns the inhabitants of the planet into a "global village," the interconnections of social life within one planetary ecosystem require of all intelligent persons a preparedness and a capability for seeing and understanding those interrelations and interdependencies. Historians, exegetes, and theologians are also the beneficiaries of this explosive "fallout."

2. Through the creative and critical use of the social sciences by exegetes, new questions concerning the salient features of the social environment of early Christianity, its institutions, networks of relations, and modes of operation have provided a more comprehensive social frame

of reference for situating the Christian movement within the crucible of ancient society and for better understanding Christianity's role in the on-going flow of interaction, conflict, and change.

3. This approach, further, has begun to clarify as well the prevailing social and cultural values, codes, and scripts according to which communication and social interaction were carried out on an everyday basis. As a result, the exegete and reader is now equipped with more adequate reading scenarios for discerning the meanings implicit as well as explicit in the writings of the early Christians.

4. Social-scientific criticism has presented an array of relevant social research, along with tested theory and models, for exposing specific features and relations of ancient society and of the biblical communities in particular. Students of the social world of the Bible and of the social dimensions and capacities of its texts may now test these models for their heuristic and explanatory power, modify or discard them as required, and add to this repertoire of theory and models through further research. An illustrative, but by no means complete, list of such models is given in appendix 4.

Through the application of a model measuring degrees of social pressure ("group") and socially constrained adherence given the symbol system ("grid"), we have been able to identify the social location of the communities of our texts and typical related features of their perceptions of the world they inhabit.

The properties and relations of total social systems are also coming into clearer focus. The dominant institutions of kinship and politics have been identified as central and contrasting orders of social organization and control and as major material bases for theological symbolization.

The importance of ancient patron-client arrangements for ordering social relations as well as symbolizing divine-human relations has become evident. We are gaining clarity on the difference between economic systems of reciprocity and redistribution and their points of conflict.

The diverse interest groups of Palestinian society are emerging more clearly, along with their respective social agendas, strategies, and ideologies. The interrelated components of composite worldviews (including issues of purity, ritual, personal identity, the body politic and personal, sin, suffering, and cosmology) are becoming apparent as elements of a coherent theological view. Restrictive Jewish codes concerning holiness and pollution and their social capacity for defining and maintaining group identity and boundaries, roles and status, diet and social relations, are now being seen as neuralgic points of social and ideological conflict within and beyond the Christian community as it develops novel strategies for its novel inclusive mission.

Dominant features of Mediterranean dyadic personality, perceptions such as those of limited good, and values such as those of honor and shame are now being appreciated as basic to the culture and behavior of the early Christian movement. This improved understanding of the social and cultural setting and scripts of Christianity in turn is resulting in a more accurate interpretation of Christian texts, their rhetorical situations and strategies, the social functions of their theological expressions, and the manner in which they constitute both reflections of and responses to their social contexts.

5. The initial conversations with social scientists and their body of research have opened up the possibility of a more fruitful dialogue in the future. The cross-disciplinary character of this endeavor is a constructive rather than destructive obliteration of the artificial walls heretofore separating complementary disciplines. Exegetes, historians, archaeologists, classicists, and social scientists, and ultimately the Bible reader, all stand to gain from this productive conversation and collaboration.

6. The immensity of the information explosion typical of the twentieth century also has made it clear that teamwork, as well as interdisciplinary collaboration, is essential. The time is past when any one scholar can individually master all the disciplines and all the information now at hand for understanding any society modern or ancient. Social-scientific criticism presumes and encourages such teamwork. Like cross-disciplinary conversation, teamwork encourages the sharing rather than the hoarding of information and fosters more effective mutual critique.

7. In the field of ancient historical and biblical research, this approach has successfully begun to demonstrate the contrast between modern, predominantly northern hemisphere social and cultural scripts and perspectives, on the one hand, and, on the other, the cognitive perspectives and behavioral scripts of the ancient world and their embodiment in its literary products. Through the construction and use of models that distinguish modern from ancient modes of organization, behavior, and thought, it enables scholars of antiquity to avoid the methodological sins of anachronism and ethnocentrism. In this way biblical readers as well as scholars become more sensitive to the danger of data contamination, of mistaking their worlds for the world of the Bible, and of practicing eisegesis rather than exegesis. Historians and exegetes informed by the social sciences are learning to become more considerate and perceptive visitors to the foreign world of the Bible and the Circum-Mediterranean.

8. This clarification of the differences between ancient and modern environments, moreover, has also enabled us to become more self-critical. Students and readers become more aware of their own social location, frames of reference, and worldviews and how they differ from those reflected in the texts they read. Readers learn to be attentive not only to the interests and ideologies inherent in texts but also to their own interests, ideologies, and agendas.

9. All of this has put us in a better position for considering and assessing the relevance of the biblical writings and their context to today's scene. That relationship is determined not simply by a perceived pertinence of biblical ideas concerning wealth or poverty, war or peace, revolt against or surrender to today's economic, social, and political "powers that be," but by analogous or dissimilar arcs of meaning generated by texts received and read in analogous or different social contexts. Social-scientific criticism provides the exegete, the theologian, the ethicist, the preacher, and the Bible reader with a more refined set of parameters and historical, literary, social, and ideological controls for assessing meaning *then* in the biblical context and meaning *now* in first, second, and third world settings. Such a contextualizing of the Bible and the biblical communities is one vital step toward a contextualization of the diversity of religious experience across the ages and the identification of visions and energies that can vitalize religious communities today (see Schreiter 1985).

From a hermeneutical perspective, the religious messages of the biblical texts are socially as well as historically conditioned. This is a principle coherent with the doctrine of the incarnation of the word of God and of God's self-revelation in, not apart from, history (see Aguirre 1985b:330–31). Social-scientific criticism aids readers in discovering and appreciating the historical, social, and cultural particularity of the biblical writings. At the same time, it treats the biblical texts as examples of the enculturation of the faith in general and stimulates thought as to how that faith is further enculturated in every age, including our own.

Such a reading of texts in their contexts and such a focus on the relation of religious experience and social situation also serve as an analogy for the contemporary contextualization of theology and spirituality. Through the perspectives of this method, contemporary believers are aided in understanding how their own faith and spirituality are shaped by social structures, social experience, and cultural values. With this awareness, we will be able to view our own place in human history with greater clarity and honesty, as Norman Gottwald has remarked (1979:705). We will be in a more advantageous position for tracing the continuities and changes that link us to and separate us from the biblical past. Rather than naively assuming a direct and unmediated connection with the inherited symbols and traditions of the past, we will seek to assess in our own time in what respects and to what degree the biblical writings as testimonies to and products of the social engagement, struggle, courage, trust, and commitment of our forebears can inspire and inform a modern spirituality and an engagement in the social and cultural struggles of our own day. Fidelity to the sacred heritage of the past will be balanced by an honest appraisal of faith in dialogue with social experience and of fidelity as tempered by the vitalities of history.

Appendix 1

COMPARISON OF THE FOCI OF THE
SOCIAL SCIENCES AND HISTORICAL CRITICISM

Social Sciences   **Historical Criticism**

Actions

regular, recurrent, repeated, routinized, common(place), ordinary, everyday, workaday	singular, occasional, rare, irregular, extraordinary, unique
actions-in-relation, patterns of actions in relation to roles and statuses	actions as cause/caused/effect
their social as well as temporal and spatial location	their temporal and spatial location

Actors

personal identity, number, social relations networks, economic, social, cultural location; self-interests and ideology	personal identity, number, origin and historical biography, individual characteristics (esp. unique features)
collectives and the intersection of biography, social structure, and history	individuals
commonalities	exceptions
generalities	specifics
actors as typical	actors as idiosyncratic

Environment, Situation

ecological, geographical, economic, social, political, cultural features of ecosystem and social system and their systemic interrelations	geographical, economic, social, political, cultural features as discrete entities; specificities—not necessarily related

107

Social Sciences	**Historical Criticism**

Society

dyads, groups, coalitions, factions, etc.; organizations, institutions	individuals, groups
society as system	component sectors
social dynamics and processes; social and cultural scripts	individual and independent behavior
prevailing, collectively shared, values, goals, norms, sanctions, standards, customs, laws	different or unique values, norms, etc.
structures and mechanisms of primary and secondary socialization	

Objects, Phenomena

properties, features, with focus on patterns of interrelationship, commonalities, typicalities	properties, features, with focus on characteristic, unusual, or unique aspects
position and capacity within the total system, or "function" of parts within totality	

Temporality

focus on present, past, and future, with stress on present	focus on present, past, and future, with stress on past
synchronic and diachronic, with stress on synchronic	diachronic primary focus

Forces, Dynamics at Work

determinative, influential *relations* of power	determinative, influential *sources, causes, and effects* of power

Knowledge, Culture, Belief System

types of knowledge; sources, use, control of science and technology; common, shared knowledge	types of knowledge; sources, use, control of science and technology; uncommon, extraordinary knowledge claimed by individuals or groups
common culture and cultural scripts	assorted but unrelated features of culture
processes and mechanisms of socialization and enculturation	educational institutions and agencies
typical meanings (manifest and latent, explicit and implicit)	different, unusual meanings manifest and explicit
systems of beliefs	specific beliefs held by individuals or group

Social Sciences	Historical Criticism
relations of beliefs to social system (ideology); embeddedness of beliefs in politics and kinship	religion, theology as phenomenon distinct from politics and kinship

Method

cross-cultural comparison and search for pattern similarities	comparisons within one culture and search for specific similarities and differences
theoretical models explicated and tested	theoretical models left implicit and unverifiable
emic/etic distinction (native vs. observer points of view)	
models used to distinguish modern from ancient perspectives and cultural scripts	Western, eurocentric perspectives and cultural scripts assumed

Appendix 2

DATA INVENTORY FOR SYNCHRONIC SOCIAL ANALYSIS OF EARLY CHRISTIAN GROUPS

A data inventory is an analytical heuristic tool or research model for identifying categories and constellations of data that are actually available or hypothetically desirable for purposes of analysis and synthesis—in this case, for a synchronic analysis of Christian groups attested in the New Testament. The various topics imply relevant issues to be investigated and questions to be asked regarding the availability of data concerning these topics. This inventory seeks to be comprehensive in scope, but, like any model, it can be expanded or modified as required. The occasional biblical references, however, are illustrative rather than comprehensive.

1. *Location*
1.1. Temporal location
1.1.1. Calendar time (imperial reigns; local time)
1.1.2. Temporal phase of existence of group (e.g., initial, intermediate, end phase)
1.2. Geographical location
1.2.1. Map location in Mediterranean basin
1.2.2. Natural environment (ecology; topography; climate; natural resources; food supply; flora and fauna; etc.)
1.2.3. Urban or rural (exclusively, predominantly, or mixed)
1.3. Social location in relation to macrosociety
1.3.1. Economic activity
1.3.1.1. Modes of land tenure; agriculture; technology; subsistence sector; modes of extraction of surplus and taxation
1.3.1.2. Modes and means of production
1.3.1.3. Household (*oikos*) management
1.3.1.4. Crafts; collective labor ("industries")
1.3.1.5. Trade; commerce; expenditures; investments; levels of money and credit; banking system; taxation

1.3.1.6. Modes of distribution and exchange of goods and services (media of exchange, exchange centers; trade and transportation; prices and wages; communications)

1.3.1.7. Relations of owners and laborers

1.3.2. Population structure (sustained by natural environment and economy)

1.3.2.1. Size and density

1.3.2.2. Morbidity, mortality rates

1.3.2.3. Population movements, displacements as results of natural catastrophes, war, migrations, etc.

1.3.3. Technology and science

1.3.3.1. Size and types of labor force (human [free, slave]; animals)

1.3.3.2. Nature and extent of scientific knowledge

1.3.3.3. Tools; processes of production

1.3.3.4. Modes of sanitation; hygiene, medicine, healing

1.3.4. Social system

1.3.4.1. Social organization

1.3.4.1.1. The private sector: institution of kinship, family, and fictive (surrogate) kin; local village communities

1.3.4.1.2 The public sector: city, state, and civic institutions

1.3.4.2. Roles and statuses

1.3.4.3. Social classes and stratification

1.3.4.4. Social relations and activities in public and private sectors, including patronage and clientism, associations (*collegia, koina*), domestic and civic cults

1.3.4.5. Social (and geographical) mobility

1.3.4.6. Consumption and standards of living

1.3.5. Political (including legal and military) organization

1.3.5.1. Political institutions for adaptation

1.3.5.1.1. Organization and administration

1.3.5.1.2. Security mechanisms (military; patrons)

1.3.5.1.3. Allocation of goods and services

1.3.5.2. Political processes for maintenance of order and control

1.3.5.2.1. Modes of extraction of surplus (tribute, taxation, booty, robbery, exploitation)

1.3.5.2.2. Modes of monopolized control of production, distribution, and consumption

1.3.5.2.3. Modes of regulation and enforcement of law

1.3.5.2.4. Modes of patronage and clientism; parasitism

1.3.5.2.5. Modes of information dissemination and control

1.3.5.3. Political culture

1.3.5.3.1. Propaganda information serving interests of elites (ideas, assumptions, expectations)

1.3.5.3.2. Cultural beliefs, values, norms, symbols, myths serving interest of elites

1.3.5.3.3. Cultural history and heritage

    1.3.6. Cultural system

    1.3.6.1. Cultural hegemony (relative autonomy yet utilization in domination process)

    1.3.6.2. Nature and extent of knowledge

    1.3.6.3. Characteristics of language, art, drama, music

    1.3.6.4. Extent of literacy; traits of orality and literacy

    1.3.6.5. Aspects of folklore, folkways, traditions, customs

    1.3.6.6. Dominant or competing perceptions of the natural and social order, human nature, time, space, the cosmos, the sacred; worldviews

    1.3.6.7. Dominant or competing values

    1.3.6.8. Dominant or competing attitudes, expectations

    1.3.6.9. Dominant or competing norms, sanctions

    1.3.6.10. Life-styles and perceived life-chances (given structural immobility)

    1.3.6.11. Distinctive features of the "great" (elite) tradition and the popular folk tradition(s) and points of similarity/dissimilarity, convergence/conflict

    1.3.6.12. Personality structure (dyadic not individualistic; authoritarian-coercive; aggressive; apathetic; conservative)

    1.3.6.13. Enculturation processes (agents and instrumentalities; information dissemination; education [formal, informal])

    1.3.7. Belief system(s) and ideologies

    1.3.7.1. Specific beliefs as interrelated components of belief systems

    1.3.7.2. Dominant or competing beliefs and belief systems

    1.3.7.3. Content of specific group myths and traditions (which tend to be past-oriented, conservative, anti-innovative; anti-empirical; anti-technological; expandable and syncretistic in nature)

    1.3.7.4. Capacity (or function) of beliefs, myths, and traditions to reinforce values of commitment, loyalty, interdependence, reciprocity, noncompetition, sociality (vs. individuality), the public (vs. the private) good, hierarchy, conformity to law and order, and the like

    1.3.7.5. Ideological utilization of beliefs, myths, traditions to serve as explanations and legitimations of group interests and political propaganda.

    2. *Christian Group Formations in Specific Localities*

    2.1. Constituency

    2.1.1. Persons (explicitly named; unnamed)

    2.1.1.1. Number; gender; ages; kin relations; ethnic origin; natives/foreigners/resident aliens (visitors, missionaries)

    2.1.1.2. Status/rank/class (according to status of family and place of origin; gender; age; personal liberty or servitude [free/freed/slave]; wealth; ethnic origin; citizenship [local; Roman]; occupation; education)

    2.1.1.3. Affiliations within and outside the group (kin relations; patrons/clients; occupational associations; friendship networks), locally and translocally (Jesus; apostles; other Christians; Jews; local residents; Greeks; Romans)

2.1.1.4. Roles (domestic; civic; within Christian group)

2.1.1.5. Occupations

2.1.2. Subgroups, coalitions, factions (size and number; basis of association [primary groups (based on kinship, surrogate kinship): families, cliques; secondary groups: coalitions, communities, associations, mobs, movements])

2.2. Group, subgroup organization

2.2.1. Mode of organization and variations over time (Jewish faction centered in Jesus; group-centered faction after Jesus' death; Jewish sect; independent group; bureaucracy after Constantine)

2.2.2. Basis and model of organization (household; synagogue; philosophic schools; collegia; cults; military; etc.)

2.2.3. Roles and statuses within Christian group (defined/undefined; ascribed/achieved) associated with specific persons

2.2.4. Agents and mechanisms of social control

2.2.4.1. Leadership roles: mode of definition; criteria of qualification

2.2.4.2. Values and norms governing exercise of authority

2.2.4.3. Mode of exercise of authority

2.2.4.4. Mechanisms for conflict management, resolution of tensions, disputes

2.2.4.5. Nature and degree of translocal influence and coercion

2.2.5. Recruitment and replacement of new members (mission strategy and tactics; conversion of households, individuals, sympathizers, clients, patrons; versions of evangelical appeal)

2.2.6. Conditions prompting modifications in form of social organization over time and nature of these modifications

2.3. Major rituals, ceremonies, and forms of worship

2.3.1. Baptism (ritual of initiation and incorporation)

2.3.2. Eucharist (ritual of integration and solidarity)

2.3.3. Sacred calendar (public and private observation)

2.3.4. Temple attendance and sacrifice

2.3.5. Prayer and domestic observances

2.4. Group identity

2.4.1. Self-definition, modes and mechanisms of

2.4.1.1. Use of collective terminology once applied to Israel or drawn from the sacred tradition (e.g., "the people of God," "the Israel of God," "the household of God," "the elect of God," "the Way," "the holy ones," *ekklēsia* [as cultic assembly], etc.)

2.4.1.2. Use of collective images and metaphors once applied to Israel or drawn from the sacred tradition (e.g., [God's] "children," "planting," "temple," "kingdom," "sheep," "progeny of Abraham [and Sarah]," etc.)

2.4.1.3. Use of terms and images adopted from macrosociety (e.g., *ekklēsia* [as assembly of citizens]; *politeuma*, "brotherhood," "*koinonia*," "*laos*" [as citizenry], "*oikos*" [as household], kingdom, "body [of Christ]," etc.)

2.4.1.4. Ideological legitimation of distinctive communal identity through, e.g.:

2.4.1.4.1. Stress on the divine initiative which called group into being and warrants its existence; claim of being divinely elected as God's special covenant community of the end time (1 Pet 1:1-2, 3-12; 2:4-10), the object of divine favor, and recipient of revelation (1 Cor 2:6-10; Gal 1:11-12, 16; 2:2; 1 Pet 1:12, 25) and the divine spirit (Acts passim; 1 Cor 6:19-20), and spiritual gifts/charisms, including spirit-endowed leaders (1 Corinthians 12 par.; 1 Pet 4:10-11); solidarity with Jesus Christ; animation by the Holy Spirit, etc.

2.4.1.4.2. Claim of being the subject of God's reversal of social status (in contrast to perceived inferior status in society at large) as illustrated in the divine reversal of the status of Jesus Christ (crucified by humans, exalted by God [Matt 19:30; 20:16 par.; Luke 1:52; 1 Pet 2:4-10, 18-25]); claim of new honor and dignity before God who stands over and above society (New Testament passim); claim of special divine favor toward the poor and powerless (Luke 1:53; Jas 2:5); demand of loyalty to God rather than to society (Acts 5:29; 1 Pet 4:2-3)

2.4.1.4.3. Claim of embodying exclusively "in Christ" the fulfillment and realization of ancient sacred promises, expectations, and hopes (in contrast to the parent body) (Gospels; Acts; Galatians; Hebrews; 1 Peter; Revelation)

2.4.1.4.4. Claim of antiquity of roots and continuity with ancient Israel; appeal to ancient Scripture and claim of its eschatological fulfillment in the sect's experience (continuity with Abraham [Galatians 3-4; Romans 4], Sarah [1 Pet 3:1-6]; and with other heroes of faith [Hebrews 11])

2.4.1.4.5. Appropriation-*cum*-modification of identity and tradition of parent body, Israel, and claim of now embodying that identity most fully as the "Israel of God" (Gal 6:16), the elect and holy covenant people of God (1 Pet 1:14-16; 2:4-10), etc., with eschatological warrant for a reinterpretation of the tradition (Rom 15:4; 1 Cor 10:1-13)

2.4.1.4.6. Reinterpretation/replacement of main institutions of parent body: the place of God's presence shifted from temple to body of Jesus (John 2:13-22) or community of the faithful (1 Cor 6:19-20); rite of initiation and incorporation shifted from circumcision to baptism (Col 2:11-14); calendar and purity rules of parent body transcended (Gal 4:8-12; 6:15; Col 2:20-23); faith in Christ replaces observance of the law (Galatians; Romans)

2.5. Group cohesion, maintenance of

2.5.1. Threats to internal group cohesion

2.5.1.1. Internal ethnic, social, cultural diversity and disagreement regarding chief values, interests, goals

2.5.1.2. External tensions and conflicts with "outsider" nonbelievers and pressures urging conformity to Jewish or macrosocietal patterns of belief and behavior

2.5.2. Mechanisms for generating and maintaining internal cohesion

2.5.2.1. Stimulation of group consciousness through ideological interpretation of salvation as divine act of incorporation, construction, collection (gathering of the dispersed and separated)

2.5.2.2. Stress on equity of access to the grace of God (Gal 3:28; 1 Pet 3:7)

2.5.2.3. Instruction and exhortation regarding necessity for internal harmony and order, social and personal integrity (Matt 5:49; James passim), mutual respect, humility, and loyalty, commitment to one another as to God and Jesus Christ; reciprocal forgiveness (Matt 18:15-18); brotherly love (1 Pet 1:22; 3:8); unity of mind and spirit (Phil 2:1-11; 1 Pet 3:8); building up of the community through love (1 Cor 8:1; 10:23; 12–13); order (1 Cor 14:40); mutual respect (1 Cor 7:4); mutual service (1 Pet 4:10-11); mutual humility (1 Pet 3:8; 5:5); mutual subordination (1 Pet 5:5); hospitality (1 Pet 4:9; 3 John); with eschatological warrant for behavior (1 Cor 7:26-31)

2.5.2.4. Establishment and enforcement of norms and sanctions governing internal and external conduct; subordination to the will of God as clarified in the teaching and exemplified in the experience of Jesus Christ; use of Decalogue, household codes clarifying domestic roles, relations, and reciprocities; lists of virtues and vices with additional christological rationale; christological, ecclesiological, and moral implications of baptism (1 Cor 1:10-16) and Lord's Supper (1 Cor 10:14-22; 11; 14); eschatological rationale (Rom 13:11-14; 1 Cor 10:1-11; Gal 6:16; 1 Pet 4:7-11; mutual humility (1 Pet 3:8; 5:5); mutual service rather than domination as criterion of leadership (1 Pet 4:10-11; 5:1-4); stress on divine impartial judgment of living and dead (Rom 14:10-23; 1 Cor 4:5; 1 Pet 1:17; 4:6, 17-19)

2.5.2.5. Maintenance of members' confidence and emotional commitment through stress on:

2.5.2.5.1. God's benevolence, fidelity, love, and providential care as basis and goal of trust, faith, obedience, hope (New Testament passim)

2.5.2.5.2. God's transforming and resurrecting power (1 Cor 15:51-52; 1 Pet 1:3-12

2.5.2.5.3. Members' solidarity with experience of Jesus Christ (rejection, suffering, and divine vindication) (Gospels; Pauline epistles; 1 Pet 2:18-25, 4:1) and experience of the larger Christian brotherhood (1 Pet 5:8-9)

2.5.2.5.4. Members' personal experience of the Spirit of God (Luke-Acts; Gal 3:2-3; 5:25)

2.5.2.5.5. Members' personal growth and maturity (Gal 3:23—4:7; Eph 4:1-16; 1 Pet 1:22—2:3)

2.5.2.5.6. The imminence and impartiality of divine judgment (1 Pet 1:17; 4:5, 7, 17-19) and divine compensation for steadfastness and fidelity (Jas 5:7-11; Revelation passim)

2.5.2.6. Promotion of rituals and ceremonies reinforcing distinctive group identity and solidarity (baptism; Lord's Supper)

2.5.2.7. Promotion of material support, hospitality, social aid; brokering of social alliances (Acts 2:44-45; Rom 12:7-8; Heb 13:1-3; 1 Pet 4:8-11)

2.5.2.8. Discipline and possible expulsion of deviants who contravene doctrinal, moral, or organizational precepts and cause internal dissension and weakening of group cohesion (Matt 18:15-17; 1 Cor 5:1-13) and its divine warrant

2.5.2.9. Stress on problems resulting from loss of group cohesion (dissension leading to defection and member loss; ill repute among outsiders and blasphemy of God leading to ineffectiveness of recruitment; denial of the indivisibility of the body of Christ)

2.5.2.10. Stressing or exaggerating threats from without as motivation for maintaining internal cohesion and group boundaries (1 Pet 3:13—4:19; 5:8-9)

2.5.2.11. Ideological provision of a plausible, coherent worldview/symbolic universe integrating values, goals, norms, patterns of belief and behavior and supplying ultimate divine legitimation for the group's interests, program, and strategies

2.6. Group boundaries, mechanisms for generating and maintaining clear, strong social boundaries

2.6.1. Vulnerability of group to "contaminating" external influences and pressures under variable conditions

2.6.1.1. Size and length of existence of group

2.6.1.2. Degree of member commitment to group values, beliefs

2.6.1.3. Degree of member and group exposure to "outsiders"

2.6.1.4. Nature of modes of interaction with "outsiders" (along a range of conformity, cooperation, exchange, competition, coercion, conflict)

2.6.1.5. Degree of political toleration of diverse groups and capacity for forcing macrosocial integration

2.6.1.6. Other external natural and social phenomena (famine; pestilence; war; migrations; etc.)

2.6.2. Strategies for generating and maintaining clear, "nonporous," strong, social and ideological boundaries

2.6.2.1. Differentiation of Christian "insiders" from "outsiders" (negative reference groups) e.g., Pharisees: (as "hypocrites") Matthew 5–7; 23; Sadducees: Mark 12:18-27 par.; Gentiles: Matthew 5:47; 6:7; 18:17; Mark 10:42-45 par.; 1 Cor 5:1; 1 Thess 4:5; 1 Pet 2:12; 4:3; Rev 16:19; 18:23; 20:8; the "world": John; 1–2 John; James 2:27; "synagogue of Satan": Rev. 2:9; 3:9

2.6.2.2. Adoption and modification of Jewish purity/pollution concept for demarcation of boundaries (1 Thess 4:1–8; 1 Pet 1:14-16; Jas 1:27; and New Testament passim)

2.6.2.3. Devaluation, vilification of the character and morals of outsiders. Negative characterization and labeling of outsiders as hostile and inferior (as wolves or lions against vulnerable sheep; sinners vs. righteous;

Gentiles vs. people of God; agents of darkness vs. light, of death vs. life; as "impure" and in league with Satan, devil, and who therefore are to be resisted (Jas 4:7, cf. 1:26-27; 1 Pet 5:8-9; 2 John 7; Revelation passim) or with the impurity or darkness of the "world" (unbelieving society) (John; Jas 1:27; 1 John; 2 John). Employment of antitheses illustrating contrasts between insiders and outsiders: earth/heaven (Matt 6:10; Phil 3:21; Hebrews passim), demonic/divine (Jas 4:7), wisdom from above (=divine)/from below (=devilish) (Jas 3:13-18); this age/age to come (Gal 1:4); then/now (1 Pet 2:10; 4:2-3); darkness/light (1 Pet 2:9); death/life, rebirth (Rom 6:1-5; 1 Pet 1:3, 22); impure/pure (1 Corinthians 5–6; 1 Thess 4:1-8; Jas 1:26-27; 4:7-8); flesh/spirit (Gal 3:3; 5:16-26); sinners/righteous (1 Pet 4:17-18); old nature/new nature (Col 3:9-10); double-minded/integral person (Jas 1:4-8; 4:8); nonbelievers/believers (1 Pet 2:4-10); inside(rs)/outside(rs) (Matt 8:12; 22:13; 25:30; Mark 4:11; 1 Cor 5:12, 13; Col 4:5; 1 Thess 4:12; 1 Tim 3:17; 1 John 4:1; 2 John 7; Rev 22:15); afflicters/afflicted (1 Thess 3:3-5; 2 Thess 1:6; 1 Pet 3:13-16; 4:12-19)

From an apocalyptic perspective, conceptual and ideological distinctions and demarcations within four correlated realms: the cosmological (heaven/earth); the temporal (this age/the age to come); the social (the righteous/unrighteous); and the personal (double-minded/whole)

2.6.2.4. Characterization of entrance into group as act of separation, dissociation, termination, movement from death to life, darkness to light, rebirth; and insistence on termination of and separation from previous associations and way of life; allegiances (social and religious); explicit imperatives ("abstain," put off, "resist," e.g., 1 Pet 2:1; 2:11; 4:2-4)

2.6.2.5. Employment of models of group definition that involve clear boundaries (household of God [surrogate family]), *ekklēsia,* kingdom, temple, planting, vine, flock, *politeuma,* etc.

2.6.2.6. Clarification of distinctive Christian values, norms, goals, interests prompted by interaction with outsiders; holiness, humility, exclusive allegiance to God and Jesus Christ; fidelity to will of God; suffering as divine test, sign of Spirit's presence, solidarity with Christ; hope; salvation (1 Peter passim)

2.6.2.7. Claim of superiority over against Judaism and Gentiles (superiority to the prophets in reception of the Christ and the gospel (Hebrews; 1 Pet 1:10-12) and claim of obsolescence of previous covenants, sacrifices, modes of worship (Hebrews); superiority over the Gentiles in knowledge of God and union with God and modes of morality (Matt 5:20; Jas 1:4; 1 Pet 1:10–12, 17; 2:4-10, 11-17, 3:15-16, 4:14-16)

2.6.2.8. Stress on debilitating effects of weak, porous boundaries (unclarity of values and norms; confusion and "contamination" of members; internal friction and fraction; loss of members; loss of clear distinctive identity as a basis for recruitment) (1 Thessalonians; James; 1–2 John; Revelation)

2.6.2.9. Promotion of good conduct toward outsiders to gain their respect, silence their slander, and possibly win their adherence (Matt 5:38-48/ Luke 6:27-30; 1 Thess 4:11-12; Col 4:5; 1 Pet 2:12, 15; 3:1-2, 8–9, 13-17; 4:12-19)

2.6.2.10. In situations of tension and conflict, turning adversity into assets— e.g.: finding a positive meaning to suffering; accentuating impression of external hostility and conflict as motivation for increased resistance and social cohesion (Mark 13 par.; Pauline letters; 1 Peter; Revelation)

2.7. Interaction of Christians with outsiders (other groups, communities, associations, mobs, movements, and macrosociety

2.7.1. Geographical and temporal locale of interaction

2.7.2. Extent and mode of interaction (exchange, cooperation, conformity, competition, coercion, conflict)

2.7.2.1. Extent and mode of interaction with Jews

2.7.2.2. Extent and mode of interaction with Gentiles, including local residents, Romans

2.7.3. Modes of depiction and assessment of outsiders

2.7.4. Principles, policies, and limits concerning types of interaction and participation in civic affairs (norms; sanctions; degrees of strictness or latitude)

2.7.5. Agents, mechanisms, and modes of regulation (communal or individual agents or both; external regulations and regulators)

2.7.6. Modes of ideological legitimation of depictions and assessments of outsiders and of regulations of interaction

2.7.7. The Christian "mission" (environmental, social, economic, political, and cultural conditions; strategies; conflicts; modes of legitimation; achievements, failures)

2.7.8. Christian interaction among local and translocal Christian groups

2.7.8.1. Geo-cultural locations of Christian groups

2.7.8.2. Extent and modes of interaction (traveling missionaries and cohorts; epistolary correspondence and sharing of letters)

2.7.8.3. Identity, constituency, interests, activities, ideologies of contending groups, coalitions, factions

2.7.8.3.1. Palestine (Jerusalem and Judea; Samaria; Galilee; the Twelve; apostles; Jesus' family; Hebrew/Hellenist factions; circles around James, Peter, Philip)

2.7.8.3.2. The Decapolis and Transjordan

2.7.8.3.3. Damascus (Paul)

2.7.8.3.4. Antioch-on-Orontes: Barnabas, Paul et al., Peter

2.7.8.3.5. Syria-Cilicia (and southern Galatia?): Paul and Barnabas

2.7.8.3.6. Asia Minor: Paul, Silvanus, Timothy; Peter? Johannine group

2.7.8.3.7. Crete, Cyprus, and Aegean Islands: Paul

2.7.8.3.8. Greece: Athens (Paul et al.); Corinth (Paul; Apollos; Cephas/Peter factions)

2.7.8.3.9. Italy and Rome: Paul et al.; Peter et al.

2.7.8.3.10. Alexandria?

2.7.8.3.11. Cyrene?

2.7.8.3.12. Carthage?

2.7.8.3.13. Spain?

2.8. Christian group interests and ideologies. (For definitions, see Glossary)

2.8.1. Christian group interests

2.8.1.1. Enabling membership access to the natural, biological, economic, social, and cultural means of sustenance and survival (collective as well as individual)—e.g.: health, food, shelter, clothing, place of belonging, protection, sociality, protection, support, information, justice, good reputation, honor, dignity); i.e., access to the limited goods of the society, "salvation" in its physical and social dimensions

2.8.1.2. Providing the membership access to a "meaningful and honorable existence," a safe and sustaining relationship with the force(s) in ultimate control of human life (God), and a plausible and coherent symbolic universe. "Salvation" as cognitive and emotional integration

2.8.1.3. Continuation and growth of the group through successful recruitment and member replacement

2.8.1.4. Maintenance of group commitment and cohesion through the effective management of internal and external tensions and the securing of group boundaries

2.8.1.5. The local and translocal consolidation of proliferating groups into an integrated, worldwide Christian movement

2.8.1.6. Competing successfully with other external interest groups for survival, expansion, influence, access to scarce and limited resources

2.8.1.7. Issues for attention/questions to be asked:

2.8.1.7.1. Who are the persons with power and authority to formulate, articulate, and secure these interests?

2.8.1.7.2. How are these interests formulated, communicated, and disseminated as ideals and goals of the group as a whole—both overtly and covertly?

2.8.1.7.3. What is the degree of group consensus regarding these interests and goals?

2.8.1.7.4. What social strategies and mechanisms (including ideology) are employed to secure these interests and goals?

2.8.1.7.5. Is there internal factional rivalry and intergroup tension reflective of competing interests? What are the focal points, conditions, processes, and consequences of this conflict? Do interests diverge and conflict according to class, gender, age, occupational, or other lines?

2.8.1.7.6. Who are the chief beneficiaries and the main "losers" in the securing of articulated interests?

2.8.1.7.7. How and by whom are these interests ideologically legitimated?

2.8.1.7.8. Which interests are realized or not realized, and under which conditions and with which consequences?

  2.8.2. Christian ideologies/theologies

  2.8.2.1. Focal points of the Christian belief system

2.8.2.1.1. God

2.8.2.1.2. The cosmos (natural and supernatural orders)

2.8.2.1.3. Time and space (and the issue of eschatology)

2.8.2.1.4. The natural and human condition (mortality, corruptibility; good and evil; conflict; sin; etc.)

2.8.2.1.5. Salvation and related metaphors

2.8.2.1.6. The mediator of salvation: Messiah-Christ and related christological concepts

2.8.2.1.7. The community of the "saved" (household of God, *ekklēsia* and related ecclesiological concepts)

2.8.2.1.8. Morality and related ethical concepts

2.8.2.1.9. Worship

  2.8.2.2. Issues for attention/questions to be asked:

2.8.2.2.1. Which beliefs and concepts are used to articulate, explain, and legitimate which personal or group interests and values?

2.8.2.2.2. How are these concepts and beliefs used in relation to group identity, organization, and action? How are they employed variously to affirm, promote group consciousness, cohesion, and commitment or to censure disapproved forms of behavior? How are they used as moral norms and sanctions?

2.8.2.2.3. Who has or assumes the power or authority to articulate these beliefs and concepts?

2.8.2.2.4. How are they promulgated and enforced?

2.8.2.2.5. What is the degree of consensus or dissensus regarding these beliefs and concepts within the group? What are the particular points of agreement and disagreement? What factors relate to and account for this agreement or disagreement?

2.8.2.2.6. By whom and by what means are disagreements over beliefs adjudicated and resolved?

2.8.2.2.7. How are these beliefs and concepts coherent with other beliefs and organized into a comprehensive conceptual or theological system?

2.8.2.2.8. How is this belief system used to integrate experience and expectation into a "comprehensive and coherent world of meaning," a "symbolic universe"?

2.8.2.2.9. Is there evidence of the existence and clash of competing belief systems and ideologies between Christian and non-Christian entities? What are the points of ideological similarity and conflict? What are the conditioning factors? What are the processes and outcomes of this conflict?

2.8.2.2.10. Under what conditions do beliefs and belief systems change over time? What are the consequences of these changes?

3. The Synchronic Situation as a Whole and the Factors and Forces Contributive toward Stability, Conflict, Change, and Transition within and among Christian Communities and within the Society at Large

Appendix 3

DATA INVENTORY FOR DIACHRONIC ANALYSIS OF
SOCIAL-HISTORICAL PHASES AND TRENDS

1. Analysis and synthesis of macrosocietal phases and trends
1.1. Identification and justification of appropriate theory, models, and research design for analyzing these phases and trends
1.2. Identification of discrete phases and criteria of demarcation (e.g., imperial reigns; procurator tenures in the provinces; phases of Herodian rule in Palestine; local calendars; specific events (death of Jesus, Stephen, James; call of Paul; first Jewish-Roman war; destruction of Jerusalem and temple; etc.)
1.3. Synchronic analysis and synthesis of each discrete phase (Appendix 2)
1.4. Identification of changes and trends ensuing from one phase to another, including consideration of internal and external interlocking conditioning factors (environmental, economic, social, political, cultural); major agents and networks; instrumentalities; relations of power; systemic contradictions; predominant causes, effects, consequences
1.5. Explanation of 1.3 and 1.4 through testing of models adopted in 1.1
2. Analysis and synthesis of microsocietal phases and trends of the early Christian movement
2.1. Identification and justification of appropriate theory, models, and research design for analyzing microsocietal group movements (and Christianity in particular). See Blasi (1988:2-11) regarding basic features of a social movement and Christianity as a social movement
2.1.1. Evaluation of models of social movements (including their specific aims and salient features; conditioning factors [environmental, economic, social, political, cultural]; agencies; instrumentalities for managing conflict; life span; etc.) and their appropriateness for modeling early Christianity
2.1.1.1. Repristination movements
2.1.1.2. Revitalization movements
2.1.1.3. Reform movements

2.1.1.4. Millenarian movements

2.1.1.5. Sectarian movements

2.1.1.6. Other models

    2.2. Identification of discrete phases of the early Christian movement (from Jewish faction to Jewish sect)

2.2.1. In specific localities

2.2.2. As a translocal movement

    2.3. Synchronic analysis of each discrete phase of each discrete group in early Christianity (see Appendix 2)

    2.4. Comparison of salient features of Christian movement groups with other contemporary movement groups, coalitions, and factions (e.g., Pharisees; Essenes; Therapeutae; baptist groups; John the Baptist group; Zealots; Sicarii; other Mediterranean movement groups) for shared and distinctive characteristics

    2.5. Analysis of interaction between Christian movement groups and outside collectivities

2.5.1. Other contemporary local and translocal groups.

2.5.2. The macrosociety

2.5.3. Checkpoints: conditioning factors of interaction; modes and extent of interaction; coexisting, competing, conflicting interests, strategies, and ideologies

    2.6. Analysis of the process of transition between phases of the Christian movement

2.6.1. Checkpoints: developments in the macrosociety (domestic and foreign relations); impact of societal interactions upon the Christian movement; internal developments with local and translocal spheres of the Christian movement; external and internal forces contributing to, limiting, or inhibiting cohesion, consolidation, and expansion of the Christian movement

2.6.2. Identification and explanation of salient areas and aspects of continuity and change between phases of the Christian movement

2.6.2.1. In specific localities

2.6.2.2. Within the encompassing translocal movement

    2.7. Synthesis of 2.3, 2.4, 2.5, and 2.6; identification and explanation of evident trends, their conditioning factors, and their consequences (short-term; long-range)

Appendix 4

MODELS FOR INTERPRETATION

Models of sociological schools of interpretation (conflict, structural-functional, symbolic interaction, ethnomethodology): Turner 1978; Elliott 1986; Malina 1988a; Neyrey 1988c; Pilch 1988b, Horsley 1989.

Models for comparison of modern industrial and ancient preindustrial, traditional societies and cultures: Romein 1958; Arensberg 1963; Augsburger 1986; Malina and Neyrey 1988:145–47; Malina 1989a, 1989b; Pilch 1991a, 1991b. See also Rohrbaugh 1987b on social location of interpreter.

Group/grid model for comparing social systems and cosmologies: Isenberg 1980; Malina 1982, 1986a, 1986e; Neyrey 1986a:129–70; L. J. White 1986b; Wire 1990:189–93. See Douglas 1973, 1978; Douglas and Isherwood 1978; and Isenberg and Owen 1977 on Douglas's work.

Scenario model for reading ancient texts: Malina 1991b:3–23.

Model of language as product of social system: Halliday 1978:11, 69.

Models of ancient social systems: Carney 1975.

Model of preindustrial agrarian societies: Redfield 1956; Sjoberg 1965; Potter 1967; Shanin 1971; Carney 1975; Rohrbaugh 1978, 1991b; Gerhard and Jean Lenski 1987. Of agrarian economies: Carney 1975; Oakman 1986, 1991a, 1991b.

Comparative models of industrial and preindustrial cities: Sjoberg 1965; Rohrbaugh 1991a, 1991b; see Stark 1991.

Models of modes of production, economic and ideological: Weber 1924; Polanyi 1957; Nash 1966; Belo 1981; Füssel 1987.

Comparative models of economic and social exchange: Mauss 1954; Sahlins 1972; Scott 1976; Houtart 1980; Belo 1981; Malina 1986a:98–138; Moxnes 1988a; Elliott 1991c.

City and countryside: Theissen 1976; Meeks 1983a:9–50; Oakman 1985, 1986, 1991b; Rohrbaugh 1991a, 1991b.

Mediterranean society as agnostic, conflict society: Gouldner 1969; Gilmore 1982; Black-Michaud 1975; Malina 1988a; Malina and Neyrey 1988, 1991d.

Mediterranean society as witchcraft society: Elliott 1988, 1990b, 1991a, 1992; Malina and Neyrey 1988; Neyrey 1988a, 1990b; cf. Derrett 1973; Evans-Pritchard 1976 (1937).

Systemic model of Palestinian social system: Elliott 1986b:13–17, following Carney 1975.

Models of social stratification: M. G. Smith 1966; Gager, in Benko and O'Rourke 1971:99–120; Theissen 1974a, 1974b, 1975c; Mayer 1983; Meeks 1983a:51–73; Rohrbaugh 1984.

Kinship (and household, family): Campbell 1964; Papajohn and Spiegel 1975; Peristiany 1976; Elliott 1981:165–266, 1991b, 1991c; Farber 1981; Malina 1981a:94–151 (including marriage strategies); Verner 1983; Todd 1985; Crosby 1988; K. C. Hanson 1989a, 1989b, 1990 (Herodian marriage strategies); Goody 1990; Bettini 1991; Elliott in Neyrey 1991:211–40.

Patronage and clientism as social and symbolical realities: Campbell 1964; Gellner and Waterbury 1977; Schmidt 1977; Eisenstadt and Roniger 1980; Malina 1980, 1988b; Roniger 1983; Eisenstadt 1984; Elliott 1987a; Moxnes 1988a, 1991a, 1991b.

Groups and modes of social obligation: Judge 1960, 1972; Wilken, in Benko and O'Rourke 1971:268–91; Meeks 1983a:74–110.

Social coalitions and factions: Boissevain 1974; Seland 1987; Malina 1988a.

Social networks: L. M. White 1988b.

Defining "rich" and "poor": Hollenbach 1987; Malina 1987.

Stereotyping and labeling "deviants": Pfuhl 1980; Malina and Neyrey 1988; Malina and Neyrey 1991d:97–122.

Christianity as a social movement: Blasi 1988.

Christianity as a millenarian movement: Isenberg 1974; Gager 1975; Jewett 1986; cf. Burridge 1969.

Christianity as a sectarian movement: Wilson 1973; Scroggs 1975; Wilde 1978; Elliott 1981, 1986a; Meeks 1983a:74–110; L. M. White 1988a.

Comparative model of Palestinian interest groups: Elliott 1986b:17–21; cf. Theissen 1978; Horsley 1986, 1987, 1989.

Internal group dynamics: Schreiber 1977.

Roles and status: Funk 1981; Blasi 1986.

Internal conflict management: Meeks 1983a:111–39.

Institutionalization: Holmberg 1980a; MacDonald 1988; cf. Schütz 1975.

Social location and social scripts (concerning perceptions of purity, rite, personal identity, body and soul, sin, cosmology based on grid/group model of Mary Douglas: Malina 1978b, 1986a; Isenberg 1980; Neyrey 1986a, 1986b, 1988c, 1990b, 1991c; from a different perspective, Robbins 1991; L. M. White 1991.

Gender distinctions and values: Pitt-Rivers 1963; Furnea 1965; Schneider 1971; Malina 1981a:25–50, 1990b; Illich 1982; Gardner 1985; Love 1987; Pilch 1991a; *BTB* 20/2 (1990) entire issue.

"Religion" embedded in kinship and politics: Malina 1986e.

First-century personality, dyadic, not individualistic: Malina 1979, 1981a:51–70, 1984a, 1989a; Malina and Neyrey 1991e:67–96.

Honor and shame, including male/female symbolizations and challenge/response: Peristiany 1965; Malina 1981a:25–50; Moxnes 1985, 1988b, 1988c; L. J. White 1986b; Abu-Lughod 1987; Gilmore 1987; Malina and Neyrey 1991f; Pilch 1991a.

Perception of limited good: Foster 1965; Malina 1981a:71–93; cf. Elliott 1990b, 1991a, 1992 on limited good, envy, and the evil eye.

Perception of time: Malina 1989b; Bettini 1991.

Systems of purity/impurity: Neusner 1973, 1975; Malina 1981a:122–52; Neyrey 1986a, 1986b, 1988c, 1991c.

Replication of physical body and social body: Douglas 1966, 1970, 1975; Malina 1981a:122–52; Neyrey 1986a:129–70, 1990b:102–46.

Illness, health, and healing: Murdock 1980; Pilch 1981, 1985, 1986, 1988c, 1989, 1991a, 1991b, 1991c; Young 1982.

Ritual and ceremonies, including meals: Van Gennep 1960; Turner 1969; Meeks 1983a:140–63; Malina 1986a:139–65; Moxnes 1986; McVann 1988, 1991; Elliott 1991b; Neyrey 1991b.

Hospitality: Malina 1986d.

Worldview and symbolic universe: Kearny 1984; Petersen 1985; Neyrey 1990b, 1991c:271–304.

Ideology and modes of ideological (and theological) legitimation: Theissen 1975a; Elliott 1981:267–95; Barton 1982, 1984; Meeks 1983a:164–92, 1983b; Petersen 1985; Esler 1987; Myers 1988:14–31.

Historians and their varying cultural scripts: Malina 1986a:166–84.

Glossary

agrarian society A generic type of society that is based on agriculture made possible by the plow and the harnessing of animal energy and that therefore generates a surplus which in turn leads to population growth and labor specialization.

anthropology The scientific study of human beings, their physical character, social relations, historical and geographical distribution, racial classification, and their cultural history, with a predominant (but not exclusive) focus on preindustrial or nonliterate societies, with two major branches:

    1. **physical anthropology**, concerned with one or more aspects of the origins, evolution, and nature of humans as a biological organism.

    2. **cultural** or **social** (Great Britain) **anthropology**, concerned with one or more aspects of the social and cultural factors in human behavior.

coalition A collectivity of persons within a larger encapsulating social structure consisting of distinct parties in temporary alliances for a limited purpose, including kin groups, cliques, gangs, action sets, and factions. See FACTION.

community An interdependent collectivity of persons living relatively permanently in a geographically limited area that serves as a focus for a major portion of the residents' daily life; usually involves people who share common institutions and a common culture. See VILLAGE.

concept An abstract generalization based on sense perception and empirical evidence. An ordered, mental image of a class of phenomena in contrast to a "percept," which is the sense impression of a single phenomenon. Associated with but also distinguished from "constructs," which are purely intellectual schemes in contrast to concepts, which must be grounded in percepts. Concepts form the basic building blocks of hypotheses, theories, and models.

culture   In the general sense: all behavior and related products that human beings, as members of human societies, acquire by means of symbolic interaction; the universal, distinctive characteristic that sets human social life apart from all other forms of social life.

As one cultural system differentiated from other cultural systems: the total, generally organized way of life, including language, knowledge, beliefs, values, norms, sanctions, institutions, art, custom, traditions, interests and ideologies, and artifacts that is proper to a given people and that is passed on from generation to generation. Compare subcultures, microcultures, and countercultures.

The "**Culture concept**" (Geertz 1973:89) "denotes an historically transmitted pattern of meanings embodied in symbols, a system of inherited conceptions expressed in symbolic forms by means of which men [*sic*] communicate, perpetuate, and develop their knowledge about and attitudes toward life."

culture, in relation to society   "A society consists of a population aggregate whose members have a particular relationship to one another; a culture consists of ways of believing, behaving and thinking" (Thomas E. Lasswell, *Class and Stratum* [Boston: Houghton Mifflin Co., 1965], 208).

cultural patterns, models, codes, or scripts   In any given society, a specific and enduring organization of culture traits and culture complexes, ethos, which give meaning, that is, objective conceptual form, to social and psychological reality both by shaping themselves to it and by shaping it to themselves (Geertz 1973:93). The prescribed patterns and processes for "playing the game of life" within a given cultural system.

cultural trait   In any given culture, one of the simplest and smallest identifiable units of a culture, a cultural element as distinguished from a culture complex, each of the latter being a set of interrelated traits.

diachronic   Literally, "through time," denoting a historical perspective that focuses on underlying and interrelated processes governing a sequence of events over time. Compare SYNCHRONIC.

dyad   A pair, a twosome, in contrast to "individual." **Dyadic relations** are those which involve two or more persons. **Dyadic personality**, in contrast to individual personality, is a sense of self determined by and dependent upon the perceptions and evaluations of others, externally rather than internally oriented, shame-based rather than guilt-based.

ecological Pertaining to the natural environment or ecosystem as a whole.

economic relations The activities of production, distribution, and consumption of goods and services embedded in the two chief social domains of public (political) and private (household) life.

embedded That which is embedded has no independent existence but is incorporated in and determined by fundamental and inclusive (social) institutions. In biblical antiquity, religion, like economics, was embedded in the basic institutions of kinship and politics (domestic and civil religion); similarly, females were embedded in the household of some male family head (*paterfamilias*). Compare such "substantive" religion and economics to the modern situation of independent, "formal" religious and economic institutions.

emic Derived from the linguistic category "phonemic" (sounds meaningful to native speakers) and denoting the viewpoint, categories of thought, and explanations of the group being studied. Compare ETIC.

etic Derived from the linguistic category "phonetic" (the science of speech sounds considered as elements of language) and denoting the perspective and classifying systems of the external investigator. Compare EMIC.

faction A coalition of persons (followers) recruited personally according to structurally diverse principles by, or on behalf of, a person in conflict with others over honor, control of resources, or "truth." See COALITION.

family or household The primary social unit, based on kinship and/or cohabitation, whose chief activities include production (of resources) and reproduction (of children) and whose internal activities are characterized by generalized reciprocity. The honor and shame of the family are symbolized by the male family head (*paterfamilias*) and his sons and by his wife and daughters, respectively.

friendship Formalized relationship between individuals based on equality of status and involving reciprocal obligations.

group The most generically inclusive term denoting a set of two or more individuals who are in reciprocal communication. **Social groups** are composed of persons whose relationships with one another are a consequence of an interrelated set of statuses and roles. Groups vary in size, duration, stability, mode of contact, objectives, manner of admission, formality, role prescriptions, degree of acquaintance among members, sanctions, etc., and can view themselves as "in-groups" in contrast to "out-groups" ("we" vs. "they") from which they distinguish themselves and for which they feel antipathy. See IN-GROUP; OUT-GROUP.

honor Socially approved and expected attitudes and behavior in areas where power, sexual status, and religion intersect. Honor is the public claim to worth and status (both ascribed and achieved) along with the social acknowledgment of such worth, status, and reputation. In ancient patriarchal societies, honor is associated primarily with male familial representatives and symbolized by blood lineage, name, and physical attributes (male testicles; strength). It is manifested in aggressiveness, daring, courage, and cunning and is constantly subject to social challenge. See SHAME.

ideal type A hypothetical idea of a phenomenon in which the phenomenon's most characteristic features are exaggerated so as to create mutually exclusive constructs and standards against which actual historical and social phenomena can be measured.

ideology An integrated system of beliefs, perspectives, assumptions, and values, not necessarily true or false, that reflect the perceived needs and interests of a group or class at a particular time in history; that contain the chief criteria for interpreting social reality; and that serve to define, explain, and legitimate collective wants and needs, interests, values, norms, and organizational goals in a continuous interaction with the material forces of history. When ideological formulations refer to God or the gods, divine representatives or agents, sacred tradition, or any instances of power and authority as ultimate or highest sources, warrants, norms, and sanctions of behavior, ideology merges with theology and theological constructs are used for ideological ends.

in-group Any set of persons whose members perceive themselves as sharing the same distinctive interests and values and as constituting a collective "we" over against nonmembers or "out-groups" designated as "they," often with negative valuation. Compare OUT-GROUP.

130

interest, self-interest, group interest An **interest** is any phenomenon that is attractive to and valued by a person or group and considered vital for meaningful existence. **Group interests** are interests that ideally are shared by a predominant number of the group's members and are considered by the membership as typical of the group as group and essential to its survival, well-being, and growth. Group interests are articulated, explained, and legitimated in the ideological/theological expressions of the group.

interest group Any group organized in terms of some distinctive interests or set of values held by its members.

kin People who are related to one another through marriage, or descent, or by sharing a common social or biological ancestor, and who therefore have special claims on and responsibility for one another. In every culture the kinship group provides its members with most of their basic adjustments, so that it forms the typical primary group. See KINSHIP, FICTIVE OR SURROGATE.

kinship, fictive or surrogate A relationship among persons giving those involved a special claim on and responsibility for one another, and based on the fiction of constituting a primary group similar to but not identical with that created by descent and blood ties. Social identity, roles, relations of a group based on and modeled after those of biological kinship, as in "household of God," "brotherhood" (of faith).

kinship system In any given society, the total complex of ideas about (*a*) methods of tracing descent for the purpose of tracing degrees and types of consanguineal relationship; (*b*) values regarding mutual rights and responsibilities; and (*c*) rewards or sanctions for relevant conforming or nonconforming behavior.

limited good, perception of The perception in peasant and small, closely knit groups that all goods and resources are in scarce and limited supply, resulting in the notion that one party's gain can occur only at another's loss and hence resulting in ongoing competition and conflict and the valorization of generosity and condemnation of miserliness and envy.

macro-level analysis Study of the general structure and interrelated institutions of total social systems.

micro-level analysis Study of segments of social systems.

model, social An abstract selective representation of the relationships among social phenomena used to conceptualize, analyze, and interpret patterns of social relations, and to compare and contrast one system of social relations with another. Models are heuristic constructs that operationalize particular theories and that range in scope and complexity according to the phenomena to be analyzed.

movement, social A loose-knit group that seeks to change the social order.

organization The process, or result of the process, wherein an assemblage of differentiated and independent units is so coordinated as to make an integrated unity consisting of parts that are, to varying degrees, interdependent. Differentiated into (a) informal (beliefs and behaviors not authoritative) and (b) formal (rules and tasks officially prescribed).

out-group Any set of persons that is perceived by members of an in-group as holding different or competing interests and values from those of the in-group and that is designated by in-group members as "they," often with negative valuation. Compare IN-GROUP.

patriarchal Traditionally used to denote (a) an older male's complete dominance over his family; and (b) societies in which such a family form predominates. Characteristic of ancient Hebrew, Greek, Roman, Islamic, Chinese, Japanese, and Indian societies.

patron-client relations Formalized relations between two parties (a superior patron and an inferior client) characterized by inequality and asymmetry in power and status, combined with the reciprocal exchange of goods and services, mutual solidarity and obligations typical of kinship relations (e.g., ruler-subjects, landlord-tenant, master–freed slave; cf. as model for God-creatures). A **broker** in this relationship is one who mediates transactions between patrons and clients.

purity-pollution system A system of order based on the social construct that categorizes phenomena and behavior into the binary opposites of clean/unclean, whole/fragmented, sacred/secular, valuated positively and negatively, respectively.

reciprocal relations Economic and social exchanges between two parties with varying interests. Exchanges of this type vary from (1) **generalized reciprocity** characterized by altruistic transactions where the "cost" is not counted, as in exchanges among kin; the ideal is the pure gift; to (2) **balanced reciprocity**, which seeks an equivalence of exchange in goods and services between kin and nonkin groups; to (3) **negative reciprocity** among strangers where maximization of gain and minimization of cost is sought, with force if necessary. Reciprocal relations contrast to a system of redistribution. Compare REDISTRIBUTION.

redistribution   A form of economic and social exchange in which the deployment of labor as a function of political power is exercised by a ruling elite who extract the agricultural surplus from its peasant producers, gather it in central storehouses, and redistribute it among themselves and others with the purpose of maintaining their power and status.Compare RECIPROCAL RELATIONS.

religion   The attitude and behavior that one is expected to display to those entities and forces which control one's existence (often synonymous with "piety," "justice," "righteousness," respect for deity [ultimate power]), and deity's various human representatives. As a cultural system (Geertz 1973:90), religion is "(1) a system of symbols which acts to (2) establish powerful, pervasive, and long-lasting moods and motivations in persons by (3) formulating conceptions of a general order of existence and (4) clothing these conceptions with such an aura of factuality that (5) the moods and motivations seem uniquely realistic." In ancient society religion is generally embedded in the two basic institutions of the city (*polis,* politically expressed religion) and kinship (*oikos,* domestically expressed religion).

roles   The behaviors expected to be manifested by particular individuals because of their position (see STATUS) and specific relations to given others, their rights and obligations; distinguished as (*a*) **ascribed roles** (assigned to individuals on the basis of kinship, gender, age, wealth, etc., irrespective of desire or accomplishment); and (*b*) **achieved roles** (attained as a consequence of having met prescribed criteria of qualification). **Reciprocal roles** are complementary behaviors in particular relationships (husband-wife, parent-child, teacher-student, etc.).

shame   The positive sensitivity for one's honor and the reputation of one's family. In ancient patriarchal societies with moralities based on shame rather than internal guilt, the physical condition and behavior of a family's females were chief indicators of this sensitivity. The sexual honor of the females and their kin group (shame in this positive sense) was preserved through their sexual purity (virginity before marriage, sexual exclusivity thereafter), submission to authority, passivity, and modesty. See HONOR.

social (From *socius* ["companion, ally, associate"] + *-alis* ["akin to"]; thus, "involving allies or confederates.") Pertaining to the properties, relations, and interactions of two or more persons (dyads, groups, collectivities, associations, communities, organizations, and the like); pertaining to relations between and among individuals and what they have in common.

socialization The process and stages (primary and secondary, within and then beyond the family) whereby individuals learn to behave willingly in accordance with the prevailing standards of their culture. Sometimes used synonymously with "enculturation."

social science(s) The branch(es) of science that deal with the institutions and functioning of human society and with the interpersonal relationships of individuals as members of society; anthropology, economics, political science, and sociology are chief branches.

social stratification The hierarchical positioning of persons and groups with varying roles and statuses relative to some continuum.

sociology The scientific study of social properties, social relations, social organizations, social institutions, and social systems. A **social system** is a group of people who are engaged in some type of collective activity and who are related to one another in various ways. **Social properties** are regularities of behavior imposed on individuals by a social system. Sociology focuses on interpersonal rather than intrapersonal phenomena, on groups rather than on individuals. Sociologists, in contrast to anthropologists, tend to focus predominantly but not exclusively on complex, modern, industrial societies. The **major sociological theoretical orientations** include structural functionalism, conflict theory, symbolic interaction, and ethnomethodology.

status The relative rank or position of an individual in a particular group with accompanying prescribed behavior (role). Differentiated as (1a) **ascribed status** (assigned to positions occupied by individuals on the basis of kinship, gender, age, wealth, etc.), irrespective of desire or accomplishment; and (1b) **achieved status** (assigned to positions occupied by individuals as a consequence of having met prescribed criteria of qualification); and (2) nominal (ungraded organizational designations such as "father-in-law") or ordered (graded continuum, as in the military or bureaucracy). Compare status groups and aggregates (persons with the same type and amount of honor), the former being exclusive and composed of persons interacting frequently with one another and the latter, inclusive and composed of persons interacting sporadically with one another. Related to honor, esteem, reputation; rank, position, social location.

status consistency or inconsistency   The degree to which an individual's vertically differentiated statuses are compatible or incompatible with one another (e.g., high status in one group, but low status in another).

status sets   A particular person's statuses (as, e.g., mother, wife, physician) considered as a group.

synchronic   Literally, "at the same time," denoting a holistic perspective on a (social) system and the interrelations of its several sectors (ecological, economic, social, political, cultural). See DIACHRONIC.

system   Any set of interrelated elements that, as they work and change together, may be regarded as a single entity, as in a **social system** composed of dynamically interrelated and interdependent individuals, groups, social structures, and cultural traits and patterns.

systemic analysis   Analysis of total systems of interrelated and interdependent elements, with the application of systems theory and models.

theory   An organized and interactive body of generalizations based on empirical evidence that purport to explain a set of phenomena and to predict the occurrence of as yet unobserved events and relationships on the basis of explanatory principles embodied in the theory. See CONCEPT; MODEL.

tradition   Relative to a particular society, either (*a*) one or more or all of the highly valued meanings and behaviors that have been transmitted from and through past generations; or (*b*) the judgment and/or assertion that given ways, customs, norms, etc., are "right" and "natural."

village   A peasant settlement that operates as a self-sufficient community and as a geographical, social, economic, and cultural unit. See COMMUNITY.

Abbreviations

ANRW	*Aufstieg und Niedergang der römischen Welt.* Edited by Hildegard Temporini and Wolfgang Haase
ASSR	*Archives des Sciences Sociales des Religions*
ATR	*Anglican Theological Review*
BET	Beiträge zur evangelischen Theologie
BJRL	*Bulletin of the John Rylands University Library of Manchester*
BTB	*Biblical Theology Bulletin*
CBQ	*Catholic Biblical Quarterly*
CurTM	*Currents in Theology and Mission*
EstBib	*Estudios Bíblicos*
ETR	*Etudes Théologiques et Religieuses*
EvK	*Evangelische Kommentare*
EvT	*Evangelische Theologie*
FRLANT	Forschungen zur Religion und Literatur des Alten und Neuen Testaments
JAAR	*Journal of the American Academy of Religion*
JAC	*Jahrbuch für Antike und Christentum*
JBL	*Journal of Biblical Literature*
JR	*Journal of Religion*
JRH	*Journal of Religious History*
JSNT	*Journal for the Study of the New Testament*
JSOT	*Journal for the Study of the Old Testament*
JTS	*Journal of Theological Studies*
NovT	*Novum Testamentum*
NTAbh	Neutestamentliche Abhandlungen
NTS	*New Testatment Studies*
RevExp	*Review and Expositor*
RSR	*Religious Studies Review*
SBL	Society of Biblical Literature
SBLDS	SBL Dissertation Series

SBLMS	SBL Monograph Series
SBS	Stuttgarter Bibelstudien
SJT	*Scottish Journal of Theology*
SNT	Studien zum Neuen Testament
SNTSMS	Society for New Testament Studies Monograph Series
TBü	Theologische Bücherei
TRE	*Theologische Realenzyklopädie*
TRu	*Theologische Rundschau*
TS	*Theological Studies*
TZ	*Theologische Zeitschrift*
VTSup	Vetus Testamentum, Supplements
ZNW	*Zeitschrift für die neutestamentliche Wissenschaft*
ZTK	*Zeitschrift für Theologie und Kirche*

Bibliographies

I. SOCIAL-SCIENTIFIC CRITICISM OF THE NEW TESTAMENT AND ITS ENVIRONMENT AND SELECTED SOCIAL-HISTORICAL STUDIES

A. Selected Earlier Social-Historical Studies

Alfaric, P. *Origines sociales du christianisme.* Paris, 1959; German translation, *Die sozialen Ursprünge des Christentums.* Darmstadt: Wissenschaftliche Buchgesellschaft, 1963.

Bitzer, Lloyd F. "The Rhetorical Situation." *Philosophy and Rhetoric* 1 (1968): 1–14.

Case, Shirley Jackson. *The Evolution of Early Christianity.* Chicago: University of Chicago Press, 1914.

Case, Shirley Jackson. *The Social Origins of Christianity.* Chicago: University of Chicago Press, 1923.

Case, Shirley Jackson. *The Social Triumph of the Ancient Church.* New York: Harper & Brothers, 1933. (On the "Chicago School," see L. Wallis, *A Sociological Study of the Bible* [Chicago, 1912]; L. E. Keck, "On the Ethos of Early Christians," *JAAR* 42 [1974]: 435–52; R. W. Funk, "The Watershed of the American Biblical Tradition: The Chicago School, First Phase, 1892–1920," *JBL* 95 (1976): 4–22; and W. J. Hynes, *Shirley Jackson Case and the Chicago School: The Socio-Historical Method* [Chico, Calif.: Scholars Press, 1981].)

Deissmann, Adolf. *Bible Studies.* Translated by A. Grieve. Edinburgh: T. & T. Clark, 1901.

Deissmann, Adolf. *Licht vom Osten: Das Neue Testament und die neuentdeckten Texte der hellenistisch-römischen Welt.* 4th ed. Tübingen: J. C. B. Mohr (Paul Siebeck), 1923 (1908). ET: *Light from the Ancient East: The New Testament Illustrated by Recently Discovered Texts of the Graeco-Roman World.* London: Hodder & Stoughton, 1910.

Deissmann, Adolf. *Das Urchristentum und die unteren Schichten.* 2d ed. Göttingen: Vandenhoeck & Ruprecht, 1908.

Engels, Friedrich. "On the History of Early Christianity." In Karl Marx and Friedrich Engels, *Basic Writings on Politics and Philosophy,* edited by L. S. Feuer. New York: Doubleday & Co., 1959. Pp. 168–94.

Grant, Frederick C. *The Economic Background of the Gospels*. London: Oxford University Press, 1926; reprinted, 1973.

Harnack, Adolf. *Die Mission und Ausbreitung des Christentums in den ersten drei Jahrhunderten*. 2 vols. Leipzig, 1902. ET: *The Mission and Expansion of Christianity*. 2 vols. London: Williams & Norgate, 1908.

Judge, Edwin A. "The Early Christians as a Scholastic Community." *JRH* 1 (1960): 4–15, 125–37. Cf. also Judge 1968 and 1972.

Judge, Edwin A. "Paul's Boasting in Relation to Contemporary Professional Practice." *Australian Biblical Review* 16 (1968): 37–50.

Judge, Edwin A. *The Social Pattern of the Christian Groups in the First Century: Some Prolegomena to the Study of New Testament Ideas of Social Obligation*. London: Tyndale Press, 1960.

Kautsky, Karl. *Foundations of Christianity*. Translated by Henry F. Mins. New York: Russell & Russell, 1953 (1908).

Kreissig, Heinz. "Zur sozialen Zusammensetzung der frühchristlichen Gemeinden im ersten Jahrhundert u. Z." *Eirene. Studia Graeca et Latina* 6 (1967): 91–100.

Lohmeyer, Ernst. *Soziale Fragen im Urchristentum*. Leipzig, 1921; reprinted, Darmstadt: Wissenschaftliche Buchgesellschaft, 1973.

Matthews, Shailer. *The Social Teaching of Jesus: An Essay in Christian Sociology*. New York: Macmillan, 1897.

Troeltsch, Ernst. *The Social Teaching of the Christian Churches*. Translated by Olive Wyon. 2 vols. New York: Harper & Brothers, 1960 (1911).

B. A Chronologically Ordered Bibliography of Studies from 1970–1992

1970 Güttgemanns, Erhardt. "Die Soziologie als methodologische Grundlage der Formgeschichte und der allgemeinen Sprach- und Literaturwissenschaft." In *Offene Fragen zur Formgeschichte des Evangeliums*. BET 54. Munich: Chr. Kaiser Verlag, 1970. Pp. 44–68; cf. 167–88.

1971 Benko, Stephen, and J. J. O'Rourke, eds. *The Catacombs and the Colosseum: The Roman Empire as the Setting of Primitive Christianity*. Valley Forge, Pa.: Judson Press.

1971 Gewalt, Dietfried. "Neutestamentliche Exegese und Soziologie." *EvT* 31 (1971): 87–99.

1972 Judge, Edwin A. "St. Paul and Classical Society." *JAC* 15 (1972): 19–36.

1972 Meeks, Wayne A. "The Man from Heaven in Johannine Sectarianism." *JBL* 91 (1972): 44–72.

1973 Derrett, J. Duncan M. *Jesus' Audience: The Social and Psychological Environment in Which He Worked*. New York: Crossroad.

1973 Neusner, Jacob. *The Idea of Purity in Ancient Judaism*. Leiden: E. J. Brill.

1973 Theissen, Gerd. "Wanderradikalismus: Literatursoziologische Aspekte der Überlieferung von Worten Jesu im Urchristentum." *ZTK* 70 (1973): 245–71. Reprinted in Theissen, *Studien*, 79–105. ET: "Itinerant Radicalism: The Tradition of Jesus Sayings from the Perspective of the Sociology of Literature." *Radical Religion* 2/2–3 (1975): 84–93.

1973 Wuellner, Wilhelm H. "The Sociological Implications of I Corinthians 1:26–28 Reconsidered." *Studia Evangelica* 6, edited by E. A. Livingstone. Berlin: Akademie-Verlag, 1973. Pp. 666–72.

1974 Belo, Fernando. *Lecture matérialiste de l'évangile de Marc: Récit-pratique—Idéologie.* Paris: Cerf; 2d ed., rev. 1975. ET 1981. Reviews: E. Poulat et al., *ASSR* 40 (1975): 119–37; A. Vanhoye, *Biblica* 58 (1977): 295–98; and R. Scroggs, *CBQ* 45 (1983): 473–74.

1974 Gülzow, Hennecke. "Soziale Gegebenheiten der altkirchlichen Mission." In *Kirchengeschichte als Missionsgeschichte,* edited by Heinzgünter Frohnes and Uwe W. Knorr. Vol. 1: *Die alte Kirche.* Munich: Chr. Kaiser Verlag. Pp. 189–226.

1974 Hengel, Martin. *Property and Riches in the Early Church: Aspects of a Social History of Early Christianity.* Philadelphia: Fortress Press.

1974 Isenberg, Sheldon R. "Millenarism in Greco-Roman Palestine." *Religion* 4 (1974): 26–46.

1974 Keck, Leander E. "On the Ethos of Early Christians." *JAAR* 42 (1974): 435–52.

1974 MacMullen, Ramsay. *Roman Social Relations 50 B.C. to A.D. 284.* New Haven: Yale University Press.

1974a Theissen, Gerd. "Soziale Integration und sakramentales Handeln." *NovT* 16 (1974): 179–206; reprinted in Theissen, *Studien* (1983), 290–317. ET: "Social Integration and Sacramental Activity: An Analysis of 1 Cor. 11:17–34." In Theissen, *Social Setting* (1982), 145–74.

1974b Theissen, Gerd. "Soziale Schichtung in der korinthischen Gemeinde." *ZNW* 65 (1974): 232–73; reprinted in Theissen, *Studien* (1983), 231–71. ET: "Social Stratification in the Corinthian Community: A Contribution to the Sociology of Early Hellenistic Christianity." In Theissen, *Social Setting* (1982), 69–119.

1974c Theissen, Gerd. "Theoretische Probleme religions-soziologischer Forschung und die Analyse des Urchristentums." *Neue Zeitschrift für systematische Theologie und Religionsphilosophie* 16 (1974): 35–56; reprinted in Theissen, *Studien* (1983), 55–76.

1974d Theissen, Gerd. *Urchristliche Wundergeschichten: Ein Beitrag zur formgeschichtlichen Erforschung der synoptischen Evangelien.* SNT 8. Gütersloh: Gütersloher Verlagshaus Gerd Mohn. ET 1983.

1974 Wilde, James Alan. *A Social Description of the Community Reflected in the Gospel of Mark.* Ph.D. dissertation, Drew University.

1975 Dahlgren, Curt. *MARANATHA: En sociologisk studie av en sektrörelses uppkomst och utveckling.* Helsingborg.

1975 Gager, John G. *Kingdom and Community: The Social World of Early Christianity.* Englewood Cliffs, N.J.: Prentice-Hall. Reviews: D. L. Bartlett, *Zygon* 13 (1978): 109–22; J. Z. Smith, *Zygon* 13 (1978): 123–30; and D. Tracy, *Zygon* 13 (1978): 131–35.

1975 Isenberg, Sheldon R. "Power through Temple and Torah in Greco-Roman Palestine." In *Christianity, Judaism and Other Greco-Roman Cults,* edited by

Jacob Neusner. Morton Smith FS. Studies in Judaism in Late Antiquity 12. Vol. 2. Leiden: E. J. Brill. Pp. 24–52.

1975 Meeks, Wayne A. "The Social World of Early Christianity." *The Council on the Study of Religion Bulletin* 6/1 (1975): 1, 4–5.

1975 Poulat, Emile, et al. "C/X ou de Marx à Marc. L' Evangile mis à ny par la subversion de l'exégèse." *ASSR* 40 (1975): 119–37.

1975 Schütz, John H. *Paul and the Anatomy of Apostolic Authority.* SNTSMS 26. Cambridge: Cambridge University Press.

1975 Scroggs, Robin. "The Earliest Christian Communities as Sectarian Movement." In *Christianity, Judaism and Other Greco-Roman Cults,* edited by Jacob Neusner. Studies in Judaism in Late Antiquity 12. Vol. 2. Leiden: E. J. Brill. P. 123.

1975 Smith, Jonathan Z. "The Social Description of Early Christianity." *RSR* 1 (1975): 19–25.

1975a Theissen, Gerd. "Legitimation und Lebensunterhalt: Ein Beitrag zur Soziologie urchristlicher Missionare." *NTS* 21 (1974/75): 192–221; reprinted in Theissen, *Studien* (1983), 201–30. ET: "Legitimation and Subsistence: An Essay on the Sociology of Early Christian Missionaries." In Theissen, *Social Setting* (1982), 27–67.

1975b Theissen, Gerd. "Die soziologische Auswertung religiöser Überlieferungen: Ihre methodologische Probleme am Beispiel des Urchristentums." *Kairos* 17 (1975): 284–99; reprinted in Theissen, *Studien* (1983), 35–54. ET: "The Sociological Interpretation of Religious Traditions: Its Methodological Problems as Exemplified in Early Christianity." In Theissen, *Social Setting* (1982), 175–200.

1975c Theissen, Gerd. "Die Starken und Schwachen in Korinth: Soziologische Analyse eines theologischen Streites." *EvT* 35 (1975): 155–72; reprinted in *Studien* (1983), 272–89. ET: "The Strong and the Weak in Corinth: A Sociological Analysis of a Theological Quarrel." In Theissen, *Social Setting* (1982), 121–43.

1976 Bailey, Kenneth E. *Poet and Peasant.* Grand Rapids: Wm. B. Eerdmans Publishing Co.

1976 Clévenot, Michel. *Approches matérialistes de la Bible.* Paris: Cerf.

1976 Funk, Robert W. "The Watershed of the American Biblical Tradition: The Chicago School, First Phase, 1892–1920." *JBL* 95 (1976): 4–22.

1976 Gottwald, Norman K., and Antoinette C. Wire, eds. *The Bible and Liberation: Political and Social Hermeneutics. A Radical Religion Reader.* Berkeley: Community for Religious Research and Publication. (A reprint of *Radical Religion* 2/2–3 [1975].)

1976 Theissen, Gerd. "Die Tempelweissagung Jesu: Prophetie im Spannungsfeld von Stadt und Land." *TZ* 32 (1976): 144–58; reprinted in Theissen, *Studien* (1983), 142–59.

1977a Berger, Klaus. "Wissenssoziologie und Exegese des Neuen Testaments." *Kairos* 19 (1977): 124–33.

1977b Berger, Klaus. "Soziologische Fragen." In *Exegese des Neuen Testaments: Neue Wege vom Text zur Auslegung.* Uni-Taschenbücher 658. Heidelberg: Quelle & Meyer. Pp. 218–41.

1977 Grant, R. M. *Early Christianity and Society.* New York: Harper & Row.

1977 Malherbe, Abraham J. *Social Aspects of Early Christianity.* Baton Rouge, La.: Louisiana State University; 2d enlarged ed. Philadelphia: Fortress Press, 1983.

1977 Messelken, K. "Zur Durchsetzung des Christentums in der Spätantike." *Kölner Zeitschrift für Soziologie und Sozialpsychologie* 29 (1977): 261–94.

1977 Rudolf, Kurt. "Das Problem einer Soziologie und 'sozialen Verortung' der Gnosis." *Kairos* 19 (1977): 33–44.

1977 Schreiber, Alfred. *Die Gemeinde in Korinth: Versuch einer gruppendynamischen Betrachtung der Entwicklung der Gemeinde von Korinth auf der Basis des ersten Korintherbriefes.* NTAbh, neue Folge 12. Münster: Aschendorff.

1977a Theissen, Gerd. *Soziologie der Jesusbewegung: Ein Beitrag zur Entstehungsgeschichte des Urchristentums.* Theologische Existenz heute 194. Munich: Chr. Kaiser Verlag. ET 1988.

1977b Theissen, Gerd. "'Wir haben alles verlassen' (Mc. X,28). Nachfolge und soziale Entwurzelung in der jüdisch-palästinischen Gesellschaft des 1. Jahrhunderts n. Chr." *NovT* 19 (1977): 161–96; reprinted in Theissen, *Studien* (1983), 106–41.

1978 Casalis, George, ed. *Introduction à la lecture matérialiste de la Bible.* Geneva: World Student Christian Federation.

1978 Elliott, John H. Review of A. Schreiber, *Die Gemeinde in Korinth* (1977), in *Biblica* 59 (1978): 589–92.

1978 Hock, Ronald F. "Paul's Tentmaking and the Problem of His Social Class," *JBL* 97 (1978): 555–64.

1978a Malina, Bruce J. "Limited Good and the Social World of Early Christianity." *BTB* 8 (1978): 162–76.

1978b Malina, Bruce J. "The Social World Implied in the Letters of the Christian Bishop-Martyr (Named Ignatius of Antioch)." In *SBL 1978 Seminar Papers,* edited by Paul J. Achtemeier. Vol. 2. Missoula, Mont.: Scholars Press. Pp. 71–119.

1978 Rohrbaugh, Richard L. *The Biblical Interpreter: An Agrarian Bible in an Industrial Age.* Philadelphia: Fortress Press.

1978 Schottroff, Luise, and Wolfgang Stegemann. *Jesus von Nazareth—Hoffnung der Armen.* Stuttgart: W. Kohlhammer.

1978 Smith, Jonathan Z. "Too Much Kingdom, Too Little Community." (Review of J. G. Gager, *Kingdom and Community,* 1975.) *Zygon* 13 (1978): 123–30.

1978 Theissen, Gerd. *Sociology of Early Palestinian Christianity.* Philadelphia: Fortress Press, 1978. ET of *Soziologie der Jesusbewegung,* 1977; published in Great Britain as *The First Followers of Jesus.* London: SCM Press, 1978. Reviews: A. E. Harvey, *JTS* n.s. 30 (1979): 279–82; B. J. Malina, *CBQ* 41 (1979): 176–78; see J. H. Elliott 1986c; R. A. Horsley 1989; T. Schmeller 1989.

1978 Wilde, James Alan. "The Social World of Mark's Gospel: A Word about Method." In *SBL 1978 Seminar Papers,* edited by Paul J. Achtemeier. Vol. 2. Missoula, Mont.: Scholars Press. Pp. 47–70.

1979 Carroll, Robert P. *When Prophecy Failed: Cognitive Dissonance in the Prophetic Traditions of the Old Testament.* New York: Seabury.

1979 Elliott, John H. *1 Peter: Estrangement and Community.* Chicago: Franciscan Herald Press.

1979 Fiorenza, Elisabeth Schüssler. "'You Are Not to Be Called Father': Early Christian History in a Feminist Perspective." *Cross Currents* 29 (1979): 301–23.

1979 Gager, John G. "Social Description and Sociological Explanation in the Study of Early Christianity. A Review Essay." *RSR* 5 (1979): 174–80; reprinted in *The Bible and Liberation: Political and Social Hermeneutics,* edited by Norman K. Gottwald. Maryknoll, N.Y.: Orbis Books, 1983. Pp. 428–40.

1979 Hock, Ronald F. "The Workshop as a Social Setting for Paul's Missionary Preaching." *CBQ* 41 (1979): 439–50.

1979 Malina, Bruce J. "The Individual and the Community: Personality in the Social World of Early Christianity." *BTB* 8 (1978): 162–76.

1979a Meeks, Wayne A. "'Since Then You Would Need to Go Out of the World': Boundaries in Pauline Christianity." In *Critical History and Biblical Faith: New Testament Perspectives,* edited by Thomas Ryan. Villanova, Pa.: College Theology Society. Pp. 4–29.

1979b Meeks, Wayne A., ed. *Zur Soziologie des Urchristentums: Ausgewählte Beiträge zum frühchristlichen Gemeinschaftsleben in seiner gesellschaftlichen Umwelt.* TBü, 62. Munich: Chr. Kaiser Verlag.

1979 Patrick, Dale. "Political Exegesis." In *Encounter with the Text: Form and History in the Hebrew Bible,* edited by Martin J. Buss. Philadelphia: Fortress Press. Pp. 139–51.

1979 Schottroff, Willy, and Wolfgang Stegemann, eds. *Der Gott der kleinen Leute: Sozialgeschichtliche Bibelauslegungen.* Vol. 1: *Altes Testament;* Vol. 2: *Neues Testament.* Munich: Chr. Kaiser Verlag; Berlin: Burckhardthaus-Laetare. ET by Matthew J. O'Connell: *God of the Lowly: Socio-Historical Interpretations of the Bible.* Maryknoll, N.Y.: Orbis Books, 1984.

1979 Stegemann, Wolfgang. "Wanderradikalismus im Urchristentum? Historische und theologische Auseinandersetzung mit einer interessanten These." In W. Schottroff and W. Stegemann, *Der Gott der kleinen Leute.* Pp. 94–120.

1979a Theissen, Gerd. *Studien zur Soziologie des Urchristentums.* Tübingen: J. C. B. Mohr (Paul Siebeck). 2d expanded ed. 1983.

1979b Theissen, Gerd. "Zur forschungsgeschichtlichen Einordnung der soziologischen Fragestellung." In Theissen, *Studien* (1979), 3–34.

1979c Theissen, Gerd. "Gewaltverzicht und Feindesliebe (Mt 5,38-48/Lk 6,27-38) und deren sozialgeschichtlicher Hintergrund." In Theissen, *Studien* (1979), 160–97.

1980 Bailey, Kenneth E. *Through Peasant Eyes: More Lucan Parables, Their Culture and Style.* Grand Rapids: Wm. B. Eerdmans Publishing Co.

1980 Freyne, Sean. *Galilee from Alexander the Great to Hadrian, 323 BCE–135 CCe: A Study of Second Temple Judaism.* Wilmington, Del.: Michael Glazier; Notre Dame, Ind.: University of Notre Dame Press.

1980 Gollwitzer, Helmut. "Historischer Materialismus und Theologie: Zum Programm einer materialistischen Exegese." In *Traditionen der Befreiung,* edited by Willy Schottroff and Wolfgang Stegemann. Vol. 1: *Methodologische Zugänge.* Munich: Chr. Kaiser Verlag. Pp. 13–59.

1980 Harrington, Daniel J. "Sociological Concepts and the Early Church: A Decade of Research." *TS* 41 (1980): 181–90.

1980 Hock, Ronald F. *The Social Context of Paul's Ministry: Tentmaking and Apostleship.* Philadelphia: Fortress Press.

1980a Holmberg, Bengt. *Paul and Power: The Structure of Authority in the Primitive Church as Reflected in the Pauline Epistles.* Philadelphia: Fortress Press.

1980b Holmberg, Bengt. "Sociological versus Theological Analysis of the Question Concerning a Pauline Church Order." In *Die paulinische Literatur und Theologie,* edited by S. Pedersen. Århus, Denmark: Åros; Göttingen: Vandenhoeck & Ruprecht. Pp. 187–200.

1980 Isenberg, Sheldon R. "Some Uses and Limitations of Social Scientific Methodology in the Study of Early Christianity." In *SBL 1980 Seminar Papers,* edited by Paul J. Achtemeier. Chico, Calif.: Scholars Press. Pp. 29–49.

1980 Judge, Edwin A. "The Social Identity of the First Christians: A Question of Method in Religious History." *JRH* 11 (1980): 201–17.

1980 Kee, Howard Clark. *Christian Origins in Sociological Perspective: Methods and Resources.* Philadelphia: Westminster Press.

1980 Malina, Bruce J. "What Is Prayer?" *The Bible Today* 18 (1980): 214–22.

1980 Meeks, Wayne A. "The Urban Environment of Pauline Christianity." In *SBL 1980 Seminar Papers,* edited by Paul J. Achtemeier. Chico, Calif.: Scholars Press. Pp. 113–22.

1980 Schottroff, Willy, and Wolfgang Stegemann, eds. *Traditionen der Befreiung. Sozialgeschichtliche Bibelauslegungen.* Vol. 1: *Methodologische Zugänge.* Vol. 2: *Frauen in der Bibel.* Munich: Chr. Kaiser Verlag; Berlin: Burckhardthaus-Laetare.

1980 Scroggs, Robin. "The Sociological Interpretation of the New Testament." *NTS* 26 (1980): 164–79.

1980 Schütz, John H. *Paul and Power: The Structure of Authority in the Primitive Church as Reflected in the Pauline Epistles.* Philadelphia: Fortress Press.

1980 Smith, Robert H. "Were the Early Christians Middle-Class? A Sociological Analysis of the New Testament." *CurTM* 7 (1980): 260–76.

1981 Allmen, Daniel von. *La famille de Dieu: La symbolique familiale dans le paulinisme.* Orbis Biblicus et Orientalis, 41. Göttingen: Vandenhoeck & Ruprecht.

1981 Belo, Fernando. *A Materialist Reading of the Gospel of Mark.* Translated by Matthew M. J. O'Connell. Maryknoll, N.Y.: Orbis Books.

1981 Drexhage, H. J. "Wirtschaft und Handel in den frühchristlichen Gemeinden (1–3 Jh. n. Chr.)." *Römische Quartalschrift* 76 (1981): 1–72.

1981 Elliott, John H. *A Home for the Homeless: A Sociological Exegesis of 1 Peter, Its Situation and Strategy.* Philadelphia: Fortress Press, 1981. 2d expanded ed., 1990. Reviews listed in 2d ed., 1990. Pp. xxxii-xxxvii.

1981 Feeley-Harnik, Gillian. *The Lord's Table: Eucharist and Passover in Early Christianity.* Philadelphia: University of Pennsylvania Press.

1981 Funk, Aloys. *Status und Rollen in den Paulusbriefen: Eine inhaltsanalytische Untersuchung zur Religionssoziologie.* Innsbrucker theologische Studien, 7. Innsbruck: Tyrolia Verlag.

1981 Hollenbach, Paul W. "Jesus, Demoniacs, and Public Authorities: A Socio-Historical Study." *JAAR* 49 (1981): 567–88.

1981 Klauck, Hans-Josef. *Hausgemeinde und Hauskirche im frühen Christentum.* Stuttgarter Bibelstudien 103. Stuttgart: Katholisches Bibelwerk.

1981a Malina, Bruce J. *The New Testament World: Insights from Cultural Anthropology.* Atlanta: John Knox Press.

1981b Malina, Bruce J. "The Apostle Paul and Law: Prolegomena for an Hermeneutic." *Creighton Law Review* 14 (1981): 1305–39.

1981 Pilch, John J. "Biblical Leprosy and Body Symbolism." *BTB* 11 (1981): 108–13.

1981 Pixley, George V. *God's Kingdom: A Guide to Biblical Study.* Maryknoll, N.Y.: Orbis Books.

1981 Rodd, Cyril S. "On Applying a Sociological Theory to Biblical Studies." *JSOT* 19 (1981): 95–106.

1981 Stegemann, Wolfgang. *Das Evangelium und die Armen: Über den Ursprung der Theologie der Armen im Neuen Testament.* Munich: Chr. Kaiser Verlag. ET by Dietlinde Elliott, *The Gospel and the Poor.* Philadelphia: Fortress Press, 1984.

1982 Barton, Stephen C. "Paul and the Cross: A Sociological Approach." *Theology* 85 (1982): 13–19.

1982a Elliott, John H., and R. A. Martin. *James, I-II Peter/Jude.* Augsburg Commentary on the New Testament. Minneapolis: Augsburg Publishing House.

1982b Elliott, John H. "Salutation and Exhortation to Christian Behavior on the Basis of God's Blessings (1 [Peter] 1:1—2:10." *RevExp* 79/3 (1982): 415–25.

1982 Feeley-Harnik, Gillian. "Is Historical Anthropology Possible? The Case of the Runaway Slave." In *Humanizing America's Iconic Book: Society of Biblical Literature Centennial Addresses 1980.* Chico, Calif.: Scholars Press. Pp. 95–126.

1982 Finn, Thomas M. "Social Mobility, Imperial Civil Service and the Spread of Early Christianity." In *Studia Patristica*, edited by E. A. Livingstone. Vol. 17. Oxford and New York: Pergamon Press. Pp. 31–33.

1982 Gager, John G. "Shall We Marry Our Enemies? Sociology and the New Testament." *Interpretation* 36 (1982): 256–65.

1982 *Interpretation* 37/3 (1982): 229–77 (articles by Bruce J. Malina, Burke O. Long, John G. Gager, Wayne A. Meeks).

1982 Kee, Howard Clark. Review of J. H. Elliott, *A Home for the Homeless*, Philadelphia: Fortress, 1981 in *Religious Studies Review* 8 (1982): 285.

1982 Lampe, Peter. "Die Apokalyptiker—ihre Situation und ihr Handeln." In *Eschatologie und Friedenshandeln: Exegetische Beiträge zur Frage christlicher Friedensverantwortung*, edited by Ulrich Luz et al. SBS 101. 2d ed. Stuttgart: Katholisches Bibelwerk. Pp. 59–114.

1982 Malina, Bruce J. "The Social Sciences and Biblical Interpretation." *Interpretation* 37 (1982): 229–42.

1982 Meeks, Wayne A. "The Social Context of Pauline Theology." *Interpretation* 36 (1982): 267–77.

1982 Remus, Harold E. "Sociology of Knowledge and the Study of Early Christianity." *Sciences Religieuses* 11 (1982): 45–56.

1982 Schirmer, Dietrich, ed. *Die Bibel als politisches Buch: Beiträge zu einer befreienden Christologie*. Stuttgart: W. Kohlhammer.

1982 Schütz, John H. "Introduction" to Gerd Theissen, *The Social Setting of Pauline Christianity*. Philadelphia: Fortress Press, 1982. Pp. 1–23.

1982 Segalla, G. "Sociologia e Nuovo Testamento—Una rassegna." *Studia Patavania* 29 (1982): 143–50.

1982 Theissen, Gerd. *The Social Setting of Pauline Christianity: Essays on Corinth*, edited and translated and with an Introduction by John H. Schütz. Philadelphia: Fortress Press.

1983 *American Baptist Quarterly* 2/2 (1983): 99–184 (seven articles on "Social Scientific Study of the Bible").

1983 Atwood, D. J., and R. B. Flowers. "Early Christianity as a Cult Movement." *Encounter* 44 (1983): 245–61.

1983 Best, Thomas F. "The Sociological Study of the New Testament: Promise and Peril of a New Discipline." *SJT* 36 (1983): 181–94.

1983 Edwards, O. C. "Sociology as a Tool for Interpreting the New Testament." *ATR* 65 (1983): 431–38.

1983 Elliott, John H. "The Roman Provinance of 1 Peter and the Gospel of Mark: A Response to David Dungan." In *Colloquy on New Testament Studies: A Time for Reappraisal and Fresh Approaches*. Edited by Bruce Corely. Macon, GA: Mercer University Press. Pp. 182–94.

1983 Fiorenza, Elisabeth Schüssler. *In Memory of Her: A Feminist Theological Reconstruction of Christian Origins*. New York: Crossroad. Reviews: W. S. Babcock 1984; J. H. Elliott 1984a; B. J. Malina 1984b; S. Heine 1990; and W. Stegemann 1991b.

1983 Füssel, Kuno. "The Materialist Reading of the Bible: Report on an Alternative Approach to Biblical Texts." In *The Bible and Liberation: Political and Social Hermeneutics*, edited by Norman K. Gottwald. Maryknoll, N.Y.: Orbis Books. Pp. 134–46.

1983a Gottwald, Norman K. "Sociological Method in Biblical Research and Contemporary Peace Studies." *American Baptist Quarterly* 2 (1983): 142–56.

1983b Gottwald, Norman K., ed. *The Bible and Liberation: Political and Social Hermeneutics*. Maryknoll, N.Y.: Orbis Books. Revised edition of *The Bible and Liberation*, 1976.

1983 Hellholm, David, ed. *Apocalypticism in the Mediterranean World and the Near East: Proceedings of the International Colloquium on Apocalypticism, Uppsala, August 12–17, 1979*. Tübingen: J. C. B. Mohr (Paul Siebeck).

1983 Herzog, William R. "Interpretation as Discovery and Creation: Sociological Dimensions of Biblical Hermeneutics." *American Baptist Quarterly* 2 (1983): 105–18.

1983 Hollenbach, Paul W. "Recent Historical Jesus Studies and the Social Sciences." In *SBL 1983 Seminar Papers*, edited by Kent H. Richards. Chico, Calif.: Scholars Press. Pp. 61–78.

1983 Kraybill, D. B., and D. M. Sweetland. "Possessions in Luke-Acts: A Sociological Perspective." *Perspectives in Religious Studies* 10 (1983): 215–39.

1983a Malina, Bruce J. "Why Interpret the Bible with the Social Sciences?" *American Baptist Quarterly* 2 (1983): 119–33.

1983b Malina, Bruce J. "The Social Sciences and Biblical Interpretation." In *The Bible and Liberation*, edited by Norman K. Gottwald, 1983. Pp. 11–25. Expanded version of same article in *Interpretation* 37 (1982): 229–42.

1983 Mayer, Anton. *Der zensierte Jesus: Soziologie des Neuen Testaments*. Olten, Switzerland: Walter-Verlag. 2d ed. 1983. Review: C. Kazmierski 1986.

1983a Meeks, Wayne A. *The First Urban Christians: The Social World of the Apostle Paul*. New Haven: Yale University Press, 1983. Reviews: J. H. Elliott 1985b; B. J. Malina 1985c; E. A. Tiryakian 1985; G. Theissen 1985.

1983b Meeks, Wayne A. "Social Functions of Apocalyptic Language in Pauline Christianity." In *Apocalypticism in the Mediterranean World*, edited by David Hellholm. 1983. Pp. 687–706.

1983 Moxnes, Halvor. "Kropp som symbol: Bruk av sosialantropologi i studiet av det Nye Testament." *Norsk Teologisk Tidsskrift* 84 (1983): 197–217.

1983 Murphy-O'Connor, Jerome, with Introduction by John H. Elliott. *St. Paul's Corinth: Texts and Archaeology*. Good News Studies 6. Wilmington, Del.: Michael Glazier. 2d ed. Collegeville, Minn.: Liturgical Press, 1990.

1983 Nickelsburg, George W. E. "Social Aspects of Palestinian Jewish Apocalypticism." In *Apocalypticism in the Mediterranean World*, edited by David Hellholm. 1983. Pp. 641–54.

1983 Pilch, John J. "Community Foundation in the New Testament." *New Catholic World* 226/1352 (1983): 63–65.

1983 Remus, Harold E. *Pagan-Christian Conflict over Miracle in the Second Century*. Patristic Monograph Series, no. 10. Cambridge, Mass.: Philadelphia Patristic Foundation.

1983 Riches, J. K. "The Sociology of Matthew: Some Basic Questions concerning Its Relation to the Theology of the New Testament." In *SBL 1983 Seminar Papers*, edited by by Kent H. Richards. Chico, Calif.: Scholars Press. Pp. 259–71.

1983 Segalla, G. "Storiografia dei tempi del Nuovo Testamento e della Chiesa primitiva." *Teologi* 8 (1983): 281–322.

1983a Theissen, Gerd. *The Miracle Stories of the Early Christian Tradition.* Translated by F. McDonagh from the German 1974 ed. and edited by J. K. Riches. Philadelphia: Fortress Press.

1983b Theissen, Gerd. *Psychologische Aspekte paulinischer Theologie.* FRLANT 131. Göttingen: Vandenhoeck & Ruprecht. ET: *Psychological Aspects of Pauline Theology.* Translated by J. P. Gavin. Philadelphia: Fortress Press, 1987.

1983c Theissen, Gerd. "Christologie und soziale Erfahrung: Wissenssoziologische Aspekte paulinischer Christologie." In Theissen, *Studien* (1983), 318–30.

1983 Tidball, Derek J. *An Introduction to the Sociology of the New Testament.* Exeter: Paternoster Press, 1983. Published in the United States as *The Social Context of the New Testament: A Sociological Analysis.* Grand Rapids: Zondervan, 1984.

1983 Verner, David C. *The Household of God: The Social World of the Pastoral Epistles.* SBLDS 71. Chico, Calif.: Scholars Press.

1984 Aguirre, Rafael. "La casa como estructura base del cristianismo primitivo: las iglesias domesticas." *Estudios Eclesiásticos* 59 (1984): 27–51.

1984 Baasland, Ernst. "Urkristendommen i sosiologiens lys." *Tidsskrift for Teologi og Kirke* 54 (1984): 45–57.

1984 Babcock, William S. "*In Memory of Her* from a 'Patristic' Perspective: A Review Article." *The Second Century* 4 (1984): 177–84.

1984 Barton, Stephen C. "Paul and the Resurrection: A Sociological Approach." *Religion* 14 (1984): 67–75.

1984 Cahill, Michael. "Sociology, the Biblical Text and Christian Community Today." *African Ecclesial Review* 26/5 (1984): 279–86.

1984 De Villiers, P. G. R. "The Interpretation of a Text in the Light of Its Socio-Cultural Setting." *Neotestamentica* 18 (1984): 66–79.

1984a Elliott, John H. Review of E. Schüssler Fiorenza, *In Memory of Her* (1983), in *New Catholic World* 227/1361 (1984): 238–39.

1984b Elliott, John H. Review of W. A. Meeks, *The First Urban Christians* (1983), in *RSR* 11 (1985): 329–35.

1984 Gallagher, Eugene V. "The Social World of Paul." *Religion* 14 (1984): 91–99.

1984 Harris, O. G. "The Social World of Early Christianity." *Lexington Theological Quarterly* 19 (1984): 102–14.

1984 Heilgenthal, Roman. "Soziologische Implikationen der paulinischen Rechtfertigungslehre im Galaterbrief am Beispiel der 'Werke des Gesetzes.'" *Kairos* 26 (1984): 38–51.

1984 Hinson, E. E. "The Sociology of Knowledge and Biblical Interpretation." *Theologia Evangelica* (Pretoria, S.A.) 17 (1984): 33–38.

1984a Judge, Edwin A. "Cultural Conformity and Innovation in Paul: Some Clues from Contemporary Documents." *Tyndale Bulletin* 35 (1984): 3–24.

1984b Judge, Edwin A. "Gesellschaft/Gesellschaft und Christentum III. Neues Testament; IV. Alte Kirche." *TRE*, vol. 12. New York and Berlin. Pp. 764–73.

1984c Judge, Edwin A. *Rank and Status in the World of the Caesars and St. Paul.* University of Canterbury Publication no. 29. Canterbury: University of Canterbury.

1984a Malina, Bruce J. "Jesus as Charismatic Leader?" *BTB* 14 (1984): 55–62.

1984b Malina, Bruce J. Review of E. Schüssler Fiorenza, *In Memory of Her* (1983), in *RSR* 10 (1984): 179.

1984a Osiek, Carolyn. *What Are They Saying about the Social Setting of the New Testament?* New York: Paulist Press. 2d expanded ed., 1992.

1984b Osiek, Carolyn. "What Social Sciences Can Do to Scripture." *National Catholic Reporter* 10–19–84, pp. 15–16.

1984 Pilch, John J. *Galatians and Romans.* Collegeville Bible Commentary, 6. Collegeville, Minn.: Liturgical Press.

1984 Richter, Philip J. "Recent Sociological Approaches to the Study of the New Testament." *Religion* 14 (1984): 77–90.

1984 Robbins, Vernon K. *Jesus the Teacher: A Socio-Rhetorical Interpretation of Mark.* Philadelphia: Fortress Press. 2d ed., 1992.

1984 Rohrbaugh, Richard L. "Methodological Considerations in the Debate over the Social Class Status of Early Christians." *JAAR* 52 (1984): 519–46.

1984 Schöllgen, Georg. *Ecclesia sordida? Zur Frage der sozialen Schichtung frühchristlicher Gemeinden am Beispiel Kathagos zur Zeit Tertullians.* Jahrbuch für Antike und Christentum E 12. Münster: Aschendorff.

1984 Schottroff, Willy, and Wolfgang Stegemann, eds. *God of the Lowly: Socio-Historical Interpretations of the Bible.* Translated by Matthew J. O'Connell from the 1979 German ed. Maryknoll, N.Y.: Orbis Books.

1984 Stegemann, Wolfgang. *The Gospel and the Poor.* Translated by Dietlinde Elliott. Philadelphia: Fortress Press.

1984 Stowers, Stanley Kent. "Social Class, Public Speaking and Private Teaching: The Circumstances of Paul's Preaching Activity." *NovT* 26 (1984): 59–82.

1984 Tidball, Derek J. *The Social Context of the New Testament: A Sociological Analysis.* Grand Rapids: Zondervan. In Great Britain: *An Introduction to the Sociology of the New Testament.* Exeter: Paternoster Press, 1983.

1984 Wire, Antoinette C. Review article on J. H. Elliott, *A Home for the Homeless* (1981), and David L. Balch, *Let Wives Be Submissive: The Domestic Code in I Peter* (SBLMS 26; Chico, Calif.: Scholars Press, 1981), in *RSR* 10 (1984): 209–16.

1985 Aguirre, Rafael. "El método sociológico en los estudios bíblicos." *Estudios Eclesiásticos* 60 (1985): 305–31.

1985 Anderson, Bernard W. "Biblical Theology and Sociological Interpretation." *Theology Today* 42 (1985): 307ff.

1985c Benko, Stephen. *Pagan Rome and the Early Christians.* Bloomington, Ind.: Indiana University Press.

1985 Duling, Dennis C. "Insights from Sociology for New Testament Christology: A Test Case." In *SBL 1985 Seminar Papers*, edited by Kent H. Richards. Atlanta: Scholars Press. Pp. 351–68.

1985a Elliott, John H. Portuguese translation and edition of *A Home for the Homeless* (1981), by J. Rezende Costa: *Um lar para quem nao tem casa: Interpretaçao sociológica da primeira carta de Pedro*. Coleçao Bíblia e sociologia. São Paulo: Ediçoes Paulinas.

1985b Elliott, John H. Review article on W. A. Meeks, *The First Urban Christians* (1983), in *RSR* 11 (1985): 329–35.

1985c Elliott, John H. "Backward and Foreward 'In His Steps': Following Jesus from Rome to Raymond and Beyond. The Tradition, Redaction, and Reception of 1 Peter 2:18-25." In *Discipleship in the New Testament*. Edited by Fernando F. Segovia. Philadelphia: Fortress. Pp. 184–209.

1985 Goell, H.-P. "Offenbarung in der Geschichte: Theologische Überlegungen zur sozialgeschichtlichen Exegese." *EvT* 45 (1985): 532–45.

1985 Gottwald, Norman K. "The Interplay of Text, Concept, and Setting in the Hebrew Bible." In *The Hebrew Bible—A Socio-Literary Introduction*. Philadelphia: Fortress Press. Pp. 595–609.

1985 Hollenbach, Paul W. "Liberating Jesus for Social Involvement." *BTB* 15 (1985): 151–57.

1985 Horsley, Richard A., and John S. Hanson. *Bandits, Prophets and Messiahs: Popular Movements at the Time of Jesus*. Minneapolis: Winston/Seabury.

1985 Kümmel, Werner Georg. "Das Urchristentum II. Arbeiten zur Spezialproblemen. b. Zur Sozialgeschichte und Soziologie der Urkirche." *TRu* 50 (1985): 327–63.

1985a Malina, Bruce J. *The Gospel of John in Sociolinguistic Perspective*. Colloquy of the Center for Hermeneutical Studies in Hellenistic and Modern Culture. Protocol Series 48. Berkeley, Calif.

1985b Malina, Bruce J. "Hospitality." *Harper's Dictionary of the Bible*, edited by Paul J. Achtemeier. San Francisco: Harper & Row. Pp. 408–9.

1985c Malina, Bruce J. Review of W. A. Meeks, *The First Urban Christians* (1983), in *JBL* 104 (1985): 346–49.

1985 Meeks, Wayne A. "Breaking Away: Three New Testament Pictures of Christianity's Separation from the Jewish Communities." In *"To See Ourselves as Others See Us": Christians, Jews, "Others" in Late Antiquity*," edited by Jacob Neusner and E. S. Frerichs. Chico, Calif.: Scholars Press. Pp. 93–115.

1985 Moxnes, Halvor. "Paulus og den norske vaerematen: 'Skam' og 'aere' i Romerbrevet." *Norsk Teologisk Tidsskrift* 86 (1985): 129–40.

1985 Neusner, Jacob, and E. S. Frerichs, eds. *"To See Ourselves as Others See Us": Christians, Jews, "Others" in Late Antiquity*. Chico, Calif.: Scholars Press.

1985 Oakman, Douglas E. "Jesus and Agrarian Palestine: The Factor of Debt." In *SBL 1985 Seminar Papers*, edited by Kent H. Richards. Atlanta: Scholars Press. Pp. 57–73.

1985 Petersen, Norman R. *Rediscovering Paul: Philemon and the Sociology of Paul's Narrative World*. Philadelphia: Fortress Press. Review: V. L. Wimbush, *RSR* 14 (1988): 121–24.

1985 Pilch, John J. "Healing in Mark: A Social Science Analysis." *BTB* 15 (1985): 142–50.

1985 Rowland, C. "Reading the New Testament Sociologically: An Introduction." *Theology* 88 (1985): 358–64.

1985 Schenk, Wolfgang. "Wird Markus auf der Couch materialistisch? Oder: Wie idealistisch ist die 'materialistische Exegese'?" *Linguistica Biblica* (1985): 95ff.

1985 Schöllgen, Georg. "Die Didache—ein frühes Zeugnis für Landgemeinden?" *ZNW* 76 (1985): 140–43.

1985 Stegemann, Wolfgang. "Zwei sozialgeschichtliche Anfragen an unser Paulusbild." *Der evangelische Erzieher. Zeitschrift für Paedagogik und Theologie* 37 (1985): 480–90.

1985 Stowers, Stanley Kent. "The Social Sciences and the Study of Early Christianity." In *Approaches to Ancient Judaism,* edited by W. S. Green. Studies in Judaism and Its Greco-Roman Context 5. Atlanta: Scholars Press. Pp. 149–81.

1985 Theissen, Gerd. Review of W. A. Meeks, *The First Urban Christians* (1983), in *JR* 65 (1985): 111–13.

1985 Tidball, Derek J. "On Wooing a Crocodile: An Historical Survey of the Relationship between Sociology and New Testament Studies." *Vox Evangelica* 15 (1985): 95–109.

1985 Tiryakian, E. A. Review of W. A. Meeks, *The First Urban Christians* (1983), in *American Journal of Sociology* 90 (1985): 1138–40.

1985 Venetz, Hermann-Josef. "Der Beitrag der Soziologie zur Lektüre des Neuen Testaments: Ein Bericht." *Theologische Berichte XIII. Methoden der Evangelienexegese.* Pp. 87–121.

1986 Balch, David L. "Hellenization/Acculturation in 1 Peter." In *Perspectives on First Peter,* edited by Charles H. Talbert. National Association of Baptist Professors of Religion Special Studies Series, 9. Macon, Ga.: Mercer University Press. Pp. 79–101.

1986 Blasi, Anthony J. "Role Structures in the Early Hellenistic Church." *Sociological Analysis* 47 (1986): 226–48.

1986a Elliott, John H. "1 Peter, Its Situation and Strategy: A Discussion with David Balch." In *Perspectives on First Peter,* edited by Charles H. Talbert. National Association of Baptist Professors of Religion Special Studies Series, 9. Macon, Ga.: Mercer University Press. Pp. 61–78.

1986b Elliott, John H., ed. *Social-Scientific Criticism of the New Testament and Its Social World.* Semeia 35. Decatur, Ga.: Scholars Press.

1986c Elliott, John H. "Social-Scientific Criticism of the New Testament and Its Social World: More on Method and Models." In *Social-Scientific Criticism of the New Testament and Its Social World,* edited by John H. Elliott. Pp. 1–33.

1986 Hollenbach, Paul W. "From Parable to Gospel: A Response Using the Social Sciences." *Forum* 2 (1986): 67–75.

1986 Horsley, Richard A. "Popular Prophetic Movements at the Time of Jesus: Their Principal Features and Social Origins." *JSNT* 26 (1986): 3–27.

1986 Jewett, Robert. *The Thessalonian Correspondence: Pauline Rhetoric and Millenarian Piety.* Foundations and Facets. Philadelphia: Fortress Press.

1986 Kazmierski, Carl. "Has the New Testament Censored Jesus?" (Review of A. Mayer, *Der zensierte Jesus,* 1983). *BTB* 16 (1986): 116–18.

1986a Malina, Bruce J. *Christian Origins and Cultural Anthropology: Practical Models for Biblical Interpretation.* Atlanta: John Knox Press. Reviews: J. H. Elliott 1987b; J. H. Neyrey 1986c; L. J. White 1986a; J. Spickard 1987.

1986b Malina, Bruce J. "Interpreting the Bible with Anthropology: The Case of the Poor and the Rich." *Listening. Journal of Religion and Culture* 21 (1986): 148–59.

1986c Malina, Bruce J. "Normative Dissonance and Christian Origins." In *Social-Scientific Criticism of the New Testament,* edited by John H. Elliott. Pp. 35–59.

1986d Malina, Bruce J. "The Received View and What It Cannot Do: III John and Hospitality." In *Social-Scientific Criticism of the New Testament,* edited by John H. Elliott. Pp. 171–94.

1986e Malina, Bruce J. "Religion in the World of Paul: A Preliminary Sketch." *BTB* 16 (1986): 92–101.

1986a Meeks, Wayne A. *The Moral World of the First Christians.* Philadelphia: Westminster Press.

1986b Meeks, Wayne A. "A Hermeneutics of Social Embodiment." In *Christians among Jews and Gentiles,* edited by George W. E. Nickelsburg and G. W. Mac-Rae. Krister Stendahl FS. Philadelphia: Fortress Press. Pp. 176–86.

1986c Meeks, Wayne A. "Understanding Early Christian Ethics." *JBL* 105 (1986): 3–11.

1986 Mosala, Itumeleng J. "Social Scientific Approaches to the Bible: One Step Forward, Two Steps Backward." *Journal of Theology for Southern Africa* 15 (1986): 15–31.

1986a Neyrey, Jerome H. "Body Language in 1 Corinthians: The Use of Anthropological Models for Understanding Paul and His Opponents." In *Social-Scientific Criticism of the New Testament and Its Social World,* edited by John H. Elliott. Pp. 129–70.

1986b Neyrey, Jerome H. "Idea of Purity in Mark's Gospel." In *Social-Scientific Criticism of the New Testament and Its Social World,* edited by John H. Elliott. Pp. 91–128.

1986c Neyrey, Jerome H. "Social Science Modeling and the New Testament." (Review of B. J. Malina, *Christian Origins and Cultural Anthropology,* 1986.) *BTB* 16 (1986): 107–110.

1986d Neyrey, Jerome H. "Witchcraft Accusations in 2 Cor 10–13: Paul in Social Science Perspective." *Listening. Journal of Religion and Culture* 21 (1986): 160–70.

1986 Oakman, Douglas E. *Jesus and the Economic Questions of His Day.* Lewiston, N.Y.: Edwin Mellen Press.

1986 Pilch, John J. "The Health Care System in Matthew: A Social Science Analysis." *BTB* 16 (1986): 102–6.

1986 Rousseau, Jacques. "A Multidimensional Approach towards the Communication of an Ancient Canonized Text: Towards Determining the Thrust, Perspective and Strategy of 1 Peter." Ph.D. diss., University of Pretoria.

1986 Schottroff, Luise, and Willy Schottroff, eds. *Wer ist unser Gott? Beiträge zu einer Befreiungstheologie im Kontext der "ersten" Welt.* Munich: Chr. Kaiser Verlag.

1986 Scroggs, Robin. "Sociology and the New Testament." *Listening. Journal of Religion and Culture* 21 (1986): 138–47.

1986 Stambaugh, John E., and David L. Balch. *The New Testament in Its Social Environment.* Philadelphia: Westminster Press.

1986 Stanley, John E. "The Apocalypse and Contemporary Sect Analysis." In *SBL 1986 Seminar Papers,* edited by Kent H. Richards. Atlanta: Scholars Press. Pp. 412–21.

1986 Stark, Rodney. "The Class Basis of Early Christianity: Inferences from a Sociological Model." *Sociological Analysis* 47 (1986): 216–25.

1986 Thompson, Leonard. "A Sociological Analysis of Tribulation in the Apocalypse of John." *Semeia* 36 (1986): 147–74.

1986 Tilborg, Sjef van. *The Sermon on the Mount as an Ideological Intervention: A Reconstruction of Meaning.* Assen: Van Gorcum. 1986.

1986 Watson, Francis. *Paul, Judaism and the Gentiles: A Sociological Approach.* SNTSMS 56. New York: Cambridge University Press.

1986a White, Leland J. "The Bible, Theology and Cultural Pluralism." (Review of B. J. Malina, *Christian Origins and Cultural Anthropology,* 1986.) *BTB* 16 (1986): 111–115.

1986b White, Leland J. "Grid and Group in Matthew's Community: The Righteousness/Honor Code in the Sermon on the Mount." In *Social-Scientific Criticism of the New Testament and Its Social World,* edited by John H. Elliott. Pp. 61–90.

1986 White, L. Michael. "Sociological Analysis of Early Christian Groups: A Social Historian's Response." *Sociological Analysis* 47 (1986): 249–66.

1987a Elliott, John H. "Patronage and Clientism in Early Christian Society: A Short Reading Guide." *Forum* 3 (1987): 39–48.

1987b Elliott, John H. Review of B. J. Malina, *Christian Origins and Cultural Anthropology* (1986), in *CBQ* 49 (1987): 512–13.

1987 Esler, Philip Francis. *Community and Gospel in Luke-Acts: The Social and Political Motivations of Lucan Theology.* SNTSMS 57. New York: Cambridge University Press.

1987 Füssel, Kuno. *Drei Tage mit Jesus im Tempel: Einführung in die materialistische Lektüre der Bible.* Münster: Edition Liberación.

1987 Hollenbach, Paul W. "Defining Rich and Poor Using Social Sciences." In *SBL 1987 Seminar Papers,* edited by Kent H. Richards. Atlanta: Scholars Press, 1987. Pp. 50–63.

1987 Horsley, Richard A. *Jesus and the Spiral of Violence.* San Francisco: Harper & Row.

1987 Kyrtatas, Dimitris J. *The Social Structure of the Early Christian Communities.* New York: Verso; London: Methuen & Co.

1987 Lampe, Peter. *Die stadtrömischen Christen in den ersten beiden Jahrhunderten: Untersuchungen zur Sozialgeschichte.* Tübingen: J. C. B. Mohr (Paul Siebeck); 2d ed. 1988.

1987 Love, Stuart L. "Women's Roles in Certain Second Testament Passages: A Macrosociological View." *BTB* 17 (1987): 50–59.

1987 Malina, Bruce J. "Wealth and Poverty in the New Testament and Its World." *Interpretation* 41 (1987): 354–67.

1987 May, David M. "Mark 3:20-35 from the Perspective of Shame/Honor." *BTB* 17 (1987): 83–87.

1987 Moxnes, Halvor. "Meals and the New Community in Luke." *Svensk Exegetisk Årsbok* 51–52 (1986–87): 158–67.

1987 Oakman, Douglas E. "The Buying Power of Two Denarii." *Forum* 3 no. 4 (1987): 33–38.

1987 Plümacher, Eckhard. *Identitätsverlust und Identitätsgewinn: Studien zum Verhältnis von kaiserlicher Stadt und frühem Christentum.* Biblisch Theologische Studien 11. Neukirchen-Vluyn: Neukirchener Verlag.

1987a Rohrbaugh, Richard L. "Models and Muddles: Discussions of the Social Facets Seminar." *Forum* 3 (1987): 23–33.

1987b Rohrbaugh, Richard L. "'Social Location of Thought' as a Heuristic Construct in New Testament Study." *JSNT* 30 (1987): 103–19.

1987 Seland, Torrey. "Jesus as a Faction Leader: On the Exit of the Category 'Sect.'" In *Context,* edited by P. W. Bokman and R. E. Kristiansen. Peder Borgen FS. Trondheim, Norway: Tapir. Pp. 197–211.

1987 Spickard, James. Review of B. J. Malina, *Christian Origins and Cultural Anthropology* (1986), in *JAAR* 55 (1987): 841–42.

1987 Stegemann, Wolfgang. "War der Apostel Paulus ein römischer Bürger?" *ZNW* 78 (1987): 200–229.

1988 Barbaglio, G. "Rassegna di studi di storia sociale e di ricerche di sociologia sulle origini cristiane. I." *Revista Bíblica* 36/3 (1988): 377–410; "Rassegna di studi di storia sociale e di recerche di sociologia sulle origini cristiane. II." *Revista Bíblica* 36/4 (1988): 495–520.

1988 Blasi, Anthony J. *Early Christianity as a Social Movement.* Toronto Studies in Religion, 5. New York: Peter Lang.

1988 Bossman, David M. "Images of God in the Letters of Paul." *BTB* 18 (1988): 67–76.

1988 Brakemeier, G. *Der "Sozialismus" der Urchristenheit: Experiment und neue Herausforderung.* Kleine Vandenhoeck Reihe 1535. Göttingen: Vandenhoeck & Ruprecht.

1988 Crosby, Michael H. *House of Disciples: Church, Economics, and Justice in Matthew.* Maryknoll, N.Y.: Orbis Books.

1988 Domeris, W. R. "Social Scientific Study of the Early Christian Churches: New Paradigms and Old Questions." In *Paradigms and Progress in Theology,* edited by J. Mouton, A. G. van Aarde, and W. S. Vorster. Pretoria: Human Sciences Research Council. Pp. 378–93.

1988 Elliott, John H. "The Fear of the Leer: The Evil Eye from the Bible to Li'l Abner." *Forum* 4 (1988): 42–71.

1988 Harrington, Daniel J. "Second Testament Exegesis and the Social Sciences: A Bibliography." *BTB* 18 (1988): 77–85.

1988 Horsley, Richard A. "Bandits, Messiahs, and Longshoremen: Popular Unrest in Galilee around the Time of Jesus." In *SBL 1988 Seminar Papers*, edited by David J. Lull. Atlanta: Scholars Press. Pp. 183–99.

1988 Joubert, Stephan S. "Die Judasbrief: 'n Simboliese universum in die gedrang." *Hervormde Teologiese Studies* 44 (1988): 613–35.

1988 Karlsaune, Erik, ed. *Religion as a Social Phenomenon: Theologians and Sociologists Sharing Research Interests.* Trondheim: Tapir.

1988 MacDonald, Margaret Y. *The Pauline Churches: A Socio-Historical Study of Institutionalization in the Pauline and Deutero-Pauline Writings.* SNTSMS 60. New York: Cambridge University Press.

1988 Mack, Burton L. *A Myth of Innocence: Mark and Christian Origins.* Philadelphia: Fortress Press.

1988 McVann, Mark. "The Passion in Mark: Transformation Ritual." *BTB* 18 (1988): 96–101.

1988a Malina, Bruce J. "A Conflict Approach to Mark 7." *Forum* 4, no. 3 (1988): 4–30.

1988b Malina, Bruce J. "Patron and Client. The Analogy behind Synoptic Theology." *Forum* 4 no. 1 (1988): 2–32.

1988 Malina, Bruce J., and Jerome H. Neyrey. *Calling Jesus Names: The Social Value of Labels in Matthew.* Foundations and Facets, Social Facets. Sonoma, Calif.: Polebridge Press.

1988 Morgan, Robert, with John Barton. "Theology and the Social Sciences." In *Biblical Interpretation.* Oxford: Oxford University Press. Pp. 133–66.

1988a Moxnes, Halvor. *The Economy of the Kingdom: Social Conflict and Economic Relations in Luke's Gospel.* Philadelphia: Fortress Press.

1988b Moxnes, Halvor. "Honour and Righteousness in Romans." *JSNT* 32 (1988): 61–78.

1988c Moxnes, Halvor. "Honor, Shame, and the Outside World in Paul's Letter to the Romans." In *The Social World of Formative Christianity and Judaism,* edited by Jacob Neusner et al. Howard Clark Kee FS. Philadelphia: Fortress Press. Pp. 207–18.

1988d Moxnes, Halvor. "Sociology and the New Testament." In *Religion as a Social Phenomenon,* edited by Erik Karlsaune. Pp. 143–59.

1988 Myers, Ched. *Binding the Strongman: A Political Reading of Mark's Story of Jesus.* Maryknoll, N.Y.: Orbis Books.

1988a Neyrey, Jerome H. "Bewitched in Galatia: Paul and Cultural Anthropology." *CBQ* 50 (1988): 72–100.

1988b Neyrey, Jerome H. *An Ideology of Revolt: John's Christology in Social-Science Perspective.* Philadelphia: Fortress Press.

1988c Neyrey, Jerome H. "A Symbolic Approach to Mark 7." *Forum* 4, no. 3 (1988): 63–91.

1988d Neyrey, Jerome H. "Unclean, Common, Polluted, and Taboo: A Short Reading Guide." *Forum* 4, no. 4 (1988): 72–82.

1988a Pilch, John J. "Interpreting Scripture: The Social Science Method." *The Bible Today* 26 (1988): 13–19.

1988b Pilch, John J. "A Structural Functional Approach to Mark 7." *Forum* 4, no. 3 (1988): 31–62.

1988c Pilch, John J. "Understanding Biblical Healing: Selecting the Appropriate Model." *BTB* 18 (1988): 60–66.

1988 Reis, Ole. "The Uses of Sociological Theory in Theology—Exemplified by Gerd Theissen's Study of Early Christianity." In *Religion as a Social Phenomenon*, edited by Erik Karlsaune. Pp. 161–78.

1988 Rensberger, David. *Johannine Faith and Liberating Community.* Philadelphia: Westminster Press.

1988 Schöllgen, Georg. "Was wissen wir über die Sozialstruktur der paulinischen Gemeinden?" *NTS* 34 (1988): 71–82.

1988a Theissen, Gerd. "Authoritätskonflikte in den johanneischen Gemeinden." Thessalonika.

1988b Theissen, Gerd. "Vers une théorie de l'histoire sociale du christianisme primitif." *ETR* 63 (1988): 199–225.

1988c Theissen, Gerd. "Wert und Status des Menschen im Urchristentum." *Humanistische Bildung* 12 (1988): 61–93.

1988 Van Staden, Pieter. "A Sociological Reading of Luke 12:35-48." *Neotestamentica* 22 (1988): 337–53.

1988a White, L. Michael. "Shifting Sectarian Boundaries in Early Christianity." *BJRL* 70 (1988): 7–24.

1988b White, L. Michael, ed. *Social Networks and Early Christianity.* Semeia 48. Decatur, Ga.: Scholars Press.

1989 Alvarez-Valdes, L. "El metodo sociologico en la investigacion biblica actual: Incidencia en el estudio la etica biblica." *Studia Moralia* 27 (1989): 541.

1989 Botha, Jan. "Sosio-Historiese en Sosiologiese Interpretasie van di Nuew Testament." *Koers. Bulletin vir Christelike Wetenskap,* 58 (1989): 480–508. Reprinted in Jan Botha, *Semeion: Inleiding tot Aspekte van die Interpretasie van die Griekse Nuew Testament.* Pretoria: N. G. Kerkboekhandel, 1990. Pp. 55–75.

1989 Clements, R. E., ed. *The World of Ancient Israel: Sociological, Anthropological and Political Perspectives.* Cambridge: Cambridge University Press.

1989 Craffert, P. F. "The Origins of Resurrection Faith: The Challenge of a Social-Scientific Approach." *Neotestamentica* 23 (1989): 331–48.

1989a Hanson, K. C. "The Herodians and Mediterranean Kinship." *BTB* 19/3 (1989): 75–84.

1989b Hanson, K. C. "The Herodians and Mediterranean Kinship: Part 2. Marriage and Divorce." *BTB* 19/4 (1989): 142–51.

1989 Hollenbach, Paul W. "The Historical Jesus Question in North America Today." *BTB* 19 (1989): 11–22.

1989 Horsley, Richard A. *Sociology and the Jesus Movement.* New York: Crossroad.

1989 Kee, Howard Clark. *Knowing the Truth: A Sociological Approach to New Testament Interpretation.* Minneapolis: Fortress Press.

1989a Malina, Bruce J. "Dealing with Biblical (Mediterranean) Characters: A Guide for U.S. Consumers." *BTB* 19 (1989): 127–41.

1989b Malina, Bruce J. "Christ and Time: Swiss or Mediterranean?"*CBQ* 51 (1989): 1–31.

1989 Osiek, Carolyn. "The New Handmaid: The Bible and the Social Sciences." *TS* 50 (1989): 260–78.

1989 Pilch, John J. "Reading Matthew Anthropologically: Healing in Cultural Perspective." *Listening* 24 (1989): 278–89.

1989a Schmeller, Thomas. *Brechungen: Urchristliche Wandercharismatiker im Prisma soziologisch orientierter Exegese.* SBS 136. Stuttgart: Katholisches Bibelwerk.

1989b Schmeller, Thomas. "Soziologisch orientierte Exegese des Neuen Testaments: Eine Bestandaufnahme." *Bibel und Kirche* 44/3 (1989): 103–10. English digest: "Sociological Exegesis of the New Testament." *Theology Digest* 37/3 (1990): 231–34.

1989 Schöllgen, Georg. "Probleme der frühchristlichen Sozialgeschichte: Einwände gegen Peter Lampes Buch über 'Die stadtrömischen Christen in den ersten beiden Jahrhunderten." *JAC* 32 (1989): 23–40.

1989 Stevenson, E. "Some Insights from the Sociology of Religion into the Origin and Development of the Early Christian Church." *Expository Times* 90 (1989): 300–305.

1989 Taylor, W. F. "Sociological Exegesis: Introduction to a New Way to Study the Bible. Part 1: History and Theory." *Trinity Seminary Review* [Columbus, Ohio] 11/2 (1989): 99–110. See Part 2: *Trinity Seminary Review* 12/1 (1990): 26–42.

1989a Theissen, Gerd. "Jesusbewegung als charismatische Wertrevolution." *NTS* 35 (1989): 343–60.

1989b Theissen, Gerd. *Lokalkolorit und Zeitgeschichte in den Evangelien: Ein Beitrag zur Geschichte der synoptischen Tradition.* Novum Testamentum et Orbis Antiquus, 8. Göttingen: Vandenhoeck & Ruprecht, 1989. ET: *The Gospels in Context: Social and Political History in the Synoptic Tradition.* Minneapolis: Fortress Press 1991.

1989 Waetjen, Herman C. *A Reordering of Power: A Socio-Political Reading of Mark's Gospel.* Minneapolis: Fortress Press.

1990 Blasi, Anthony J. "On Precision in Studying Ancient Palestine." *Sociological Analysis* 51 (1990): 395–99.

1990a Elliott, John H. *A Home for the Homeless: A Social-Scientific Criticism of 1 Peter, Its Situation and Strategy, with a New Introduction.* Minneapolis: Fortress Press (1981).

1990b Elliott, John H. "Paul, Galatians, and the Evil Eye." *CurTM* 17 (1990): 262–73.

1990 Garmus, L., ed. *Sociologia das Comunidades Paulinas.* Estudios Bíblicos 25. Petrópolis, Brazil: Vozes.

1990 Hamel, G. *Poverty and Charity in Roman Palestine, First Three Centuries C.E.* University of California Publication: Near Eastern Studies, 23. Berkeley and Los Angeles: University of California Press.

1990 Hanson, K. C. "The Herodians and Mediterranean Kinship. Part III. Economics." *BTB* 20 (1990): 10–21.

1990 Heine, S. "Brille der Parteilichkeit: Zur einer feministischen Hermeneutik." *EvK* [Stuttgart] 23 (1990): 354–57.

1990a Holmberg, Bengt. *Sociology and the New Testament: An Appraisal.* Minneapolis: Fortress Press.

1990b Holmberg, Bengt. "Sociologiska perspektiv pa Gal 2:11–14 (21)." *Svensk Exegetisk Årsbok* 55 (1990): 71–92.

1990a Malina, Bruce J. "Does the Bible Mean What It Says?" *Window* (Creighton University) 6/2 (1989–90): 10–13.

1990b Malina, Bruce J. "Mother and Son." *BTB* 20 (1990): 54–64.

1990 Murphy-O'Connor, Jerome, with an Introduction by John H. Elliott. *St. Paul's Corinth: Texts and Archaeology.* Good News Studies 6. 2d expanded ed. Collegeville, Minn.: The Liturgical Press.

1990a Neyrey, Jerome H. "Mother and Maid in Art and Literature." *BTB* 20 (1990): 65–75.

1990b Neyrey, Jerome H. *Paul, In Other Words: A Cultural Reading of His Letters.* Louisville, Ky.: Westminster/John Knox Press.

1990 Nineham, D. E. "Cultural Relativism." In *A Dictionary of Biblical Interpretation,* edited by R. J. Coggins and J. L. Houden. London: SCM Press; Philadelphia: Trinity Press International. Pp. 155–59.

1990 Pilch, John J. "Marian Devotion and Wellness Spirituality: Bridging Cultures." *BTB* 20 (1990): 85–94.

1990 Rodd, Cyril S. "Sociology and Social Anthropology." In *A Dictionary of Biblical Interpretation,* edited by R. J. Coggins and J. L. Houden. London: SCM Press; Philadelphia: Trinity Press International. Pp. 635–39.

1990 Rogerson, J. W. "Anthropology." In *A Dictionary of Biblical Interpretation,* edited by R. J. Coggins and J. L. Houden. London: SCM Press; Philadelphia: Trinity Press International. Pp. 26–28.

1990 Smith, Jonathan Z. *Drudgery Divine: On the Comparison of Early Christianities and the Religions of Late Antiquity.* Chicago Studies in the History of Judaism. Chicago: University of Chicago Press.

1990 Stevens, Maryanne. "Paternity and Maternity in the Mediterranean: Foundations for Patriarchy." *BTB* 20 (1990): 47–53.

1990 Taylor, W. F. "Sociological Exegesis: Introduction to a New Way to Study the Bible. Part 2: Results." *Trinity Seminary Review* 12/1 (1990): 26–42.

1990 Weiner, E., and A. Weiner. *The Martyr's Conviction: A Sociological Analysis.* Brown Judaic Studies 203. Atlanta: Scholars Press.

1991 Atkins, Robert A., Jr. *Egalitarian Community: Ethnography and Exegesis.* Tuscaloosa, Ala.: University of Alabama Press.

1991 Balch, David L., ed. *Social History of the Matthean Community: Cross-Disciplinary Approaches*. Minneapolis: Fortress Press.

1991 Bravo Aragón, J. M. "Congreso Internacional sobre la interpretación socio-histórica del Nuevo Testamento." *EstBib* 49 (1991): 399–402.

1991 Crossan, John Dominic. *The Historical Jesus: The Life of a Mediterranean Jewish Peasant*. San Francisco: Harper & Row.

1991a Elliott, John H. "The Evil Eye in the First Testament: The Ecology and Culture of a Pervasive Belief." In *The Bible and the Politics of Exegesis: Essays in Honor of Norman K. Gottwald on His Sixty-fifth Birthday*, edited by David Jobling et al. Cleveland, Ohio: Pilgrim Press, 1991. Pp. 147–59.

1991b Elliott, John H. "Household and Meals vs. Temple Purity: Replication Patterns in Luke-Acts." *BTB* 21 (1991): 102–8. Published also in *Hervormde Teologiese Studies* 47/2 (1991): 386–99.

1991c Elliott, John H. "Temple versus Household in Luke-Acts: A Contrast in Social Institutions." In *The Social World of Luke-Acts: Models for Interpretation*, edited by Jerome H. Neyrey. Pp. 211–40. Published also in *Hervormde Teologiese Studies* 47/1 (1991): 88–120.

1991 Fiensy, David A. *The Social History of Palestine in the Herodian Period: The Land Is Mine*. Studies in the Bible and Early Christianity 20. Lewiston, N.Y.: Edwin Mellen Press.

1991 Frick, Frank S. "Sociological Criticism and Its Relation to Political and Social Hermeneutics in South African Liberation Theology." In *The Bible and the Politics of Exegesis: Essays in Honor of Norman K. Gottwald on His Sixty-fifth Birthday*, edited by David Jobling et al. Cleveland, Ohio: Pilgrim Press. Pp. 225–38.

1991 Gowler, David B. *Host, Guest, Enemy and Friend: Portraits of the Pharisees in Luke and Acts*. Emory Studies in Early Christianity, 2. New York: Peter Lang.

1991 Jobling, David; Peggy L. Day; Gerald T. Sheppard, eds. *The Bible and the Politics of Exegesis: Essays in Honor of Norman K. Gottwald on His Sixty-fifth Birthday*. Cleveland, Ohio: Pilgrim Press.

1991 McVann, Mark. "Rituals of Status Transformation in Luke-Acts: The Case of Jesus the Prophet." In *The Social World of Luke-Acts: Models for Interpretation*, edited by Jerome H. Neyrey. Pp. 333–60.

1991a Malina, Bruce J. "Interpretation: Reading, Abduction, Metaphor." In *The Bible and the Politics of Exegesis: Essays in Honor of Norman K. Gottwald on His Sixty-fifth Birthday*, edited by David Jobling et al. Pp. 253–66.

1991b Malina, Bruce J. "Reading Theory Perspective: Reading Luke-Acts." In *The Social World of Luke-Acts: Models for Interpretation*, edited by Jerome H. Neyrey. Pp. 3–23.

1991c Malina, Bruce J. "Scienze sociali e interpretazione storica: La questione della retrodizione." *Revista Biblica* 39 (1991): 305–23.

1991d Malina, Bruce J. [with Jerome H. Neyrey]. "Conflict in Luke-Acts: Labelling and Deviance Theory." In *The Social World of Luke-Acts: Models for Interpretation*, edited by Jerome H. Neyrey. Pp. 97–122.

1991e Malina, Bruce J. [with Jerome H. Neyrey]. "First Century Personality: Dyadic, Not Individualistic." In *The Social World of Luke-Acts: Models for Interpretation*, edited by Jerome H. Neyrey. Pp. 67–96.

1991f Malina, Bruce J. [with Jerome H. Neyrey]. "Honor and Shame in Luke-Acts: Pivotal Values of the Mediterranean World." In *The Social World of Luke-Acts: Models for Interpretation*, edited by Jerome H. Neyrey. Pp. 25–65.

1991a Moxnes, Halvor. "Patron-Client Relations and the New Community in Luke-Acts." In *The Social World of Luke-Acts: Models for Interpretation*, edited by Jerome H. Neyrey. Pp. 241–68.

1991b Moxnes, Halvor. "Social Relations and Economic Interaction in Luke's Gospel: A Research Report." In *Luke-Acts: Scandinavian Perspectives*, edited by Petri Luomanen. Publications of the Finnish Exegetical Society, 54. Helsinki: Finnish Exegetical Society; Göttingen: Vandenhoeck & Ruprecht. Pp. 58–75.

1991a Neyrey, Jerome H., ed. *The Social World of Luke-Acts: Models for Interpretation*. Peabody, Mass.: Hendrickson Publishers.

1991b Neyrey, Jerome H. "Ceremonies in Luke-Acts: The Case of Meals and Table Fellowship." In *The Social World of Luke-Acts: Models for Interpretation*, edited by Jerome H. Neyrey. Pp. 361–87.

1991c Neyrey, Jerome H. "The Symbolic Universe of Luke-Acts: They Turn the World Upside Down." In *The Social World of Luke-Acts: Models for Interpretation*, edited by Jerome H. Neyrey. Pp. 271–304.

1991d Neyrey, Jerome H. [with Bruce J. Malina]. "Conflict in Luke-Acts: Labelling and Deviance Theory." In *The Social World of Luke-Acts: Models for Interpretation*, edited by Jerome H. Neyrey. Pp. 97–122.

1991e Neyrey, Jerome H. [with Bruce J. Malina]. "First Century Personality: Dyadic, Not Individualistic." In *The Social World of Luke-Acts: Models for Interpretation*, edited by Jerome H. Neyrey. Pp. 67–96.

1991f Neyrey, Jerome H. [with Bruce J. Malina]. "Honor and Shame in Luke-Acts: Pivotal Values of the Mediterranean World." In *The Social World of Luke-Acts: Models for Interpretation*, edited by Jerome H. Neyrey. Pp. 25–65.

1991a Oakman, Douglas E. "The Ancient Economy in the Bible." BTB Readers Guide. *BTB* 21 (1991): 34–39.

1991b Oakman, Douglas E. "The Countryside in Luke-Acts." In *The Social World of Luke-Acts: Models for Interpretation*, edited by Jerome H. Neyrey. Pp. 151–79.

1991a Pilch, John J. *Introducing the Cultural Context of the Old Testament*. Hear the Word. Vol. 1. New York and Mahwah, N.J.: Paulist Press.

1991b Pilch, John J. *Introducing the Cultural Context of the New Testament*. Hear the Word. Vol. 2. New York and Mahwah, N.J.: Paulist Press.

1991c Pilch, John J. "Sickness and Healing in Luke-Acts." In *The Social World of Luke-Acts: Models for Interpretation*, edited by Jerome H. Neyrey. Pp. 181–209.

1991 Robbins, Vernon K. "The Social Location of the Implied Author of Luke-Acts." In *The Social World of Luke-Acts: Models for Interpretation*, edited by Jerome H. Neyrey. Pp. 305–32.

1991a Rohrbaugh, Richard L. "The City in the Second Testament." BTB Readers Guide. *BTB* 21 (1991): 67–75.

1991b Rohrbaugh, Richard L. "The Pre-Industrial City in Luke-Acts: Urban Social Relations." In *The Social World of Luke-Acts: Models for Interpretation*, edited by Jerome H. Neyrey. Pp. 125–49.

1991 Saldarini, Anthony J. "The Gospel of Matthew and Jewish-Christian Conflict." In *Social History of the Matthean Community: Cross-Disciplinary Approaches*, edited by David L. Balch. Pp. 38–61.

1991 Stark, Rodney. "Antioch as the Social Location for Matthew's Gospel. " In *Social History of the Matthean Community: Cross-Disciplinary Approaches*, edited by David L. Balch. Pp. 189–210.

1991a Stegemann, Wolfgang. *Zwischen Synagoge und Obrigkeit: Zur historischen Situation der lukanischen Christen.* FRLANT 152. Göttingen: Vandenhoeck & Ruprecht.

1991b Stegemann, Wolfgang. "Rezension von: Elisabeth Schüssler Fiorenza, Zu ihrem Gedächtnis . . . Eine feministisch-theologische Rekonstruktion der christlichen Ursprünge (München: Kaiser, 1988)." *EvT* 51 (1991): 383–95.

1991a Van Staden, Piet. *Compassion—The Essence of Life: A Social-Scientific Study of the Religious Symbolic Universe Reflected in the Ideology/Theology of Luke. Hervormde Teologiese Studies,* Supplement 4. Pretoria: University of Pretoria Press.

1991b Van Staden, Piet, and A. G. Van Aarde. "Social Description or Social-Scientific Interpretation? A Survey of Modern Scholarship." *Hervormde Teologiese Studies* 47 (1991): 55–87.

1991 White, L. Michael. "Crisis Management and Boundary Maintenance: The Social Location of the Matthean Community." In *Social History of the Matthean Community: Cross-Disciplinary Approaches*, edited by David L. Balch. Pp. 211–47.

1991 Wire, Antoinette C. "Gender Roles in a Scribal Community." In *Social History of the Matthean Community: Cross-Disciplinary Approaches*, edited by David L. Balch. Pp. 87–121.

1992 Barton, Stephen C. "The Communal Dimension of Earliest Christianity: A Critical Survey of the Field." *JTS* 43 (1992): 399–427.

1992 *BTB* 22/2 and 3 (1992). Special Issue on the International Conference on the Social Sciences and Second Testament Interpretation. (Seven essays and introductions by David M. Bossman and Carlos del Valle.)

1992 Bloomquist, L. G.; N. Bonneau; and J. K. Coyle. "Prolegomena to a Sociological Study of Early Christianity: The Example of the Study of Early Christian Leadership." *Social Compass* [Louvain] 39/2 (1992): 221–39.

1992 Duhaime, J. "L'univers social des premiers ehrétiens d'apres J. G. Gager." *Social Compass* [Louvain] 39 (1992): 207–19.

1992 Duhaime, J., and M. St.-Jacques. "Early Christianity and the Social Sciences: A Bibliography." *Social Compass* [Louvain] 39 (1992): 275–90.

1992 Duling, Dennis C. "Matthew's Plurisignificant 'Son of David' in Social Science Perspective: Kinship, Kingship, Magic, and Miracle." *BTB* 22 (1992): 99–116.

1992 Ebertz, Michael N. "Le stigmate du mouvement charismatique autour de Jésus de Nazareth." *Social Compass* [Louvain] 39 (1992): 255–73.

1992 Elliott, John H. "Matthew 20:1-15: A Parable of Invidious Comparison and Evil Eye Accusation." *BTB* 22 (1992): 52–65.

1992a Elliott, John H. "Peter, First Epistle of." *Anchor Bible Dictionary* 5 (1992): 267–78.

1992 Esler, Philip Francis. "Glossolalia and the Admission of Gentiles into the Early Christian Community." *BTB* 22 (1992): 136–42.

1992 Garrett, Susan R. "Sociology of Early Christianity." *Anchor Bible Dictionary* (1992), 6:89–99.

1992 Gottwald, Norman K. "Sociology of Ancient Israel." *Anchor Bible Dictionary* (1992), 6:79–89.

1992a Malina, Bruce J. "Is There a Circum-Mediterranean Person? Looking for Stereotypes." *BTB* 22 (1992): 66–87.

1992b Malina, Bruce J., and Richard L. Rohrbaugh. *Social-Scientific Commentary on the Synoptic Gospels*. Minneapolis: Fortress Press.

1992 Matthews, V. H. "Hospitality and Hostility in Genesis 19 and Judges 19." *BTB* 22 (1992): 3–11.

1992 Oakman, Douglas E. "Was Jesus a Peasant? Implications for Reading the Samaritan Story (Luke 10:30–35)." *BTB* 22 (1992): 117–25.

1992a Osiek, Carolyn. "The Social Sciences and the Second Testament: Problems and Challenges." *BTB* 22 (1992): 88–95.

1992b Osiek, Carolyn. *What Are They Saying about the Social Setting of the New Testament?* Expanded and fully revised ed. New York and Mahwah, N.J.: Paulist Press (1984).

1992a Pilch, John J. "Understanding Healing in the Social World of Early Christianity." BTB Readers Guide. *BTB* 22 (1992): 26–33.

1992b Pilch, John J. "Lying and Deceit in the Letters to the Seven Churches. Perspectives from Cultural Anthropology." *BTB* 22 (1992): 126–35.

1992 Robbins, Vernon K. *Jesus the Teacher: A Socio-Rhetorical Interpretation of Mark*. 2d ed. Philadelphia: Fortress Press (1984).

1992 Rogerson, J. W. "Anthropology and the OT." *Anchor Bible Dictionary* (1992), 1:258–62.

1992 Theissen, Gerd. *Social Reality and the Early Christians: Theology, Ethics, and the World of the New Testament*. Minneapolis: Fortress Press.

II. SELECTED BIBLIOGRAPHY ON THE SOCIAL SCIENCES, THE SOCIAL HISTORY OF ANTIQUITY, CIRCUM-MEDITERRANEAN STUDIES, AND RELATED FIELDS

The titles listed are those cited or those recommended for general orientation or for the pursuit of research along social-scientific lines. See also the rich bibliography in Norman K. Gottwald, *The Hebrew Bible—A Socio-Literary Introduction* (Philadelphia: Fortress Press, 1985, pp. 611-65).

A. Dictionaries, Reference Works

Bart, Pauline, and Linda Frankel. *The Student Sociologist's Handbook.* 3d ed. Glenview, Ill.: Scott, Foresman & Co., 1981.

Seymour-Smith, C. *Dictionary of Anthropology.* Boston: G. K. Hall & Co., 1986.

Sills, D. L., ed. *International Encyclopedia of the Social Sciences.* 17 vols. New York: Macmillan Co., 1968.

Winthrop, Robert. *Dictionary of Concepts in Cultural Anthropology.* New York: Greenwood Press, 1991.

Woodson, Linda. *A Handbook of Modern Rhetorical Terms.* Urbana, Ill.: National Council of Teachers of English, 1979.

B. Social Theory and Method

Barbour, Ian G. *Myths, Models, and Paradigms: A Comparative Study in Science and Religion.* New York: Harper & Row, 1974.

Black, Max. *Models and Metaphors: Studies in Language and Philosophy.* Ithaca, N.Y.: Cornell University Press, 1962.

Buckley, Walter. *Sociology and Modern Systems Theory.* Englewood Cliffs, N.J.: Prentice-Hall, 1967.

Carney, Thomas F. *Content Analysis: A Technique for Systematic Inference from Communications.* Winnipeg: University of Manitoba Press, 1972.

Diesing, Paul. *How Does Social Science Work? Reflections on Practice.* Pittsburgh: University of Pittsburgh Press, 1991; see esp. "Hermenuetics: The Interpretation of Texts," pp. 104-45.

Durkheim, Emile. *The Rules of Sociological Method.* 8th ed. New York: Free Press, 1966 (1895).

Eagleton, Terry. *Ideology: An Introduction.* London: Verso, 1991.

Eisenstadt, Shmuel, and M. Curelaru. *The Form of Sociology—Paradigms and Crises.* New York: John Wiley & Sons, 1976.

Gill, Robin. *The Social Context of Theology: A Methodological Enquiry.* London and Oxford: Alden & Mowbray, 1975.

Hodge, Robert, and Gunther Kress. *Social Semiotics.* Ithaca, N.Y.: Cornell University Press, 1988.

Inkeles, Alex. *What Is Sociology? An Introduction to the Discipline and the Profession.* Englewood Cliffs, N.J.: Prentice-Hall, 1964.

Kinloch, Graham C. *Sociological Theory: Its Development and Major Paradigms.* New York: McGraw-Hill Book Co., 1977.

Kuhn, Thomas S. *The Structure of Scientific Revolutions. International Encyclopedia of Unified Science,* vol. 2, no 2. 2d ed., enlarged. Chicago: University of Chicago Press, 1970.

Laszlo, Ervin. *Introduction to Systems Philosophy.* New York: Gordon & Breach Science Publishers, 1969.

Laszlo, Ervin. *The Systems View of the World: The Natural Philosophy of the New Developments in the Sciences.* New York: George Braziller, 1972.

Lenski, Gerhard and Jean. *Human Societies: An Introduction to Macrosociology.* 5th ed. New York: McGraw Hill Book Co., 1987 (1970).

Lofland, John, and Lyn H. Lofland. *Analyzing Social Settings: A Guide to Qualitative Observation and Analysis.* 2d ed. Belmont, Calif.: Wadsworth Publishing Co., 1984.

Lowry, S. Todd. *The Archaeology of Economic Ideas: The Classical Tradition.* Durham, N.C.: Duke University Press, 1987.

Mouton, J., and H. C. Marias. *Basic Concepts in the Methodology of the Social Sciences.* Pretoria: Human Sciences Research Council, 1988.

Peacock, James. *The Anthropological Lens: Harsh Light, Soft Focus.* New York: Cambridge University Press, 1986.

Peirce, Charles. "The Laws of Nature and Hulme's Argument against Miracles." In *Values in a Universe of Chance.* Edited by P. P. Wiener. Garden City, N.Y.: Doubleday, 1958.

Richardson, Jacques, ed. *Models of Reality: Shaping Thought and Action.* Mount Airy, Md.: Lomond Publications, 1984.

Riley, Matilda White, ed. *Sociological Research.* 2 vols. Vol. 1: *A Case Approach.* New York: Harcourt, Brace & World, 1963.

Rosaldo, Renato. *Culture and Truth: The Remaking of Social Analysis.* Boston: Beacon Press, 1989.

Sartori, Giovanni, ed. *Social Science Concepts: A Systematic Analysis.* Beverly Hills, Calif.: Sage Publications, 1984.

Segal, Robert A. *Religion and the Social Sciences.* Atlanta: Scholars Press, 1989.

Turner, Jonathan H. *The Structure of Sociological Theory.* Rev. ed. Homewood, Ill.: Dorsey Press, 1978; 3d ed., 1982.

Wallis, Roy. "Relative Deprivation and Social Movements: A Cautionary Note." *British Journal of Sociology* 26 (1975): 360–63.

Weber, Max. *Economy and Society: An Outline of Interpretive Sociology.* Edited by Guenther Roth and Claus Wittich. 2 vols. Berkeley and Los Angeles: University of California Press, 1978.

Williams, Robin M., Jr. *American Society: A Sociological Interpretation.* 3d ed. New York: Alfred A. Knopf, 1977.

Zeitlin, Irving M. *Ideology and the Development of Sociological Theory.* Englewood Cliffs, N.J.: Prentice-Hall, 1968.

C. Sociolinguistics, Literary Theory

Burke, Kenneth. *The Philosophy of Literary Form: Studies in Symbolic Action.* 2d ed. Baton Rouge, La.: Louisiana State University Press, 1967.

Eagleton, Terry. *Criticism and Ideology: A Study on Marxist Literary Theory.* London: Verso, 1978.

Eagleton, Terry. *Literary Theory: An Introduction.* Minneapolis: University of Minnesota Press, 1983.

Eco, Umbert. *A Theory of Semiotics*. Bloomington, Ind.: Indiana University Press, 1976.

Fowler, Roger. *Linguistic Criticism*. Oxford and New York: Oxford University Press, 1986.

Halliday, M. A. K. *Language as Social Semiotic: The Social Interpretation of Language and Meaning*. Baltimore: University Park Press, 1978.

Louw, J. P., ed. *Sociolinguistics and Communication*. London: United Bible Societies, 1986.

Plett, H. F. *Textwissenschaft und Textanalyse: Semiotik, Linguistik, Rhetorik*. Heidelberg: Quelle & Meyer, 1975.

Said, Edward W. *The World, the Text, and the Critic*. Cambridge: Harvard University Press, 1983.

Sapir, Edward. *Culture, Language, and Personality: Selected Essays*, edited by D. C. Mandelbaum. Berkeley and Los Angeles: University of California Press, 1956.

D. Sociology of Knowledge

Berger, Peter L., and Thomas Luckmann. *The Social Construction of Reality: A Treatise in the Sociology of Knowledge*. Garden City, N.Y.: Doubleday & Co., 1967.

Mannheim, Karl. *Ideology and Utopia*, with a preface by L. Wirth. New York: Harcourt, Brace & World, 1936.

Phillips, Charles Robert. "The Sociology of Religious Knowledge in the Roman Empire to A.D. 284." *ANRW* 2.16.3 (1986), 2711–73.

E. Specific Issues

Carrier, Hervé. *The Sociology of Religious Belonging*. New York: Herder & Herder, 1965.

Farber, Bernard, *Conceptions of Kinship*. New York: Elsevier, 1981.

Lenski, Gerhard. *Power and Privilege: A Theory of Social Stratification*. New York: McGraw Hill Book Co., 1966; 2d ed. Chapel Hill, N.C.: University of North Carolina Press, 1984.

Nader, L., and H. F. Todd, Jr., eds. *The Disputing Process—Law in Ten Societies*. New York: Columbia University Press, 1978.

Papajohn, John, and John Spiegel. *Transactions in Families*. San Francisco: Jossey-Bass, 1975.

Pfuhl, E. H., Jr. *The Deviance Process*. New York: Van Nostrand Reinhold Co., 1980.

Rogers, Everett M. *Diffusion of Innovations*. 3d ed. New York: Free Press, 1983.

Simmel, Georg. *Conflict and the Web of Group-Affiliations*. New York: Free Press, 1955.

Snow, D. A.; L. A. Zurcher; and S. Ekland-Olson. "Social Networks and Social Movements: A Microstructural Approach in Differential Recruitment." *American Sociological Review* 45 (1980): 787–801.

Todd, Emmanuel. *The Explanation of Ideology: Family Structures and Social Systems.* Translated by David Garrioch. Oxford: Basil Blackwell, 1985.

Tumin, Melvin M. *Social Stratification: The Forms and Functions of Inequality.* Englewood Cliffs, N.J.: Prentice-Hall, 1967.

Westhues, Kenneth, ed. *Society's Shadow: Studies in the Sociology of Countercultures.* Toronto: McGraw-Hill Ryerson, 1972.

F. Anthropology: Cultural, Economic, Social, Political

Arensberg, Conrad M., and Arthur H. Niehoff. "American Cultural Values." In *Introducing Social Change,* edited by C. M. Arensberg and A. H. Niehoff. 2d ed. Chicago: Aldine-Atherton, 1971. Pp. 363–78.

Bettini, Maurizio. *Anthropology and Roman Culture: Kinship, Time, Images of the Soul.* Translated by John Van Sickle. Baltimore: Johns Hopkins University Press, 1991 (1988).

Boissevain, Jeremy. *Friends of Friends: Networks, Manipulators and Coalitions.* New York: St. Martin's Press, 1974.

Burridge, Kenelm. *New Heaven, New Earth: A Study of Millenarian Activities.* New York: Schocken Books, 1969.

Cohen, Ronald, and Elman R. Service., eds. *Origins of the State: The Anthropology of Political Evolution.* Philadelphia: Institute for the Study of Human Issues, 1978.

Douglas, Mary Tew. *Purity and Danger: An Analysis of Concepts of Pollution and Taboo.* London: Routledge & Kegan Paul; New York: F. A. Praeger, 1966.

Douglas, Mary Tew. *Natural Symbols: Explorations in Cosmology.* London and Boston: Routledge & Kegan Paul, 1970.

Douglas, Mary Tew. *Implicit Meanings: Essays in Anthropology.* London and Boston: Routledge & Kegan Paul, 1975.

Douglas, Mary Tew. *Cultural Bias.* Occasional Paper no. 34 of the Royal Anthropological Institute of Great Britain and Ireland. London, 1978.

Douglas, Mary Tew, ed. *Rule and Meanings: The Anthropology of Everyday Knowledge.* New York: Penguin Books, 1973.

Douglas, Mary Tew, ed. *Witchcraft Confessions and Accusations.* New York: Tavistock Publications, 1970.

Douglas, Mary Tew, and Baron Isherwood. *The World of Goods.* New York: Basic Books, 1978.

Evans-Pritchard, Edward E. *A History of Anthropological Thought,* edited by André Singer, with Introduction by E. Gellner. New York: Basic Books, 1981.

Evans-Pritchard, Edward E. *Social Anthropology.* Glencoe, Ill.: Free Press, 1952.

Evans-Pritchard, Edward E. *Theories of Primitive Religion.* Oxford: Clarendon Press, 1965.

Evans-Pritchard, Edward E. *Witchcraft, Oracles and Magic among the Azande.* Oxford: Clarendon Press, 1937; abridged reprint, 1976.

Farber, Bernard. *Comparative Kinship Systems: A Method of Analysis.* New York: John Wiley and Sons, 1968.

Feleppa, R. "Emics, Etics and Social Objectivity." *Current Anthropology* 27 (1986): 243–55.

Geertz, Clifford. *The Interpretation of Cultures: Selected Essays.* New York: Basic Books, 1973.

Geertz. Clifford. "'From the Native's Point of View.' On the Nature of Anthropological Understanding." In *Meaning in Anthropology,* edited by K. H. Basso and H. A. Selby. Albuquerque: University of New Mexico Press, 1976. Pp. 221–37.

Grunlan, Stephen A., and Marvin K. Mayers. *Cultural Anthropology: A Christian Perspective.* Grand Rapids: Zondervan, 1979.

Harris, Marvin. *Cultural Materialism: The Struggle for a Science of Culture.* New York: Vintage Books, 1979.

Harris, Marvin. "History and Significance of the Emic/Etic Distinction." *Annual Review of Anthropology* 5 (1976): 329–50.

Harris, Marvin. *The Rise of Anthropological Theory: A History of Theories of Culture.* New York: Thomas Y. Crowell, 1968.

Henderson, George. *A Practitioner's Guide to Understanding Indigenous and Foreign Cultures.* Springfield, Ill.: Charles C. Thomas, 1989.

Hobsbawm, E. J. *Primitive Rebels.* New York: W. W. Norton, 1959.

Hsu, Francis L. K. "American Core Value and National Character." In Francis L. K. Hsu, *Psychological Anthropology.* Cambridge, Mass.: Schenkman Publishing Co., 1972. Pp. 241–62.

Illich, Ivan. *Gender.* New York: Pantheon Books, 1982.

Isenberg, Sheldon R., and Dennis E. Owen. "Bodies, Natural and Contrived: The Work of Mary Douglas." *RSR* 3 (1977): 1–17.

Kearny, Michael. *World View.* Novato, Calif.: Chandler & Sharp Publications, 1984.

Kluckholm, F. R., and F. L. Strodtbeck. *Variations in Value Orientations.* New York: Harper & Row, 1961.

Kottak, Conrad Phillip. *Cultural Anthropology.* 4th ed. New York: Random House, 1987.

Leach, Edmund. *Culture and Communication: The Logic by Which Symbols Are Connected.* Cambridge: Cambridge University Press, 1976.

Lessa, William A., and Evon Z. Vogt., eds. *Reader in Comparative Religion: An Anthropological Approach.* 3d ed. San Francisco: Harper & Row, 1972.

Lévi-Strauss, Claude. *The Savage Mind.* Chicago: University of Chicago Press, 1966.

Lévi-Strauss, Claude. *Structural Anthropology.* Translated by Monique Layton. New York: Basic Books, 1986.

Lewellen, Ted C. *Political Anthropology: An Introduction.* South Hadley, Mass.: Bergin & Garvey Publishers, 1983.

Mair, Lucy. *An Introduction to Social Anthropology.* 2d ed. Oxford: Clarendon Press, 1972.

Naroll, Raoul, and Ronald Cohen, eds. *A Handbook of Method in Cultural Anthropology.* Garden City, N.Y.: Natural History Press, 1970.

Nida, Eugene. *Customs and Cultures: Anthropology for Christian Missions.* New York: Harper & Row, 1954.

O'Laughlin, Bridget. "Marxist Approaches in Anthropology." *Annual Review of Anthropology* 4 (1975): 341–70.

Radcliffe-Brown, A. R. *Structure and Function in Primitive Society: Essays and Addresses.* New York: Free Press, 1965 (1952).

Samovar, Larry A., and Richard E. Porter, eds. *Intercultural Communication: A Reader.* Belmont, Calif.: Wadsworth, 1985.

Shanin, Teodor, ed. *Peasants and Peasant Societies: Selected Readings.* Baltimore: Penguin Books, 1971.

Thrupp, Sylvia L., ed. *Millennial Dreams in Action: Studies in Revolutionary Religious Movements.* The Hague: Mouton Publishers; New York: Schocken Books, 1970.

Turner, Victor W. *Dramas, Fields and Metaphors.* Ithaca, N.Y.: Cornell University Press, 1974.

Turner, Victor W. *The Ritual Process: Structure and Anti-Structure.* Chicago: Aldine Publishing Co., 1969.

Van Gennep, Arnold. *The Rites of Passage.* Chicago: University of Chicago Press, 1960 (1908).

Wallace, Anthony F. C. *Religion: An Anthropological View.* New York: Random House, 1966.

Watson, Graham. "The Social Construction of Boundaries between Social and Cultural Anthropology in Britain and North America." *Journal of Anthropological Research* 40 (1984): 351–66.

G. The Relation between the Historical and Social Sciences

Barraclough, Geoffrey. *Main Trends in History.* New York: Holmes & Meier, 1979.

Block, Marc. *The Historian's Craft.* Translated by Peter Putnam. New York: Alfred A. Knopf, 1963.

Burke, Peter. *Sociology and History.* Controversies in Sociology 10. London: Allen & Unwin, 1980.

Leff, Gordon. *History and Social Theory.* Garden City, N.Y.: Doubleday & Co., 1971.

Romein, J. M. "The Common Human Pattern (Origin and Scope of Historical Theories)." *Journal of World History* 4 (1958): 449–63.

Skocpol, Theda, ed. *Vision and Method in Historical Sociology.* Cambridge: Cambridge University Press, 1984.

H. Historical and Cross-Cultural
Social Science and Social History
(including antiquity, preindustrial, and third world)

Alföldy, Géza. *Römische Sozialgeschichte.* 3d fully revised ed. Wiesbaden: Franz Steiner Verlag, 1984.

Arensberg, Conrad M. "The Old World Peoples. The Place of European Cultures in World Ethnography." *Anthropological Quarterly* 36 (1963): 75–99.

Augsburger, David W. *Pastoral Counseling across Cultures.* Philadelphia: Westminster Press, 1986.

Aune, David E. "Magic in Early Christianity." *ANRW* 2.23.2 (1980). Pp. 1507–57.

Austin, M. M., and P. Vidal-Naquet. *Economic and Social History of Ancient Greece: An Introduction.* Berkeley and Los Angeles: University of California Press, 1977.

Bengtson, Hermann. *Introduction to Ancient History.* Berkeley and Los Angeles: University of California Press, 1970.

Bradley, Keith. *Discovering the Roman Family: Studies in Roman Social History.* Oxford: Oxford University Press, 1991.

Brunt, P. A. "A Marxist View of Roman History." *Journal of Roman Studies* 72 (1982): 156–63 (review of G. E. M. de Ste. Croix, *Class Struggle in the Ancient World,* 1981).

Carney, Thomas F. *The Shape of the Past: Models and Antiquity.* Lawrence, Kans.: Coronado Press, 1975.

de Ste. Croix, G. E. M. *The Class Struggle in the Ancient World from the Archaic Age to the Arab Conquests.* Ithaca, N.Y.: Cornell University Press, 1981.

DeVaux, Roland. *Ancient Israel.* 2 vols. New York: McGraw-Hill Book Co., 1965.

Eilberg-Schwartz, Howard. *The Savage in Judaism: An Anthropology of Israelite Religion and Ancient Judaism.* Bloomington, Ind.: Indiana University Press, 1990.

Eisenstadt, S. N., and René Lemarchand, eds. *Political Clientalism, Patronage and Development.* Beverly Hills: Sage Publications, 1981.

Eisenstadt, S. N. and Louis Roniger. *Patrons, Clients and Friends: Interpersonal Relations and the Structure of Trust in Society.* Cambridge and New York: Cambridge University Press, 1984.

Eisenstadt, S. N., and Louis Roniger. "Patron-Client Relations as a Model of Structuring Social Exchange." *Comparative Studies in Society and History* 22 (1980): 42–77.

Finley, Moses I. *The Ancient Economy.* Berkeley and Los Angeles: University of California Press, 1973.

Finley, Moses I. *Economy and Society in Ancient Greece.* Edited by Brent D. Shaw and Richard P. Saller. New York: Penguin Books, 1983.

Finley, Moses I. *The World of Odysseus.* 2d rev. ed. New York: Penguin Books, 1979.

Foster, George M. "The Anatomy of Envy: A Study in Symbolic Behavior." *Current Anthropology* 13 (1972): 165–202.

Foster, George M. "Peasant Society and the Image of Limited Good." *American Anthropologist* 67 (1965): 293–315.

Frank, Tenney, ed. *An Economic Survey of Ancient Rome*. 5 vols. Baltimore: Johns Hopkins University Press, 1933–40.

Gardner, Jane F. *Women in Roman Law and Society*. Bloomington, Ind.: Indiana University Press, 1985.

Garnsey, Peter, and Richard P. Saller. *The Roman Empire: Economy, Society and Culture*. Berkeley and Los Angeles: University of California Press, 1987.

Goody, Jack. *The Oriental, the Ancient and the Primitive: Systems of Marriage and the Family in the Pre-industrial Societies of Eurasia*. New York: Cambridge University Press, 1990.

Gottwald, Norman K. "Bibliography on the Social Scientific Study of the Old Testament." *American Baptist Quarterly* 2 (1983): 142–56.

Gottwald, Norman K., ed. *Social Scientific Criticism of the Hebrew Bible and Its Social World: The Israelite Monarchy*. Semeia 37. Decatur, Ga.: Scholars Press, 1986.

Gottwald, Norman K. "Sociological Method in the Study of Ancient Israel." In *Encounter with the Text: Form and History in the Hebrew Bible*, edited by Martin J. Buss. Philadelphia: Fortress Press, 1979. Pp. 69–81.

Gottwald, Norman K. *The Tribes of Yahweh: A Sociology of the Religion of Liberated Israel 1250–1050 B.C.E.* Maryknoll, N.Y.: Orbis Books, 1979.

Gouldner, Alvin W. *The Hellenic World: A Sociological Analysis*. New York: Harper & Row, 1969. [Part 1 of *Enter Plato: Classical Greece and the Origins of Social Theory*. New York: Basic Books, 1965.]

Green, Henry Alan. *The Economic and Social Origins of Gnosticism*. SBLDS 77. Atlanta: Scholars Press, 1985.

Hengel, Martin. *Judaism and Hellenism*. 2 vols. Philadelphia: Fortress Press, 1974.

Houtart, François. *Religion et modes de production précapitalistes*. Brussels: University of Brussels Press, 1980.

Humphreys, Sally C. *Anthropology and the Greeks*. London: Routledge & Kegan Paul, 1983.

Kautsky, John. *The Politics of Aristocratic Empires*. Chapel Hill, N.C.: University of North Carolina Press, 1982.

Kimbrough, S. T. Jr. *Israelite Religion in Sociological Perspective: The Work of Antonin Cuasee*. Wiesbaden: Verlag Otto Harrassowitz, 1978.

Kippenberg, Hans G. *Religion und Klassenbildung im antiken Judäa: Eine religionssoziologische Studie zum Verhältnis von Tradition und gesellschaftlicher Entwicklung*. Göttingen: Vandenhoeck & Ruprecht, 1978.

Koester, Helmut. *Introduction to the New Testament*. 2 vols. Berlin and New York: W. de Gruyter; Philadelphia: Fortress Press, 1982.

Kramer, Ross S. "Women in the Religions of the Graeco-Roman World." *RSR* 9 (1983): 127–39.

Lang, Bernhard, ed. *Anthropological Approaches to the Old Testament*. Philadelphia: Fortress Press; London: SPCK, 1985.

Lanternari, Vittorio. *The Religions of the Oppressed: A Study of Modern Messianic Cults*. New York: New American Library, 1963.

Leach, Edmund. "Anthropological Approaches to the Study of the Bible during the Twentieth Century." In *Humanizing America's Iconic Book: Society of Biblical Literature Centennial Addresses 1980*. Chico, Calif.: Scholars Press, 1982. Pp. 73–94.

Lemche, N. P. *Early Israel: Anthropological and Historical Studies on the Israelite Society before the Monarchy*. VTSup 37. Leiden: E. J. Brill, 1985.

Long, Burke O. "The Social World of Ancient Israel." *Interpretation* 37 (1982): 243–55.

Mauss, Marcel. *The Gift: Forms and Functions of Exchange in Archaic Societies*. (Translation of *Essai sur le don*, 1925.) London: Cohen & West, 1954.

Mayes, Andrew D. H. *The Old Testament in Sociological Perspective*. London: Pickering & Inglis, 1989.

Murdock, George Peter. *Theories of Illness: A World Survey*. Pittsburgh: University of Pittsburgh Press, 1980.

Nash, Manning. *Primitive and Peasant Economic Systems*. San Francisco: Chandler Publishing Co., 1966.

Parsons, Talcott. *Societies: Evolutionary and Comparative Perspectives*. Englewood Cliffs, N.J.: Prentice-Hall, 1966.

Pedersen, Johannes. *Israel, Its Life and Culture*. 4 vols. London: Oxford University Press, 1926–40.

Petit, Paul. *Pax Romana*. Berkeley and Los Angeles: University of California Press, 1976.

Polanyi, Karl. *The Great Transformation: The Political and Economic Origins of Our Time*. Boston: Beacon Press, 1957.

Potter, Jack M., May N. Diaz; and George M. Foster, eds. *Peasant Society: A Reader*. Boston: Little, Brown & Co., 1967.

Rawson, Beryl. "The Roman Family." In *The Family in Ancient Rome: New Perspectives*. London: Croom Helm, 1986. Pp. 1–57.

Redfield, Robert. *Peasant Society and Culture*. Chicago: University of Chicago Press, 1956.

Rieche, Anita. *Das antike Italien aus der Luft*. Bergisch Gladbach: Gustav Lübbe Verlag, 1978.

Rogerson, J. W. *Anthropology and the Old Testament*. Atlanta: John Knox Press, 1978.

Roniger, Luis. "Modern Patron-Client Relations and Historical Clientalism: Some Clues from Ancient Republican Rome." *Archives Européennes de Socilogie* 24 (1983): 63–95.

Rostovtzeff, Michael I. *The Social and Economic History of the Hellenistic World.* 3 vols. Oxford: Clarendon Press, 1953.

Rostovtzeff, Michael I. *The Social and Economic History of the Roman Empire.* 2 vols. 2d rev. ed. by P. M. Fraser. Oxford: Clarendon Press, 1957.

Rowland, Michael; Mogens Larsen; and Kristian Kristiansen, eds. *Center and Periphery in the Ancient World: New Directions in Archeology.* New York: Cambridge University Press, 1987.

Sack, Robert David. *Human Territoriality.* Cambridge Studies in Historical Geography 7. Cambridge: Cambridge University Press, 1987.

Sahlins, Marshall. *Stone Age Economics.* Chicago: Aldine-Atherton, 1972.

Saller, Richard P. "Familia, Domus and the Roman Conception of the Family." *Phoenix* 38 (1984): 336–55.

Schmidt, Steffen W., et al., eds. *Friends, Followers, and Factions: A Reader in Political Clientism.* Berkeley and Los Angeles: University of California Press, 1977.

Schreiter, Robert J. *Constructing Local Theologies.* Maryknoll, N.Y.: Orbis Books, 1985.

Scott, James C. *Domination and the Arts of Resistance: Hidden Transcripts.* New Haven: Yale University Press, 1990.

Scott, James C. *The Moral Economy of the Peasant: Rebellion and Subsistence in South-East Asia.* New Haven: Yale University Press, 1976.

Scott, James C. *Weapons of the Weak: Everyday Forms of Peasant Resistance.* New Haven: Yale University Press, 1985.

Sjoberg, Gideon. *The Preindustrial City, Past and Present.* New York: Free Press, 1965.

Smith, Daniel L. *The Religion of the Landless: The Social Context of the Babylonian Exile.* Bloomington, Ind.: Meyer-Stone Books, 1989. (Re sociological exegesis and its critics, 1–14.)

Smith, M. G. "Pre-Industrial Stratification Systems." In *Social Structure and Mobility in Economic Development,* edited by Neil J. Smelser and Seymour M. Lipset. Chicago: Aldine Publishing Co., 1966. Pp. 141–76.

Smith, W. Robertson. *Lectures on the Religion of the Semites.* London: A. & A. Black, 1894; reprinted as *The Religion of the Semites: The Fundamental Institutions.* New York: Schocken Books, 1972.

Stavenhagen, Rodolfo. *Social Classes in Agrarian Societies.* Garden City, N.Y.: Anchor Press, 1975. (Spanish original 1970.)

Veyne, Paul. *Bread and Circuses: Historical Sociology and Political Pluralism.* Translated by Brian Pearce. Baltimore: Penguin Books, 1990.

Veyne, Paul, et al., eds. *A History of Private Life.* Vol. 1: *From Pagan Rome to Byzantium.* Translated by Arthur Goldhammer. Cambridge: Harvard University Press, 1987.

Wallace-Hadrill, A., ed. *Patronage in Ancient Society.* London and New York: Routledge & Kegan Paul, 1990 (1989).

Weber, Max. "Agraverhältnisse im Altertum." In *Gesammelte Aufsätze zur Sozial-und Wirtschaftsgeschichte*. Tübingen: Mohr, 1924. Pp. 1–288.

Wendland, Ernst R. *The Cultural Factor in Bible Translation*. New York: United Bible Societies, 1987.

Wilson, Bryan R. *Magic and the Millennium: A Sociological Study of Religious Movements of Protest among Tribal and Third-World Peoples*. San Francisco: Harper & Row, 1973.

Wilson, Robert R. *Sociological Approaches to the Old Testament*. Philadelphia: Fortress Press, 1984.

Wolf, Eric R. *Peasants*. Foundations of Modern Anthropology. Englewood Cliffs, N.J.: Prentice-Hall, 1966.

Young, Allan. "The Anthropologies of Illness and Sickness." *Annual Review of Anthropology* 11 (1982): 257–85.

I. Mediterranean and Middle East Social Studies

Abu-Lughod, Lila. *Veiled Sentiments: Honor and Poetry in a Bedouin Society*. Berkeley and Los Angeles: University of California Press, 1987.

Black-Michaud, Jacob. *Cohesive Force: Feud in the Mediterranean and the Middle East*. New York: St. Martin's Press, 1975.

Braudel, Fernand. *The Mediterranean and the Mediterranean World of Philip II*. 2 vols. New York: Harper & Row, 1972.

Campbell, John K. *Honour, Family, and Patronage*. Oxford: Oxford University Press, 1964.

Davis, John. *People of the Mediterranean*. London: Routledge & Kegan Paul, 1977.

Eickelman, D. F. *The Middle East: An Anthropological Approach*. 2d ed. Englewood Cliffs, N.J.: Prentice-Hall, 1989.

Furnea, Elizabeth W. *Guests of the Sheik: An Ethnography of an Iraqi Village*. Garden City, N.Y.: Doubleday & Co., 1965.

Gellner, E., and Waterbury, J. *Patrons and Clients in Mediterranean Societies*. London: Gerald Duckworth & Co., 1977.

Gilmore, David D. "Anthropology of the Mediterranean Area." *Annual Review of Anthropology* 11 (1982): 175–205.

Gilmore, David D., ed. *Honor and Shame and the Unity of the Mediterranean*. American Anthropological Association Special Publication 22. Washington, D.C.: American Anthropological Association, 1987.

Goitein, Solomon Dob. *A Mediterranean Society: The Jewish Communities of the Arab World as Portrayed in the Documents of the Cairo Geniza*. 4 vols. Berkeley and Los Angeles: University of California Press, 1967–83.

Grant, Michael, and Rachel Kitzinger, eds. *Civilization of the Ancient Mediterranean*. 3 vols. New York: Charles Scribner's Sons, 1988.

Nieuwenhuijze, C. A. O. Van. *Sociology of the Middle East: A Stocktaking and Interpretation*. Leiden: E. J. Brill, 1971.

Patai, Raphael. *The Arab Mind.* Rev. ed. New York: Charles Scribner's Sons, 1983 (1973).

Peristiany, Jean G., ed. *Contributions to Mediterranean Sociology.* Paris: Mouton, 1965.

Peristiany, Jean G., ed. *Honour and Shame: The Values of Mediterranean Society.* London: Weidenfeld & Nicolson, 1965; Chicago: University of Chicago Press, 1966.

Peristiany, Jean G., ed. *Mediterranean Family Structure.* Cambridge: Cambridge University Press, 1976.

Pitt-Rivers, Julian A. *The Fate of Shechem; or, the Politics of Sex: Essays in the Anthropology of the Mediterranean.* New York: Cambridge University Press, 1977.

Pitt-Rivers, Julian A., ed. *Mediterranean Countrymen: Essays in the Social Anthropology of the Mediterranean.* Paris: Mouton, 1963.

Pitt-Rivers, Julian A. *The People of the Sierra.* 2d ed. Chicago: University of Chicago Press, 1971 (1954).

Pitkin, Donald S. "Mediterranean Europe." *Anthropological Quarterly* 36 (1963): 120–29.

Pryce-Jones, David. *The Closed Circle: An Interpretation of the Arabs.* San Francisco: Harper & Row, 1989.

Schneider, Jane. "Of Vigilance and Virgins: Honor, Shame and Access to Resources in Mediterranean Societies." *Ethnology* 9 (1971): 1–24.

Schneider, Jane, and Peter Schneider. *Culture and Political Economy in Western Sicily.* New York: Academic Press, 1976.

Semple, Ellen C. *The Geography of the Mediterranean Region: Its Relation to Ancient History.* New York: H. Holt & Co., 1931.

Walker, D. S. *The Mediterranean Lands.* 3d ed. London: Methuen, 1965.

Wolf, Eric R., ed. *Religion, Power and Protest in Local Communities: The Northern Shore of the Mediterranean.* Religion and Society 24. New York, Berlin, and Amsterdam: Mouton, 1984.